£4·20

The Court Wits
of the Restoration

The Court Wits of the Restoration

AN INTRODUCTION

BY JOHN HAROLD WILSON

FRANK CASS & CO. LTD.

1967

Published in Great Britain by
FRANK CASS AND COMPANY LIMITED
67 Great Russell Street
London, W.C. 1, England

Printed in U.S.A.

Preface

WITHIN recent years there has been a considerable revival of interest in the literary rakes who flourished at the Court of Charles II. Biographical and critical studies have been made of Buckingham, Dorset, Etherege, Rochester, Sedley, and Wycherley, and the "works" of the last four have been studiously, if not always successfully, edited. In addition, the major literary rakes have been the subjects of numerous research articles, which have already outmoded some biographies and critical editions.

Essays on the Court Wits as individuals, however well done, have always been somewhat unsatisfactory because of a natural tendency to treat the subject of the essay as a phenomenon taken bodily from his cultural environment. This singling out of the individual has sometimes resulted in a further tendency to minimize his faults as a man and to magnify his work as a poet. However, the Court Wits constituted a unique group of writers; they were, in effect, a little "school," and each of them, to some degree at least, spoke for the group as much as for himself. They were close friends; they wrote often in collaboration; they submitted their work to each other for correction and approval; they even tended to write in the same style. It is difficult to study one Wit without studying all of them.

Therefore they can be seen best as individuals if they are seen first as a cohesive group. This essay is planned as an introduction to the Wits as men and writers. It is not aimed at completeness in biography or bibliography; rather it is designed to present a unified study of the human and literary activities of the coterie.

Merely to list the names of those friends and colleagues who have read and corrected these pages is a poor return for their generosity, but it is all I can offer. Therefore, like any dedicating poet, I humbly acknowledge the wit and wisdom of William Charvat, Robert M. Estrich, Charles F. Harrold, Frederick J. Hoffman, William R. Parker, and Francis L. Utley, and the painstaking editorial assistance of Mrs. Myra McCrory. Timidly I may say to them of this book, as Dryden did to his patron, the Earl of Mulgrave, "Some things in it have passed your approbation, and many your amendment."

J.H.W.

March 12, 1947

Contents

List of Illustrations

The Court Wits

IN the spring of 1660, England abandoned its abortive experiment in republicanism, and on May 29, while bells rang and bonfires flared, London flocked to welcome home its exiled King. With typical irony, Charles II remarked that it must have been his own fault that he had stayed away so long; nowhere could he find a subject who did not profess happiness at his return. Significant of the new reign is the fact that the King's first night in London was spent, not at his palace, but at the house of Sir Samuel Morland, scientist and inventor. Typical also is the fact that Charles slept that night with his favorite mistress, Barbara Palmer.

Whitehall Palace was scoured and disinfected of the last taints of Puritanism. The nasal whine and sober dress of the godly gave way to the careless laughter and gaudy plumes of the cavalier. A new Parliament, dominated by royalists, did all in its power to make it seem that the Interregnum had never been, even to dating the reign of Charles II from the death of Charles I. Regicides were executed; the bodies of Cromwell, Ireton, and Bradshaw were dug up and hung in chains; nonconformists were persecuted; the sumptuary laws of Cromwell's regime were repealed or ignored. Sin, which had flourished openly in the days of James and Charles I, came jauntily out of hiding.

After eighteen years of turbulence, the English people relapsed almost happily into their old ways and customs. Society rearranged itself into the familiar pyramid of classes. The broad base of the pyramid and its solid body were made up chiefly of farmers, for agriculture was still the dominant industry. The inhabitants of the towns—particularly of London—looked down upon the country folk. The gentry—esquires, knights and baronets—were, of course, superior to all yeomen. Above the gentry were the nobility, in the ascending order of baron, viscount, earl, marquis, and duke, the "my lords" of the titled world. Above them all, at the peak of the pyramid, were the royal family and the King.

London, the capital, was the center of commerce, finance, art, society, and practically everything else. It too had its divisions and castes. The inhabitants of the City (the old, walled section of London) were merchants and craftsmen —"citizens," suspected of lingering republican sympathies, to be scorned and distrusted by all good royalists. In the newer western section of London (Westminster and its environs) was the Town, where the gentry and the nobility constituted a tight, self-conscious society of their own. Still farther along the bank of the Thames were Whitehall Palace and the Houses of Parliament, the political center of the nation. Living in or near the palace was the Court, the inner circle of gentry and nobility—ministers, privy councillors, gentlemen and ladies in waiting, secretaries, functionaries, and numerous lesser courtiers and courtesans. The Court ruled the King, Parliament, and the nation. Court favor made men or broke them, determined laws, taxes, and fashions, affected science, art, literature, religion, and foreign policy. The galleries of Whitehall buzzed with intrigues and counter-intrigues, in which noblemen (often with noble motives) took part, bribing, spying, flattering, and employing ladies of easy virtue as tools to work their wills.

While faction strove with faction, and ministers quarreled, while the Established Church warred to destroy dissent, while republicans fought to limit the monarchy and monarchists to limit Parliament, King Charles sat on the

lid of the national kettle and cocked a humorous eye at
Fate. A man of practical mind and genial, kindly disposition, he had no convictions and only one aim—to stay
where he was. For all the arguments he cared not a fig; so
that he did not have to go on his travels again, he was content to maintain things as they were. He had few illusions.
People he loved individually—especially pretty women;
for mankind at large he had only good-humored contempt.
He was fond of music, plays, poetry, pageants, dogs, ducks,
and chemistry. He liked to walk, talk, hunt, fish, drink,
and make love. He was well-read, intelligent, lazy, and
according to his lights a pretty good king. By virtue of both
rank and temperament, he was the first of the Wits.[1]

Shortly after the Restoration, the serious-minded cava-
liers at Court noted with dismay that the King was to be
found more and more often in company with the "men of
mirth," as dour old Chancellor Hyde called them.[2] These
were sprightly young fellows who had no respect for the
Chancellor's dignity and gray hairs, who cared nothing for
laws civil or ecclesiastical, and who could and did droll at
anything under Heaven, including the King's own Majesty. These men formed the nucleus of the group that
came to be known as the Court Wits.

The name was as loose as the morals of the assemblage.
A Wit was anyone from wild, malicious Harry Killigrew
or George Bridges ("created a Wit for hard drinking")[3]
to George Villiers, Duke of Buckingham, the last splendid
playboy of the fading Renaissance, or William Wycherley,
the finest dramatic genius of the Restoration Court. A Wit
was not necessarily one skilled at jest and repartee, nor
need he be a poet, playwright, or maker of libels and lampoons. In the Restoration meaning of the term, a Wit was
simply anyone who pretended to intellectuality, and (especially if he were a lord) he was often taken at his own
valuation.

The nature of wit as a quality of art was much discussed;

it was well defined by two of the leading poets of the age, Cowley and Dryden. According to Cowley (in his ode "Of Wit"), it was not jests, "florid Talk," metrical skill, poetical adornments, puns, obscenity, rant, bombast, or an "odd similitude." To Cowley, wit was completeness and perfection in any artistic effort,

> In a true piece of Wit all things must be,
> Yet all things there agree.

Dryden was more specific. To him, wit was the perfect blend of fancy and judgment. It was also, at times, "sharpness of conceit," and it could even be mere pleasantry. But finally, said Dryden, "Wit . . . is a propriety of thought and words; or, in other terms, thoughts and words elegantly adapted to the subject."[4] Since Dryden did not limit his several discussions of the subject to literature, we may take it that wit spoken had its values as well as wit written. Thus a dedicating poet might address his noble patron as a Wit (deceiving no one but the complacent lord who was the subject of his eulogy) and mean thereby that his hoped-for Maecenas was a clever conversationalist when his money did the talking.

In general practice, the label Wit was attached only to one who made some real pretense to distinction as a poet, critic, translator, raconteur, or man of learning. Most of the Court Wits could boast of some achievement in the literary arts, although the importance of their work was, of course, greatly exaggerated by their admiring contemporaries. The Court Wits differed from wits in general in one important respect: they were all gentlemen amateurs. Dryden and Shadwell were wits, and closely attached to the Court circle, but they earned their bread by their pens. Etherege and Wycherley were successful playwrights, but they were gentlemen and courtiers by profession, and dramatists for fun.

While there were many courtiers who claimed the title

of Wit, there are only fourteen who at one time or another were members of the charmed inner circle. In the order of their social rank (which was very important to the Restoration reader) they are the following:

First was George Villiers, Duke of Buckingham, boon companion to the King from early childhood, politician, playwright, chemist, poet, fiddler, and buffoon, a man of ability, but cursed with too much imagination, and fundamentally unstable. Next in rank was phlegmatic Charles Sackville, Lord Buckhurst, Earl of Dorset and Middlesex, an easy-going rake, with a talent for light verse. He was not only a Wit himself, but, as a generous patron of poets, the cause of wit in other men. John Sheffield, Earl of Mulgrave, was Dorset's social equal, but his inferior as a man of letters. He fancied himself as a soldier and politician; at intervals he was also a mediocre poet and critic. Proud and quarrelsome, he was referred to variously as "Bajazet" and "King John." Lord John Vaughan, who later became Earl of Carbery, was an able but undistinguished gentleman, who was a Court Wit more by virtue of rank and patronage than by achievement in literature. John Wilmot, Earl of Rochester, had the newest title, the handsomest face, and the greatest poetic gift of all the noble Wits. He was dissipated, but not vicious, and his reputation as a frantic rake and libertine is largely undeserved.*

Among the gentry, Sir Charles Sedley deserves first place. A man of wealth and good family, he was a painstaking poet and playwright, and some of his work has considerable merit. Because of his slight stature, he was affectionately known as "Little Sid" to his circle of friends. Sir Carr Scroope is sometimes confused with Sedley be-

---

* Some confusion because of the changes in titles of these noble poets is unavoidable. Buckhurst was known by that title during his younger days. For about three years he signed his name "Middlesex." In 1677, he became "Dorset." Mulgrave became, in 1694, Marquis of Normanby and, in 1703, Duke of Buckinghamshire, and is sometimes confused with Villiers, Duke of Buckingham. Vaughan did not become Earl of Carbery until 1685.

cause of their common initials, "Sir C. S." Scroope was a squint-eyed, conceited versifier; although he had some small ability he had the misfortune to quarrel with Rochester, and suffered thereafter under a torrent of abuse. Sir George Etherege, lazy, good-humored and convivial, was known as "gentle George." He has an excellent claim to the title of originator of the Restoration comedy of manners. "Brawny" William Wycherley, the best comic dramatist of the age, was known for two generations as "The Plain Dealer," after the title of his most famous play. He drifted quietly through an unhappy life, hardly aware of his greatness.

The lesser Court Wits (gentlemen, but with little pretense to literary fame) were Henry Savile, a fat, red-faced diplomat, one of the most eloquent letter writers of his generation; Fleetwood Shepherd (knighted toward the end of the century), a ribald wit and farceur; Henry Bulkeley, known for his critical discernment; Henry Killigrew, a distinguished liar; and Henry Guy, financier and politician. These last four are mentioned not because of their literary productions (most of which are lost or unidentifiable), but because as members of the circle of Court Wits, they shared in influencing literary taste.*

From the Wits' own poems and letters we get the impression of a kind of loose fraternity of men of kindred tastes. Rochester wrote a verse poem to Mulgrave "Upon Their Mutual Poems." (Later they became bitter enemies.) In the 1680's, exiled Etherege in a letter to Buckingham spoke sadly of losing the company of his Grace, and of his other friends, Sir Charles Sedley and the Earl of Dorset.[5] The letters of Henry Savile refer in intimate terms to such Wits as Bulkeley, Etherege, Dorset, Guy,

---

* There were others who were more loosely attached to the group; for example, Charles, Lord Middleton, Sidney Godolphin, Baptist May, Francis Newport, and the poets Samuel Butler and Edmund Waller. Because of the accidents of friendship, age, or interest, they never became permanent members of the coterie.

Killigrew, Shepherd and Vaughan. And Rochester, in his "Allusion to Horace," mentions with approval Etherege, Wycherley, Buckhurst, Sedley, Shepherd and Buckingham, among other men of poetic skill and good taste.

Contemporary and later observers also bore witness to the existence of the fraternity. For example, Marvell referred to the Wits as "the merry gang," which had Buckingham, Rochester, and Middlesex as its leaders.[6] Anthony à Wood listed Killigrew, Savile, Guy, Baptist May, Lord Buckhurst, and the Earls of Rochester and Mulgrave as those courtiers who were most intimate with the King.[7] In the next century, John Dennis asserted that the best critics at the Restoration Court were the Duke of Buckingham, the Earls of Dorset, Mulgrave, and Rochester, Sir John Denham, and Messrs. Bulkeley, Savile, and Waller.[8] The Wits' circle was well-known.

The fraternity flourished from about 1665 to 1680. In 1665, the young Earl of Rochester joined the group and quickly became its leader in literature and deviltry. At that time the Wits consisted of the Duke of Buckingham (at thirty-seven, the oldest), Sir Charles Sedley (aged twenty-six), Charles, Lord Buckhurst (aged twenty-two), and the recently acquired George Etherege (aged thirty), who had made a great hit the year before with his first play. To this quintet was added, within the next few years, youthful John Sheffield, Earl of Mulgrave, Henry Savile, Sir Carr Scroope, and (about 1671) William Wycherley. The lesser members of the circle, John, Lord Vaughan, Henry Killigrew, Henry Guy, Henry Bulkeley, and Fleetwood Shepherd, also drifted into the group during the years 1665 to 1670.

By the end of 1680 the Wits had disintegrated as a group. Rochester and Scroope were dead; Sedley had retired to domestic life in the country; Buckingham, in political disgrace, was allied with the anti-Court party; Mulgrave had quarreled with his associates and turned to war and politics; Etherege and Wycherley wrote no more plays. But if the Wits' dance in the sun was ephemeral, their music lingered on. Their influence on English letters lasted well into the Augustan age. Their reputations as libertines have lasted to the present. But they were no more than products of their age, talented men, no doubt, but typical in their ways of living, working, playing, and thinking.

I

THE Court Wits were all gentlemen, and some of them had large incomes derived from landed properties. Buckingham, Mulgrave, Sedley, Vaughan, and Buckhurst were wealthy, although before his death Buckingham had dissipated one of the largest properties in England. Rochester and Etherege inherited little, but both married heiresses and got along comfortably. In addition, Buckingham, Mulgrave, Rochester, Buckhurst and Vaughan all drew considerable sums from the Treasury as Court appointees. Savile, an impecunious younger brother, drew a good living from his Court and diplomatic posts, and scheming Henry Guy became very wealthy from his. Killigrew and Bulkeley also held minor Court posts, and enjoyed the financial favor of the King. Shepherd lived on the bounty of the Earl of Dorset, for whom he acted as a kind of superior steward. Only Wycherley, whose income for the greater part of his life depended on the whims of his father, was ever seriously in need. He spent four years in prison for a debt of five hundred pounds.

In spite of the conventional gentlemanly horror of marriage, all but four of the Wits submitted to matrimony—some of them more than once. The fact that they usually married ladies with sizeable dowries should not be held against them; it was the custom of the century. Marriage for love only was as uncommon in rural England as it was in the sophisticated circles of the Court.[9] The large-hearted

King Charles II. About 1664
By Michael Wright. Courtesy of the National Portrait Gallery

GEORGE VILLERS DUKE OF BUCKINGHAM.

George Villiers, Duke of Buckingham. About 1679
By Sir Peter Lely. Courtesy of the National Portrait Gallery

Wits found it quite within their powers to love their wives as well as their mistresses.

Buckingham married Mary Fairfax, daughter of the Parliamentary general, and thereby saved his estates from the Committee of Sequestration. Sedley married Katherine Savage, daughter of John, Earl Rivers. His sister-in-law, Mary, became the wife of Henry Killigrew. Rochester captured Elizabeth Malet, who had an income (according to Pepys) of £2500 a year. Etherege's circumstances are obscure, but it is thought that he bought a knighthood in order to get a rich widow as his wife. Dorset married in succession two wealthy ladies of noble birth, and finally a commoner, his housekeeper. Vaughan married twice; his second wife was Anne Savile, Henry's niece. Mulgrave collected the relicts of earls. His first wife was Ursula, widow of the Earl of Conway; his second was Katherine, widow of the Earl of Gainsborough; his third was Catherine, illegitimate daughter of James II and Katherine Sedley, and divorced wife of the Earl of Anglesey. Henry Bulkeley married "Lady" Sophia Stewart, younger sister of the Duchess of Richmond and Lennox. Wycherley had an unhappy year and a half as the husband of Laetitia, widow of the Earl of Drogheda. On his deathbed, to spite his heirs, the famous dramatist took as his second wife a woman of low degree.

Some of the Wits had country houses, where they spent the hot months of summer. When they were in town they had houses or lodgings in fashionable Drury Lane, Covent Garden, Lincoln's Inn Fields, at Charing Cross, or in King Street, conveniently near Whitehall. The Palace was the center of genteel life. There those Wits who held Court appointments had rooms, and were periodically on duty in the bedchambers of the King, or at near-by St. James's Palace, in attendance on the Duke of York. The great galleries of Whitehall were places of daily resort for gallants, politicians, men of business, and ladies of pleasure. At times the Wits were invited to the King's own chambers for convivial gatherings, or they met His Majesty at midnight supper parties in the apartments of the royal mistresses: Barbara Palmer, Duchess of Cleveland, Louise Keroualle, Duchess of Portsmouth, or "pretty, witty" Nell Gwyn.

Other favorite places of resort were the taverns and ordinaries which abounded within a short distance of the palace. The popular houses were Locket's Ordinary at Charing Cross, The Rose in Russell Street (otherwise known as Long's from the name of its proprietor), the Dog and Partridge in Fleet Street, the Cock Tavern in Bow Street (kept by the famous Oxford Kate), and Will's Coffee-house. At these places the Wits dined, drank, gambled, talked, and touseled the barmaids. Occasionally the lesser wits of the town—the professionals, Dryden, Shadwell, Crowne, and Settle, and the minor literary gentry, Wolseley, Duke, Higgons, Ayloffe, and their sort—were permitted to enjoy the conversation of their betters.

In the afternoons, the Wits were often to be found at either of the two playhouses, the King's House in Drury Lane or the Duke's Theatre in Lincoln's Inn Fields. For outdoor amusements, they rode or drove in Hyde Park, walked in the Mall, or strolled with the King by Rosamund's Pond in St. James's Park. The Wits with athletic inclinations played bowls or tennis. At night, there was almost always music, dancing, or cards at Whitehall, heavy gambling at the Groom Porter's, heavy drinking at a tavern, or a light affair of the heart to be carried to its consummation. There was no lack of amusements in London. When all else failed, there was always the frail sisterhood of Whetstone Park, Lewkenor's Lane, or Dog-and-Bitch Yard. Regrettably, this last amusement often led the disillusioned Wits to the sweating-tubs and mercury treatments of Leather Lane.

However, the Wits' lives were not all gaiety, gambling, drink, and love. Some of the Wits were members of Parliament (by right of peerage or election), and now and then they took their legislative duties seriously. Buckingham and Mulgrave were politically ambitious, and they worked hard at cabals and committees. Sedley and Savile were sometimes sent on minor diplomatic missions, in which they usually managed to combine business with pleasure. Dorset and Rochester found their duties as Gentlemen of the Bedchamber to the King tedious, if not onerous. Vaughan spent over three years (December, 1674, to March, 1678) as Governor of Jamaica. Etherege and Wycherley were elegant idlers. But as the Wits grew older they took their responsibilities more seriously. In the post of envoy to France from 1679 to 1683, Savile performed able diplomatic service. From 1685 to 1689 Etherege served faithfully as English observer at the Diet of the Empire. Dorset and Mulgrave held important offices as Lord Chamberlains and Privy Councillors in the reigns of James II, William, and Anne. Most of the Wits were intelligent fellows, and able enough, once they had outgrown the follies and idleness of youth.

The Wits were the leaders of fashion; like Etherege's Dorimant they loved to be well-dressed, and they spent considerable sums to decorate their persons. Sometimes they did so for politic reasons, as when Henry Savile, in France, spent two hundred pistoles (about $800) to appear to advantage at a state wedding.[10] More often, their extravagances were to please themselves. According to a tailor's bill which has survived (presumably unpaid), the Earl of Rochester, in something over three years, spent £232, 18s, 4½d "for clothes, made for his lordships person, and also for his servants costume."[11] This, of course, would not include the cost of such items as boots (30s), sword and belt (20s to 40s), silk stockings (15s), two or three periwigs (40s to £10 each), a dressing gown (35s), gloves (2s to 10s), and underwear, cravats, hats, lace bands, handkerchiefs, perfumes and jewels. A Wit's garments were made of fine wool or silk, beribboned, laced, and embroidered with gold and silver at incredible cost.*

To be in the mode, a Wit kept servants (labor was very cheap), a coach (£50 to £60), four to six coach horses (at not less than £30 apiece), one or more riding horses (about £50), and a mistress (Buckhurst gave Nell Gwyn £100 a year). In addition, a gentleman of fashion made expensive presents to friends of both sexes or to the King, had his portrait painted often (£25 to £60), sat in the pit or an upper box at the theatre (2s, 6d, to 4s), and bought oranges from the orange women at 3d apiece. Dinner at an ordinary was rarely less than a shilling. Wine cost approximately 2s a quart, and an evening's drinking at a tavern, with brimmers going around, must have been expensive. It is hardly to be wondered that the country members of Parliament, in 1667, were incensed at the sneering statement of Bab May, Keeper of the King's Privy Purse, that "£300 a year is enough for any country gentleman."[12]

II

THE Wits were the leaders of fashion in thought as well as in dress. According to the standards of their class, most of them were well-educated. Their formal education was usually brief, although several held degrees from Oxford. Buckingham's residence at Cambridge had been interrupted by the Civil War. Dorset had a year at Westminster School, followed by two years of foreign travel with a tutor. Sedley was a student at Wadham College, Oxford, for a year, but he took no degree. Rochester and Scroope were also Wadhamites, and each received his M.A., Rochester at fourteen (after a year and a half in residence), Scroope at eighteen (after two years and a half

---

* For a rough comparison with modern prices in the United States consider a shilling approximately equivalent to a dollar in purchasing power. A pound, then, would be equivalent to twenty dollars.

as a student). Neither was an infant prodigy. Guy, sometime of Christ Church, had an Oxford M.A. and much
learning in the law, acquired at Gray's Inn and the Inner
Temple. Shepherd, B.A. and M.A. from Oxford, was also
a Gray's Inn student for a time. Vaughan and Savile each
spent brief periods at Christ Church, Oxford. Wycherley,
in his youth a student at Angoumois, France, later spent
a few months at Queen's College, Oxford, and then dallied
at the Inner Temple for years. Bulkeley was a resident at
Cambridge for a short time; he took no degree. Etherege's
slim education appears to have been acquired in France.
Mulgrave, dissatisfied with his tutors, educated himself.

Restoration gentlemen learned their letters and figures
at the knee of a private tutor or the local clergyman, and
rarely went to a grammar school. They began the study of
Latin almost as soon as they could read English, and thereafter their education was largely restricted to what they
could learn from the classic poets, philosophers, and
historians. A few of the gentry learned a little Greek. All
of them, perforce, became intimately acquainted with the
Bible, which influenced their style of writing, if not of
living. At a very early age—twelve to sixteen years—a
scion of the gentry was usually sent to Oxford or Cambridge. In a year or so he left the university, with or without a degree, and went on the foreign tour which completed
his education. With his tutor and his servants, he traveled
in leisurely fashion through France into Italy, perhaps
with a side trip into Spain. He stayed some time in Rome
or Florence, then wandered back to France again, perhaps
by way of Germany. He always ended up in Paris, and
had to be pried loose from that delightful city. Paris was
the center of all pleasures, sensual and intellectual.

At the universities, skill in the reading and writing of
Latin was almost an entrance requirement. The under-
graduate was lectured to on Greek and Latin authors, and
he heard daily the sonorous roll of Latin speech, even in

the dining halls. The traditional curriculum included lectures on logic, on philosophy (Aristotle, Pliny, and Plato), on rhetoric (Cicero and Quintilian), on mathematics (Strabo and Ptolemy), on the Greek classics (Homer, Demosthenes, and Euripides). If a student elected the natural sciences, he studied Aristotle (except, perhaps, at Wadham College, where the "new" science was getting a foothold). If he was interested in medicine, he studied Hippocrates and Galen, and never, by any chance, the human body.[13]

In all probability, most of the Wits took their education lightly. If they were the sons of noblemen they were exempt from many duties and responsibilities, and their degrees were rarely earned. The arduous regimen of sober learning was all very well for the would-be parson or pedagogue, but budding Wits had little taste for elaborate prolusions, theological disputations, and hard study of the crabbed page. However, they brought away from the halls of Oxford and Cambridge something more than a smattering of learning and a brisk competence at the writing of Latin verse. They had lived for a time in the climate of opinion, of sharp contradictions and oppositions of thought, of new philosophies clashing with old. They had been exposed to orthodox theology, to Platonic idealism, to Aristotelian science, to Pyrrhonic skepticism, and to some, at least, of the new experimental science. They came out well on the way toward the easy materialism which most of them eventually affected.[14]

The Wits have been variously labeled cynics, skeptics, libertines, Epicureans, pagans, and atheists. To a certain extent, some of the terms apply, yet none is strictly accurate. They were cynical (as the King, their master, was cynical) because their limited experience demonstrated that no man was honest and no woman chaste. Their credo was that of Congreve's Lady Wishfort, "What's integrity to an opportunity?"[15] and for the society in which they moved, the epigram was true. Yet they put their faith in each other, and agreed that "if there bee a reall good upon earth, 'tis in the name of friend."[16] They were not true skeptics, for they accepted the materialism of Lucretius and Hobbes. They were libertines by instinct (as most young male animals are), but they were libertines by conviction as well, for they saw no ethical values in their world, and no purpose in living save the gratification of their senses. They were Epicureans, not in the philosophical meaning of the term, but only as that title has become confounded with hedonism; they were addicted to the unholy trinity: wine, women, and song. Pagans they were not, for they worshiped no idols and took no joy in Nature. They were atheists only in the eyes of the scandalized clergy, who were prone to use the term to describe any deviation from orthodoxy. Yet they were all members of the Church of England, and gave an easy lip service to its dogmas. Rochester's famous conversion by Dr. Burnet was only from heterodoxy to orthodoxy. Mulgrave's reasons for the King's being a Deist might serve as well for any of the Wits: *epilogue — p 205.*

And this uncommon opinion he owed more to the liveliness of his parts, and carelessness of his temper, than either to reading or much consideration; for his quickness of apprehension at first view could discern through the several cheats of pious pretences; and his natural laziness confirm'd him in an equal mistrust of them all, for fear he should be troubled with examining which Religion was best.[17]

Experimental science, the "new philosophy" of Bacon and Descartes, was rapidly destroying the authoritarianism of the past. The speculative minds of the Restoration turned their energies to the problems of matter and motion, and no longer sought to

Dive into Mysteries, then soaring pierce
The flaming limits of the Universe.[18]

Speculative reason, the dialectic of opinionated philosophers and divines (as one of the Wits saw it), had resulted in "little better in reality than meer Romances, finely contrived and made to cohere well together, mixed with a vast deal of wit and fancy."[19] The Court Wits had no use for such nonsense. On the other hand, they were not particularly interested in science, although the King played at dissecting in his private laboratory, Buckingham and Rochester amused themselves with chemistry, and Lord Vaughan, in his graver days, was elected president of the Royal Society. In their headlong fashion, the young Wits seized upon the findings of science, mixed them recklessly with the materialism of their friend Hobbes, and used the result as a justification of their way of life. As opposed to speculation, they upheld "Right Reason," which was their name for common sense. Their only truth was that which could be proved by the test of the senses; their only good was the action which brought about the satisfaction of the senses. They were downright empiricists.

III

AS the Wits lived to amuse themselves, they wrote for the same purpose. They wrote plays to please themselves and the theatre-loving king; songs to please themselves and some timid Phyllis who needed encouragement; and satires to vent their spleen. They were not interested in the mechanic art of bookmaking, nor (they insisted) in popular fame. Their plays, however, were snapped up by booksellers and published, and some of their songs, satires, and occasional verses appeared in broadsides or in various miscellanies while the authors were still alive. In his old age, Wycherley submitted to the guidance of Pope and published a volume of *Miscellany Poems* (1704). Mulgrave's *Works*, supposedly "published by his Grace in his Lifetime," actually appeared after his death in February,

1721, and it is very doubtful that Mulgrave authorized the publication. Two years later, Pope produced a corrected edition at the request of Mulgrave's widow. The poems and sketches of Buckingham, Dorset, Rochester, and Sedley were assembled and published only after the deaths of those Wits, and not always by honest editors.

The Wits were as gregarious in their writing as they were in their lives; there are numerous indications of collaboration and mutual aid and criticism. Buckingham and Rochester, for example, are supposed to have worked together on "Timon, a Satyr," and "A Session of the Poets." Buckhurst, Sedley, Waller, Godolphin and Sir Edward Filmore collaborated on a translation of Corneille's *Pompey*—one act per man. Buckingham was supposed to have had the assistance of Butler, Clifford and Sprat in the writing of *The Rehearsal*. Sedley was accused by Dryden of larding with wit Shadwell's "hungry *Epsom* prose."[20] Kept in London by his duties, while Dorset, Buckingham, and Shepherd were visiting Rochester at Woodstock, Harry Savile reported on a new libel against the poets, which was much commended by the Town, "and therefore the more probably thought to be composed att Woodstock, especially considering what an assembly either is yett or att least has been there."[21] We get the impression of a group of jovial Wits, sitting about a table and composing collectively over their wine. One Esau might do the actual writing, with several Jacobs to inspire him.

Verses written in privacy were quickly made public. In all probability even love poems were shown about among the authors' friends before being sent to the nymphs for whom they were written. Etherege represents his Sir Fopling Flutter (a fair image of a little, or half, Wit) as producing a song, his "Coup d'Essay in English," for the judgment of his friends Dorimant and Medley. It was a light thing, but "passionate and well turn'd" "after the French way."[22] Satires, too, were passed about from hand

to hand, or sent "by the post" to a coffeehouse or tavern, to
be read aloud by a waiter to the assembled company. Thus
the author, secure in his anonymity, could learn the
opinions of the critics without venturing his reputation.[23]
Songs and satires so publicized were often copied, fell
into the hands of unscrupulous booksellers, and were
printed, anonymously and without authorization. Harry
Savile's "Advice to a Painter to Draw the Duke By," once
"went about" from hand to hand, and some years later was
printed without Savile's permission. His only concern was
that the satire was "very falsely printed."[24]

Many coffeehouse habitués kept commonplace books,
into which they copied those songs, satires, and epigrams
which pleased them. Sometimes they changed a phrase or
so, or added an impromptu couplet or quatrain; consequently many Restoration poems have as many variant
readings as there are sources. Because of the careless affectation of anonymity, the same copy of verses was often
attributed to two or more poets, and when the transcriber
was in doubt, the credit was given to that most prolific of
writers, "Anon."

It was usually from commonplace books, plus other
casual manuscript copies (rarely the originals), that the
booksellers made up their editions of the Wits' poems.
Various advertisements would beg gentlemen who owned
"valuable Pieces" "in print or manuscript" to send them in
to the publisher, who promised to take pains "to have them
correctly printed."[25] In the hands of a careless or dis-
honest publisher, the results of such undiscriminating
collection could be chaotic. An extreme example is the 1680
edition of Rochester's poems, avowedly published at Antwerp, and lacking any bookseller's name. The volume contains sixty-one poems, all attributed to Rochester. Of these,
fifteen were certainly written by other poets: three by
Aphra Behn, two by Alexander Radcliffe, two by Etherege,
three by Buckhurst, two by Scroope, and three by Oldham.

At least two more are almost certainly not by Rochester, and for the rest we must take the word of the nameless publisher.[26]

Even reputable booksellers make mistakes. Samuel Briscoe, in his foreword to Buckingham's *Miscellaneous Works* (1704), boasted of his care in printing his Grace's "Miscellaneous Tracts" from the genuine originals "which were luckily procured from one of his intimate Domesticks." He had taken care, also, to correct false attributions:

I might add, that several Copies of Verses in this Edition are now restored to their proper Authors, which were attributed before to Persons, to whom they [n]ever belong'd; the Transcribers of the last Age, as well as those of the former, either following common Report, which is often mistaken, or else setting any plausible Names before their Copies (no matter with what justice this was done) provided that it would but promote the value of their manuscript.

However, in spite of Briscoe's honest concern, he attributed to Buckingham two poems which were either written by Rochester alone or by the two friends in collaboration, and one that was certainly written by Sir Carr Scroope.[27]

It follows that no modern editor can prepare an edition of any of the major Wits with even fair assurance that he has not made several wrong attributions, or that he has recovered all the pieces extant.* With the lesser Wits, the

* Thus John Hayward's *Collected Works of John Wilmot, Earl of Rochester* (1926) is a hodgepodge of poems by Rochester, Aphra Behn, Etherege, Oldham and others. It even contains two poems by Thomas Randolph (first printed in 1638). Mr. Hayward attributes all to Rochester. Sedley's works have been ably edited by V. de Sola Pinto, who found it necessary to include a lengthy appendix of "Works ascribed to Sedley on doubtful authority." Editions of Dorset and of Etherege are now being prepared by Brice Harris and H. F. B. Brett-Smith, respectively. Montague Summers had no particular problems of ascription to deal with in editing Wycherley. There are no modern editions of either Buckingham or Mulgrave.

task of identification and editing is nearly impossible. For example, Anthony Wood said of Sir Carr Scroope, "And as divers satyrical copies of verses were made on him by other persons, so he hath divers made by himself on them, which to this day go from hand to hand."[28] And Aphra Behn wrote with admiration of the "little chance things [songs] of Sir Carr Scroope," as if they were numerous.[29] Yet the only remnants of Sir Carr's work that can be positively identified are two lyrics, one prologue, one long satire, one epigram, two translations from Ovid, and one from Montemayor's *Diana*. Scroope is not an unusual example. Fleetwood Shepherd was described as a man of "fluent Stile and coherent Thought,"[30] yet he has left, under his name, only five short satires and one prose burlesque, "The Calendar Reformed," in which various saints are joyfully exposed as frauds.[31] Lord Vaughan left only two evidences of his skill, a short satire on Edward Howard[32] and a commendatory poem prefixed to Dryden's *Conquest of Granada*. Henry Bulkeley may have been (as some said) one of the best critics of the Court, but the only product of his pen is a solitary letter to Rochester—witty, but not critical.[33] Henry Guy's claim to consideration rests upon a nonextant "Pastoral" which once gained him some fame.[34] Killigrew had a talent for description, and his letters were highly valued by Savile, but none has survived.[35] We must take the literary skills of the lesser Wits on trust.

In addition to their own literary productions, the Wits are important in the history of letters as patrons of professional poets and playwrights. In the seventeenth century, writers lived much better by subsidies than by the sale of their wares. Patronage took many forms: gifts of cash, pensions, or clerical livings, appointments to posts under the government, or recommendations to important officials or prospective benefactors.

With few exceptions, Restoration plays were dedicated to members of the royal family (including the royal

mistresses) or to munificent noblemen, who were supposed
to acknowledge the compliment with a gift of five or ten
guineas. Among noble patrons, the Wits are well represented. To choose only from the major dramatists of the
period: Dryden dedicated *Marriage-à-la-Mode* to Rochester, *The Assignation* to Sedley, *Aurenge-Zebe* to Mulgrave, and *Limberham* to Lord Vaughan. Otway dedicated
Alcibiades and *Friendship in Fashion* to Dorset, and *Titus
and Berenice* to Rochester. Crowne dedicated his *History
of Charles the Eighth* to Rochester, the *Country Wit* to
Dorset, and *The Married Beau* to Mulgrave. Lee dedicated
The Tragedy of Nero to Rochester, *The Rival Queens* to
Mulgrave, and *Mithridates*, *Lucius Junius Brutus*, and
The Princess of Cleve to Dorset. Shadwell likewise dedi-
cated three plays to Dorset: *The Miser*, *The Squire of
Alsatia*, and *Bury Fair*. To Buckingham he dedicated
Timon of Athens, and to Sedley *A True Widow*. The qual-
ity of all such dedications may be illustrated by a sentence
from Dryden's fulsome address to Rochester:

. . . the best comic writers of our age, will join with me to acknowledge, that they have copied the gallantries of courts, the delicacy
of expression, and the decencies of behaviour, from your lordship.

In addition, the Wits patronized (and influenced)
numerous other dramatists, poets, critics, and essayists.
The Maecenas of the Restoration was the Earl of Dorset.
For forty years he read manuscripts, gave advice and
money, subscribed to expensive books, and promoted and
encouraged every kind and quality of literary effort. At his
two country houses, Copt Hall and Knole, needy men of
letters could always find bed and board for any period
from a day to a month, and the more worthy were likely
to find bank notes under their plates at dinner. Butler,
Dryden, Lee, Prior, Tom Brown, and D'Urfey had many
reasons to be grateful to their noble patron. Nahum Tate,
Robert Gould, John Dennis, Sir Francis Fane, Thomas

Rymer, Peter Motteux, and William Congreve were among the host of men of letters who in eulogistic dedications and prefaces acknowledged their various debts to the Earl of Dorset. In the swelling chorus of flattery, Dorset was "the Favorite of Mankind," "the Noble Patron of Wit and Poetry," "the most correct and Judicious writer, the truest Judge, and the most disinterested Patron," "whose judgment never Errs." "Your single Suffrage," wrote Henry Higden (a person of no importance), "weighs more with me, and the thinking part of Mankind, than the repeated acclamations of a numerous assembly." Even poetasters must eat.[36]

Taken as a group, the Wits formed a circle of poets and patrons which was small but very important in the development of Restoration literature. None of them was prolific as a writer, yet together they were responsible for the writing or rewriting of sixteen plays, more than five hundred songs, satires, prologues, and other occasional poems, and more than three hundred essays, letters, and scattered prose pieces, besides, no doubt, many more fugitive compositions now lost or unidentified. Furthermore, the courtiers were not only wits themselves, but the leaders of wit in their generation. Their taste in art and poetry became that of the cultured coteries which hung upon the fringes of Whitehall and played the sedulous ape to their social betters. The great body of the English people hardly knew that the Wits existed, except as some of their more scandalous exploits were reported with lively exaggeration. To Puritans and to godly people in general, they were truly "the sons of Belial, flown with insolence and wine." About them has grown up a considerable body of lurid tradition, nourished by the gossip mongers of the eighteenth century, and by the errors and credulities of modern biographers. Their private lives must be scanned to see how much of the noise of riot in the streets of Sodom was real and how much was the clack of scandalous tongues.

The Wits in Private Life

JOHN DRYDEN liked to think of himself as a member of the Court Wits in full standing. In 1673, when he dedicated *The Assignation* to Sir Charles Sedley, he wrote,

I have often laughed at the ignorant and ridiculous descriptions which some pedants have given of the wits, as they are pleased to call them; which are a generation of men as unknown to them, as the people of Tartary, or the Terra Australis, are to us. And therefore, as we draw giants and anthropophagi in those vacancies of our maps, where we have not travelled to discover better; so those wretches paint lewdness, atheism, folly, ill-reasoning, and all manner of extravagancies amongst us, for want of understanding what we are.[1]

In spite of Dryden's stricture, it must be admitted that the Court Wits, at least in their younger days, were guilty of numerous follies and extravagancies. They all wore swords and occasionally used them. They kept mistresses—ladies of fashion, actresses, and miscellaneous willing wenches. Occasionally they drank too much, scoured the town, broke windows, and fought with the watch. They lived in a Godless world and sought their pleasure where it was to be found, certain of being able to "jump the life to come." Nor were they fearful of "judgment here"; their master, the King, was indulgent to their follies and sure to remit their fines.

Because historians and biographers have made so much of the Wits' exploits in taverns and boudoirs, we think of them today as rakes rather than as men of letters. Therefore we must first deal with them as rakes in order to clear away some of the wild growth of misconception which hides their leaves of verse. Admitting that they were a pretty bad lot, just how bad were they? Of which sins were they guilty?

According to the standards of the Restoration court, the Wits were no more dissipated than other courtiers, and less so than some. Had they not been rakes, and had they not kept mistresses, they would have been conspicuous in a raking, keeping age.* Because they were both libertines and poets, the gaudy light of publicity (then and now) has thrown their faults into high relief. Their more sober contemporaries were shocked by their wicked doings, but they were shocked also by the even more vicious actions of many non-literary debauchees, men like Jermyn, May, Bruncker, Blood, the Duke of Monmouth, and the half-mad Earl of Pembroke—men who, with almost complete immunity, committed assault, theft, rape, or even murder. By comparison with such scoundrels, the Court Wits seem little more than gay dogs with an itch for trouble. Nevertheless, because the Wits were poets, later generations have edited their works, written their biographies, and gloated over their escapades. Isolated from the referential frame of Restoration morals, the peccadilloes of the Wits have been magnified into crimes, and their sins have been outlined in scarlet. Moreover, they have been given full credit for sins which they never committed.

The seventeenth century, like most centuries, was quick to believe evil of people in high places. Because the Wits were courtiers, noblemen, and members of Parliament, their doings were news, and many a letter and diary was spiced with items about them. Fact and rumor were set down without distinction. "Mulgrave and Rochester went away on Monday in order to fight and no news of either of

* Francis North, Lord Guildford, a sober lawyer, was seriously advised to "keep a whore," because "he was ill looked upon (at Court) for want of doing so . . ." (Roger North, *Lives of the Norths*, London, 1826, II, 164).

John Sheffield, Earl of Mulgrave. About 1680
By Sir Godfrey Kneller. Courtesy of the National Portrait Gallery

them since."[2] "Fleetwood Sheppard was either hanged or broke upon the wheel at Parys for some roguery that he had committed."[3] "Buckingham runs out of all with the Lady Shrewsbury, by whom he believes he had a son."[4] "The pleasant story of H. Killigrew is, that he opiated the mother and daughter, and then ravished the daughter, for which he was condemned to the gallows, but by the great mediation of the Queen Mother and Madame he is only banished [from France]."[5] "Sheapherd . . . was runn with a sword under the eye, endeavouring to part Buckly and Etheridge squabbling in a taverne."[6] "Savel being very drunk, fel so fowly on Ld:·Molgrave that Kg: commanded Savel to be gonne out of his presence. However, the next day Mollgrave sent him a challenge by Ld: Middleton; Rochester was 2d to the other side. There was noe harm done."[7]

These are typical of the hundreds of items about the Wits to be found in contemporary records. Since most news stories came to recorders like Pepys, Evelyn, Aubrey, Wood, and Muddiman only at second hand, it was inevitable that fiction should be mingled with fact. Sometimes the recorders themselves garbled the stories, or confused names. Not infrequently, they were guilty of padding their yarns with invented details, or, lacking complete information, they made wild guesses, and attributed an episode to the wrong parties. The Wits had very bad reputations; if a treasonable lampoon was written, a watchman beaten up, or a maid of honor seduced, a Wit was always blamed. In June, 1677, for example, while Rochester and Lord Lumley were dining at a cook shop in the Mall, a French cook belonging to the place was stabbed in a kitchen brawl. All next day the good nature of the town reported that Rochester was the stabber. Rochester begged his friend Savile to write the truth to Lord Halifax in the country, saying that if the report "once get as far as York, the truth will not be believed under two or three years."[8]

If the accounts of the Wits' contemporaries are question-
able, those of following generations are even more so. The
venal publishers and hackwriters of the early eighteenth
century were responsible for dozens of ugly stories, most
of them fashioned from whole cloth. The number and the
scurrility of such fables were directly proportional to the
rank and to the literary reputation of the dead Wit;
Rochester, an earl and a much reprinted poet, was a popular
subject for fictional biography. Unfortunately, modern
scholars have all too often accepted as facts the inventions
of plausible liars. The Wits were wicked enough, in all
conscience; they needed no gossip or invention to embellish
their reputations as brawlers, wenchers, and troublemakers.

I

LIKE almost all of their class, the Wits were belligerent
men, given to explosions of temper, to duels fought
according to the code of the day, and to sudden brawls in
streets and taverns. Every gentleman wore a sword and
was touchy about his "honor." The King did his best to
stamp out the practice of dueling, with little success. Gentry
and nobility engaged in pitched battles almost daily, often
in the sacrosanct purlieus of Whitehall itself. In such
fights, the Wits had their proportionate share.

Only two of the duels in which Wits were involved
resulted in fatalities. In 1668, while Henry Bulkeley was
still an ensign in the King's Guards in Ireland, he fought
with and killed one Stephen Radford. Found guilty of
manslaughter, Bulkeley was condemned to be burned in the
hand. However, because of the intercession of friends in
high places, even that comparatively mild sentence was
never executed.[9] Bulkeley appears to have been a pug-
nacious young rake. Four years before the fatal duel with
Radford, he had been dangerously wounded while acting
as second to a superior officer.[10] After his return to England,

he continued to get into broils. In July, 1673, Bulkeley, Lord Buckhurst, and Colonel Strode fought a skirmish with three antagonists in the street before the King's Theatre. Bulkeley was wounded in the neck, Buckhurst in the body, and Strode in the hand and ear.[11] In October, 1674, Bulkeley was again wounded, this time while he was acting as second to Lord Mulgrave.[12] In February, 1675, he was sent to the Tower for daring to challenge the Earl of Ossory. In December, 1677, he challenged Ossory again and fought with him—"The old quarrel about Mr. B. wiffe" whispered the town gossips—but no harm was done to either contestant.[13] Two weeks later he engaged in a brawl with Etherege in a tavern, presumably only a falling-out between friends.[14] Thereafter, except for one unimportant skirmish in 1691, Bulkeley appears to have lived in peace.[15]

The only other battle in which a Wit killed his opponent was the famous duel in 1668 between Buckingham and the Earl of Shrewsbury, the outcome of Buckingham's liaison with the Countess of Shrewsbury. This, oddly enough, seems to have been the only duel in which Buckingham ever engaged. He was constantly quarreling with men of quality and was often challenged, but something always happened to prevent the actual duel. Usually the King had notice in advance and sent the challenger to the Tower, or else he dispatched a file of musketeers to the appointed meeting place to seize both belligerents. It became almost a custom for men who dared to challenge Buckingham to wind up in the Tower (sometimes the Duke was sent there too). There were murmured charges of cowardice; however, Buckingham had quite sufficiently demonstrated his courage years earlier, in the wars between Roundhead and Cavalier. He had no love for casual encounters, and it is quite possible that he avoided them by seeing to it that His Majesty received notice in time.[16]

The other duelists among the Wits were Henry Killi-

grew and the Earl of Mulgrave. Killigrew fought a duel
at Heidelberg in 1660; no casualties.[17] Thirty-three years
later he fought with "one Mr. Chamberlain"; again no
casualties.[18] Killigrew was a troublesome rogue, and often
in hot water, but he was no great fighter.

Haughty Mulgrave was as quarrelsome as he was
proud. However, contemporary stories of his brushes with
Rochester and Savile (neither of whom was a warrior)
must not be taken too seriously.[19] One of his more dangerous escapades involves a sequence of events which began in
September, 1674. In that month he wooed and won Mall
Kirke, one of her Royal Highness's Maids of Honor, who
seems to have been mistress to both the Duke of York
and the Duke of Monmouth at the time. Young Monmouth, warned of his new rival, set a guard about the
lady's lodgings in Whitehall, caught Mulgrave as he was
making a guilty exit and had him sent to spend a night in
the guardhouse like any common miscreant. Mulgrave could
not challenge the King's son, of course, even though he
wore the bar sinister; but it was easy to fasten the quarrel
upon one of Monmouth's adherents. The gossip who first
spread the story of the scandal added in the same breath,
"Lord Moulgrave and Mr. Felton have fought; Lord
Middleton and Mr. Buckley the Seconds slightly wounded."[20]

Nine months later the gossips had another tidbit. Mrs.
Mary Kirke "had ye ill fortune to become a mother of a
brave boy," which, however, "died within 3 or 4 houres."
It was "not said yet to wt father it belongs."[21] One could
choose, of course, between two dukes and an earl.

But Mall had a brother who was determined that someone should pay for her dishonor. Captain Percy Kirke (who
was to become infamous in 1685 as the commander of
"Kirke's Lambs") had recently distinguished himself by
taking an heiress from her friends by force. With the lady
under his arm, he had "fought it through the streets to the

waterside and lodged her in Whitehall" as his mistress. Apparently the heiress was willing.[22]

On July 4, 1675, this moral gentleman challenged Mulgrave "for haveing debauch'd and abus'd his sister." In spite of the fact that "ye Earle purg'd himself before hand of any injury he had done of yt nature, & though shee herself does not accuse him either of getting ye child or any other act that we heare of," Mulgrave had to go through with the duel. The earl had as his aid Lord Middleton, "his old accustomed second." Kirke was seconded by Captain Charles Godfrey. Mulgrave was severely wounded.[23] On July 8, Harry Savile wrote drily, "My Lord Mulgrave yet keeps his chamber of his wounds, and Mrs. Kirke persists to protest that she does not know whether he be man or woman."[24] Mulgrave recovered, of course; his narrow escape left but small impression on his boundless conceit. Fifty years later, when he was writing his memoirs, he moralized on the affair in speaking of the intimacy between the Duke of York and his nephew, Monmouth. The bond between the two dukes had been very strong, wrote Mulgrave, "yet a little inconstancy in one of their Mistresses, tho' in favour of a third person, was the accidental cause of such a division between them, as never ceas'd till it cost one of them the hazard of his Crown, and the other that of his life on a Scaffold."[25] Mulgrave was merely the third person.

The affairs in which other Wits were involved were all abortive, stopped by higher authority, or by the combatant's natural timidity. For example, Dorset, a peaceable man, was once challenged by the maniacal Earl of Pembroke. The House of Lords had word (perhaps Dorset, quite sensibly, told); the House summoned the two nobles, confined them for a brief period to their respective dwellings, and enforced a peace.[26] The gossips had Rochester mixed up in duels at least three times in his short life, but none of them ever came off, and one—when Rochester was too sick to fight—gave his opponent, Mulgrave, a chance to boast of an empty victory.[27] Harry Savile was too fat to fight, but not to run. At a country houseparty, he made a midnight foray into the bedchamber of Lady Northumberland, an heiress whom he hoped to marry. She was so unappreciative as to scream and rouse the household. Savile fled to London, pursued by the lady's kinsmen, with swords drawn and challenges ready. Again the King had notice and prevented the duel. But Savile was taking no chances; he crossed over into France and left no forwarding address.[28]

There were other Wits who had no love for dangerous weapons. Etherege's mild scuffle with Bulkeley seems to have been his only essay with the sword. Guy, Scroope, Sedley, Shepherd, and Wycherley, it appears, were never challenged to the field of honor. Perhaps they were more circumspect than their colleagues; perhaps they had less courage.

I I

HAD all the relatives of approachable females been as bloody-minded as Captain Kirke, few of the Wits would have survived their youthful years. They were an amorous lot, and their frail ladies were not infrequently of high rank and good families. The King himself set the example of promiscuity, and the Wits did their best to better his instructions.

Marriage was no check to their libertine ways. According to custom, infidelity in a husband was to be expected, and the perfect wife was one who endured with patience. The Marquis of Halifax, while deploring the double standard, advised the betrayed wife to suffer her husband's faults in silence. To his daughter he wrote,

Remember That next to the danger of committing the Fault yourself, the greatest is that of seeing it in your husband. Do not seem to look or hear that way: If he is a Man of Sense, he will reclaim himself; the Folly of it, is of itself sufficient to cure him: if he is not so, he will be provok'd, but not reform'd.[29]

The Countess of Rochester and the Duchess of Buckingham are good examples of such long-suffering wives, and there is evidence that the Duchess not only endured her husband's waywardness but even remained friendly with his acknowledged mistress, the Countess of Shrewsbury.[30] Some wives were less patient (the virago Dame Etherege,[31] for example, and Wycherley's jealous spouse, the Countess Drogheda),[32] and some acquired scandalous reputations for their own reputed misdeeds. The first Countess of Dorset (Mary Bagot) was certainly an indiscreet woman, if not a sinner,[33] and "Lady" Sophia Bulkeley was notorious for her affairs.[34] With such complaisant or incontinent mates, there was little domestic pressure to keep the Wits virtuous.

The beauties of the Court of Charles II—actresses, Maids of Honor, heiresses, and courtesans—in accordance with the mode, cultivated plump bosoms and languorous airs, and had themselves painted in loose robes. Nudes were not in vogue, but Sir Peter Lely was once commissioned to paint Nell Gwyn naked, and, while the work was in progress, the King himself came to the studio to look on beauty bare.[35] Lely was very successful in depicting provocative flesh, but his greatest achievement with the Restoration beauties was in catching their drowsy, seductive glances. As Pope wrote,

> Lely on animated canvas stole
> The sleepy eye, that spoke the melting soul.

These deliquescent charmers were ever ready to meet a handsome Wit at least halfway; some of them were as libertine as their companions in sin, and at least one, the raffish Duchess of Cleveland, was an insatiable cyprian.[36] Any attempt to sort out the tangled threads of Court intrigue is complicated by the usual confusion of fact and fiction. Let a Wit be attentive to an actress or write her a paper of verses, and—presto!—the busybodies had her with child by him. The King could acknowledge his mistresses and his illegitimate offspring publicly; Samuel Pepys recorded his own amorous affairs in shorthand; the Court Wits wrote of their conquests with gentlemanly caution and rarely mentioned names.

According to numerous romancers, Rochester was the Casanova of the Restoration. No doubt he made a number of conquests (he had the face of an angel, and very winning ways), but he has been credited with amazing incontinence. We are told that he kept several mistresses in play at the same time, that he was a frequent patron of various brothels, and that once, at least, he was guilty of rape. The stories may all be true, but there is a remarkable lack of circumstantial support for most of them. We can be certain only that Rochester was intimate with Elizabeth Barry, the actress, by whom he had a daughter. Other probable mistresses were two famous demi-mondaines, Jane Roberts and Nell Gwyn.[37]

The volatile Duke of Buckingham had a reputation as a lover second only to Rochester's, although he appears to have been faithful to one mistress, the Countess of Shrewsbury, for about nine consecutive years. By her he had a son who died in infancy.[38] While it is possible that he was fairly consistent in his marital infidelity, his other mistresses remain anonymous. It is significant, not only of Buckingham's reputation but also of the charity of the times, that whenever he was absent from public view for a few days, it was noised abroad that he "had been with his wenches."[39]

The Earl of Dorset had low tastes. His known mistresses include such undistinguished women as Doll Chamberlain, a shopkeeper in the New Exchange, and the otherwise unidentified Laetitia Child and Phillipa Waldegrave; by the last he had a daughter and perhaps a son. His claim to fame in the history of Restoration intrigue rests on the fact that he succeeded the actor Charles Hart in the affections of Nell Gwyn, becoming her "Charles the Second," and in turn passed her on to the King—Nell's "Charles the Third."[40]

The Earl of Mulgrave boasted of being "learn'd in those ill arts that cheat the fair." However, one of his anonymous biographers informs us smugly that "none of his mistresses could ever prevail upon him to marry foolishly, or ever gained too great an ascendancy over him"— a matter much more important than morality. Upon his numerous wenches, we are told, he begot "many natural children, which he had and own'd before his third Marriage"—as a gentleman should.[41] At the Restoration Court, his only known mistress was Mall Kirke. There is, however, good evidence that he was once in the stable of the insatiable Duchess of Cleveland, and he may have been the father of one of her numerous children.[42]

In his graceless youth, Sir Charles Sedley also found safety—if not satiety—in numbers. Among his reputed wenches (said Pepys, who professed to be shocked) was a kinswomen of Archbishop Sheldon.[43] Sir Charles was also rumored to be on intimate terms with two well-known actresses, Mary Knipp and Peg Fryer.[44] His most serious affair came after his insane wife, the former Katherine Savage, had been safely shut up in a nunnery at Ghent. Sir Charles fell in love with Ann Ayscough, daughter of a poverty-stricken Yorkshire gentleman. Divorce and remarriage were legally impossible; nevertheless, in 1672, Sedley went through a form of marriage with Ann, and thereafter lived happily and decently in his bigamous relationship. By Mistress Ayscough, he had one son, named after his father, and known by the surname of Sedley. The antiquaries have recorded their belief that Sir Charles had two other natural children, "daughters named L. and E. Charlot," evidently by still another mistress.[45]

Rochester, Buckingham, Dorset, Mulgrave, and Sedley

were the most famous Wits; because they were men of high rank their amours were publicized by the gossips. It is possible that the untitled Wits, who lacked the attractions of rank and wealth, may have been less promiscuous. We know of their erotic exploits only from their own references, or from the chance remark of a gossip who had nothing more interesting to write about. So, for example (in a letter to Dorset), we have Etherege's obscure allusion to the "draggle-tailed nymphs," whom the two rakes had carried "one bitter, frosty night over the Thames to Lambeth."[46] So (in a letter to Savile) we have Rochester's cryptic comment on Fleetwood Shepherd, who "appears very obdurate to the complaints of his own best Concubine, and your fair Kinswoman M—— who now starves."[47]

Harry Savile was accused, with apparent reason, of being the Duchess of Cleveland's "lover and agent," while, at much the same time, another correspondent wrote sadly of Lady Scroope (Sir Carr's witty and still handsome mother) as being in the "ill hands" of Mr. Savile, as his mistress.[48] Wycherley, too, seems to have been caught for a while in the avid grasp of the Duchess of Cleveland.[49] Henry Killigrew claimed intimacy with the Countess of Shrewsbury, and was well basted for his boast.[50] Etherege, exiled at Ratisbon, had to content himself with an actress, "a plain Bavarian with her sandy coloured locks, brawny limbs, and a brick complexion." Although he remarked in his letters that he often found himself "very hearty," he bemoaned his absence from "the kind, charming creatures London affords."[51]

From a modern point of view, the record of debauchery is sufficiently complete, and there is not much that can be said in defense of the dissolute Wits. Even in their own day there were outcries from respectable people, who wondered why Heaven withheld its fire. Yet one who is tempted to pass judgment should remember that the Wits were young, high-spirited, relatively free from all social and religious restraints, and subject to innumerable temptations. Whitehall was like a splendid brothel; the King's mistresses were treated with vast respect, and there were many unattached ladies who would gladly have traded places with the Duchesses of Portsmouth or Cleveland. Within the Court circles, gallantry was fashionable, and liaisons were socially proper. Finally, due allowance must be made for the exaggerations of gossips and the inventions of romancers. Even the Wits' own letters must not be trusted too far; as gentlemen they were discreet with the names of their mistresses, but they were young enough to magnify their own prowess.

I I I

THE Wits' addiction to wine and revelry, coupled with their freedom from moral or legal restraints, sometimes resulted in deviltry—horseplay and fun for the most part, usually harmless if sometimes shocking. They were not given to malicious mischief, yet at times their riots involved vandalism or worse. Here are two fairly well substantiated stories of madcap doings which had sad results.

In the Privy Garden at Whitehall stood a sundial, "the rarest in Europe," an elaborate structure of glass spheres grouped in the form of an erect cone. Late on a June night in 1675, a gang of riotous courtiers, including the Earl of Rochester, Lord Buckhurst, and Fleetwood Shepherd, came back to Whitehall "from their revels" and passed through the Privy Garden. Inspired by wine, Rochester suddenly perceived the phallic significance of the dial in relation to a feminine personification of time. "What!" he cried, "Dost thou stand there to ——— Time?" At once he drew his sword; his drunken companions followed suit in chivalric defense of the rosy-bosomed Hours, and in a moment the sundial was a melancholy ruin.[52]

The second story has a more tragic conclusion. In July, 1676, Rochester, Etherege, George Bridges, and one Captain Downes were reveling at Epsom. They were amusing themselves one night with the mild sport of tossing a fiddler in a blanket (fiddlers were fair game), when a barber appeared on the scene, lured by the noise. The Wits seized upon him as their next victim. To free himself the wily barber offered to direct them to the most beautiful woman in Epsom. They accepted, but the house they were sent to was that of the chief constable. Ignorant of his identity, the Wits broke into the house, found no women, and therefore beat the constable. That worthy finally escaped and called his watch. Confronted by superior forces, the Wits were tamed, and Etherege made a "submissive oration." The appeased watchmen had started to return to their beds, and all would have been well had it not been for Rochester's drunken demon of irresponsibility. On impulse, he drew his sword and made a pass at the chief constable. Downes seized the earl's arm; the constable cried out. The watchmen returned, mistook the aggressor, and struck at Downes with pikes and staves, while the other rioters fled. A few days later, Downes died of his wounds. There was much talk that his companions would be charged with the responsibility for his death—talk which, as usual, came to nothing.[53]

Few contemporary accounts of the Wits' escapades can be accepted as completely reliable. Misunderstandings, the garblings of gossips, the exaggeration and embroidery of letter writers more eager to entertain than to inform, often turned harmless pranks into debauches and less innocent revels into monstrosities.

The Wits were frequently charged with nudism, and perhaps with some cause. In the heat of riot, tight and elaborate clothing was likely to be shed with the rioter's inhibitions. Pepys, who was not an eye witness, reports a story of Buckhurst and Sedley rambling through the streets in a semi-nude condition, and at last fighting, being beaten by the watch and jailed for the night.[54] It seems an odd sort of amusement for gentlemen to be running through the streets in late October without their breeches. However, Pepys' informant, Dr. James Pierce, was a male gossip, whose scandalous yarns were often false. A comparable story about Sir George Etherege's dancing "stark naked" in his chamber with two young women, and afterwards going about the streets of Ratisbon with a male companion "having nothing on but their shirts"* must be considered unsubstantiated also. The teller of the tale was Etherege's malicious secretary, Hugh Hughes, who was scheming to supplant his superior as envoy.[55]

A similarly unpleasant accusation was fired at Lords Lovelace and Rochester in September, 1677, when Robert Harley wrote of their "beastly prank" of "running along Woodstock Park naked."[56] That story grew until in the next century the antiquarian Hearne recorded it as an attempt to impress "several of the female sex," who, however, failed to appear to witness the fleshly spectacle.[57] As usual, the truth was something different. Rochester wrote to Savile:

> For the hideous Deportment, which you have heard of, concerning running naked, so much is true, that we went into the River somewhat late in the Year and had a frisk for forty yards in the Meadow, to dry ourselves.

That such a sequel to a dip in Woodstock waters was not uncommon, Rochester proceeded to prove in the same letter, reminding fat Harry of the year 1676 and another

---

* It must be remembered that "naked" might differ from "stark naked," since a "naked" man might be wearing undergarments. Similarly, the phrase "in his shirt" or "nothing but his shirt" usually meant that one had divested himself only of coat and waistcoat, and was appearing in shirt and breeches—an unconventional attire for an ambassador, but hardly indecent.

nude procession, when Savile himself "led the Coranto around Rosamund's fair Fountain," with a notable steato-pygous display.[58] Innocent goings-on, no doubt, but scan-dalous to staid folk who rarely bathed.

A less innocent case of reported nudism was the famous brawl at the Cock Tavern on June 16, 1663. Of this, the only *facts* available are those given in the formal accounts of the trial which followed. According to Keble's reports of cases in the Court of the King's Bench, in late June, 1663, Sir Charles Sedley was brought before the Court, fined two thousand marks, committed without bail for a week, and bound to his good behavior for a year. Evidently he had confessed guilty to "showing himself naked on a Balcony" and throwing down bottles "*vi et armis*" among the people in Covent Garden, "*contra pacem* and to the scandal of the Government."[59]

On July 1, Pepys first heard of the affair from his fellow gossip, Sir William Batten, who had not witnessed the episode and probably had not been at the trial. The details recorded by Pepys were so gross that Wheatley could not bring himself to transcribe all of them in his edition of the *Diary*.[60] Pepys' report, like all others, follows the trial, and is evidently based upon Batten's account of "information" brought in by witnesses. Restoration lawyers and judges were as credulous as Mr. Pepys; the laws of evidence ad-mitted anything in the way of hearsay, elaboration or ex-aggeration, and a prisoner was considered guilty until he could prove himself innocent. Nevertheless, Sir Charles was formally charged only with breach of the peace; to that he confessed, and made no answer to other accusations.

Anthony à Wood, less squeamish than Mr. Wheatley, printed full details—based as usual on secondhand and much embellished information from the trial, and recorded months after the date of the affair.* According to Wood's

---

* He called the presiding justice Sir Robert Hyde. Actually he was Sir Robert Foster, who died on October 4, 1663, and was succeeded by Hyde.

story, Sedley, Lord Buckhurst, and Sir Thomas Ogle had
dined at the Cock Tavern on the night of June 16, and
afterward, full of wine, food, and deviltry, had adjourned
to the balcony, stripped themselves naked and harangued
the passers-by in obscene and blasphemous language. A riot
followed, but the mob was baffled by locked doors, and the
three revelers withdrew in safety.[61]

The affair was so widely commented upon (by the
"fanatics," said Wood) that a lurid version of it reached
saintly Philip Henry in far-off Flintshire; it came by way
of "a letter from Mr. Joshua Hotchkis to his brother-in-
law Ralph Eddon." In his diary, the trusting Reverend
Philip noted that the three rakes had "had six dishes of
meat [i.e., six courses] brought in by six naked women"—
a nice touch. After dinner (presumably ignoring the dis-
robed damsels), the Wits "went forth in their shirts into
the balcony" and there were blatantly blasphemous. Finally
they went back in, saying, "Come now, let us go in and
make laws for the nation." Buckhurst was a member of
Parliament.[62]

By putting together all the details from Pepys, Wood,
and Henry, with some moral additions by the great Dr.
Johnson,[63] modern biographers have been able to make
the affair into a ripsnorting scandal. One even added a
little embroidery of his own, concluding

. . . even the low denizens of the neighboring slums, who formed
the larger part of their audience, were scandalized and disgusted
at the scene, and a rush was made at the tavern-door with the
object of wreaking vengeance on the three performers. So determined was the mob that it was only after a long and desperate
fight that Sedley, Buckhurst and Ogle were rescued from its
clutches; indeed all three nearly lost their lives as they had successfully lost their characters.[64]

Canceling the contradictions in evidence, and making
due allowance for the snowball growth of scandal, we are
left with a story of three brash young men (Sedley, the

oldest, was twenty-four) dining and drinking at a disreputable tavern. After dinner, the rakes (probably "brave and boosy") repaired to the balcony, perhaps for a breath of fresh air, perhaps to carry out a dare or wager agreed upon at table. Sir Charles, the chief, if not the only, public offender (he was the only one haled into court), proceeded to preach a kind of mountebank sermon, meanwhile, perhaps, showing his "nakedness,"* either to illustrate a point in his discourse, or simply to free himself from some of his over-warm clothing. A crowd gathered, mocking; some one threw a stone. The Wits replied with their only available weapons, wine bottles thrown *vi et armis*. No doubt the windows of the tavern as well as the King's peace were broken; Sir Charles was held responsible and properly punished by a fine and imprisonment. The numerous details added to the basic story may be taken as the embroidery of angry citizens at the trial, plus the embellishments of rumor.

While the Restoration proper was certainly gullible and much given to scandal and false report, the reputations of the Wits suffered less at the hands of their contemporaries than at those of the antiquarians, anecdote collectors, and Grub Street hacks of the following century. Most of the yarns collected by Oldys, Hearne, and Spence, for example, are based on the dubious authority of oral tradition, while the romantic stories of such fabulists as Grammont,† Oldmixon, Captain Alexander Smith, John Langhorne, and their anonymous kin are either fictions added to some authentic incident or pure fabrications standing alone.

* According to Pepys, only Sedley stripped; Wood accused all three, but was sure only of the nudity of Sedley; Henry left all three "in their shirts." The court reporters accused Sedley only.

† Although Philibert, Comte de Grammont, was a contemporary of the Wits, his famous *Memoirs* (1713) must be classed both in time and unreliability with the romances of the early eighteenth century scandalmongers. A noted liar all his life, he related his memoirs to Anthony Hamilton (the actual writer of the book) in his extreme old age, and he drew upon his fertile imagination when memory failed.

Sir Charles Sedley
Courtesy of the Harvard Theatre Collection, Harvard University

Anna-Maria, Countess of Shrewsbury. About 1668
By Sir Peter Lely. Courtesy of the National Portrait Gallery

An example of fiction added to fact is the story of Lady Shrewsbury's supposed conduct at the duel between her husband and her lover, the Duke of Buckingham, on January 16, 1668. The duel itself was as futile and bloody an affair as any to be found in the annals of gallantry. The liaison between Anna-Maria, Countess of Shrewsbury, and George, Duke of Buckingham was so well known that Pepys could write, the day after the duel, "Lady Shrewsbury . . . is at this time, and hath for a great while been, a whore to the Duke of Buckingham."[65] Apparently, the Earl of Shrewsbury was himself well aware of the affair, and quite unconcerned. He seems to have challenged Buckingham because of pressure by members of his own and Anna-Maria's families, and then only after Anna-Maria, fleeing from the gossip stirred up by Henry Killigrew, a rejected suitor, had deserted her husband (in September, 1667), and fled to France. At the time of the duel she was still in France, hibernating in a nunnery.[66]

The duel was fought in a close near Barn Elms, outside of London. Each contestant had two seconds who fought also. Buckingham's friends were Sir Robert Holmes and Captain William Jenkins; Shrewsbury's were Sir John Talbot and Bernard Howard. The fight was long and desperate. Finally Shrewsbury fell, fatally wounded. The duke sprang to help Jenkins, but Howard, the latter's opponent, put aside the duke's sword, and with a wild lunge laid Jenkins dead. Talbot was seriously wounded, and the others were all somewhat damaged.

These are the known facts in the case. The fictions began to accumulate a half century later when Pope told Spence that the duel had been concerted between Buckingham and Lady Shrewsbury, and that the buxom countess, dressed as a page and holding her lover's horse, had witnessed the battle. "All that morning she was trembling for her gallant, and wishing the death of her husband; and, after his fall, 'tis said the duke slept with her in his bloody shirt."[67]

To this story Langhorne added more details in 1769, in a fictitious letter purporting to be from the philosopher St. Evremonde to the poet Waller. We are told that the lady "had pistols concealed, and that she had pledged her honour to shoot both Shrewsbury and herself, if her husband proved victorious."[68] Finally, Macaulay summarized matters in his usual sensational fashion: "Some said that the abandoned woman witnessed the combat in man's attire, and others that she clasped her victorious lover to her bosom while his shirt was still dripping with the blood of her husband."*[69]

This is all synthetic romance, of course; there is no contemporary confirmation of any part of the incredible story. Even Grammont, who says some vicious things about Lady Shrewsbury,[70] makes no mention of it. And there is almost certain evidence that Lady Shrewsbury was not even in England at the time. Yet nearly all modern biographers and historians have accepted the fable as fact, and united in condemning the wicked duke and his "abandoned" countess as brazen and heartless sinners.

A good example of pure fabrication is a story told in a memoir attributed by the booksellers to St. Evremonde and prefixed to a reprint of Rochester's poems in 1707.[71] It has long been accepted as true, and it has been retold with shocked horror by almost every modern writer who has dealt with the period. Once upon a time (we are told) Buckingham and Rochester were banished together from the court for certain unmentioned misdemeanors. With nothing better to do, they hired an inn on the road to Newmarket, set themselves up as innkeepers, and proceeded to fuddle the neighborhood swains in the taproom, while wantoning with their wives in the bedroom. One beautiful nymph they knew of only by report; her husband was a

* Buckingham's most recent biographer, R. P. T. Coffin (*The Dukes of Buckingham*, New York, 1931, p. 282), has added a cruel speculation of his own: "She probably kept the shirt as a souvenir of a completely happy day."

miserly curmudgeon, and she was closely guarded by a dragon of a spinster, whose only weakness was a love of strong drink. One day, while Buckingham entertained the husband at the tavern, handsome Rochester, disguised in woman's weeds, went to visit the nymph; under his garments he bore a bottle of spirits, well qualified with opium. By a simple ruse he gained entrance, introduced the dragon to the "somniferous liquor," seduced the pretty Phyllis, and fled with her over the fields to the inn. While the two rakes by turns took their fill of the wife's charms, the miserly husband, returning to find his nest robbed, went out and hanged himself. Some days later, the noblemen dismissed the widow with a gift of money and the kindly advice to go to London and get herself a husband of a better leer.

So far as I can discover there is not a word of truth in this charming tale. There is nothing circumstantial about it, and it is not confirmed by a scrap of contemporary evidence. Furthermore, we may be certain that the actual author was not St. Evremonde, who knew both Rochester and Buckingham, and who was reasonably reliable as a narrator.* That it was pretty certainly written by a hack is indicated first by the fact that the biographical account of Rochester in the "Memoir" is taken with little change from Bishop Burnet's *Life* of the poet, and second by the fact that the "Memoir" was first printed as a joint publication by two booksellers of bad repute, Benjamin Bragge and "the unspeakable" Edmund Curll, who specialized in anonymous and fictitious biographies.[72]

It is impossible to say who the writer of the spurious "Memoir" might have been—perhaps John Oldmixon, one of Curll's most prolific hacks, or possibly even Curll

---

* Imitations and forgeries of St. Evremonde's work were numerous in the early eighteenth century. St. Evremonde himself, before his death, employed his editor, Des Maiseaux, to collect his work and sift out the forgeries. The "Memoir" was not admitted into the list of authentic articles. See St. Evremonde's *Works* (1728), I, 22.

himself—but the authorship is not important.[73] The important fact is that the Buckingham-Rochester episode has been so long accepted as valid and used to further defame the two Wits. The most cursory acquaintance with the French and Italian literature of gallantry should enable a reader of the "Memoir" to identify the stock devices used—the amorous gallants at an inn, the suspicious old husband, the beautiful young wife and the duenna, the lover disguised as a woman, and the use of drugs—all old tricks, used by Aretino, Boccaccio, Masuccio, Sansovino, and a dozen others, even including the seventeenth century La Fontaine.[74] As a romance, the story is in the right erotic vein, but it is not biography.

It would be fruitless and tedious to deal individually with all the additions to the Wits' apocrypha as they accumulated during the seventeenth and eighteenth centuries. Granted that the Wits were a raffish fraternity, who fought duels, made love not wisely but too much, and engaged in riots and debauches, yet they were not devils of indecency. Too much has been made of their private lives; they have been pictured consistently as elegant loafers, spendthrifts, rakes, and wastrels. The other side of the picture, their public lives, is not scandalous; therefore it is less interesting and has been largely ignored.

The Wits in Public Life

EVEN in their riotous youth, some of the Court Wits were useful citizens, holding various posts in the hierarchy of the state and discharging important duties. As they grew older, almost all of them held from time to time one or more offices of trust, varying in responsibility from the small cares of the Master of the King's Household (Henry Bulkeley) to the great tasks of the chief minister of England (the Duke of Buckingham). Nine of them were members of Parliament, some for many years. No doubt some of them sought public office only for personal or pecuniary reasons. Nevertheless, all the Wits were members of the upper class, steeped in the tradition of *noblesse oblige*, and trained to accept the duty of the English gentleman: to lead and govern the masses.

Few courtiers would have agreed with the Earl of Rochester that "they who would be great in our little Government, seem as ridiculous to me as School-boys, who with much endeavour, and some danger, climb a Crab-tree, venturing their Necks for Fruit which solid Piggs would disdain if they were not starving."[1] Most of them had a very human desire for prestige and power, although, like Henry Savile, they might hate the slow process of Court advancement, the "fawning, creeping and serving on in offices troublesome and servile enough in themselves, however gilded by the fancies of men."[2] There is every evidence that they welcomed the responsibilities of their class, whether those responsibilities were thrust upon them by the accident of birth, or acquired by assiduous courtship. With varying degrees of enthusiasm, most of the Wits (including the cynical Rochester) served their King and country at Court, in the army and navy, in foreign lands as envoys and governors, and in the Houses of Parliament. If, in the course of such service, they managed to line their pockets comfortably, they merely followed the immemorial custom of courtiers and politicians.

I

PLACES at the Restoration Court were in such demand that (with His Majesty's consent) they were bought and sold freely, often at very high prices,* and fortunate was the favorite who was appointed to a post without having to pay a large sum to its previous incumbent. Such places were often "troublesome and servile," but they carried with them some power, a deal of prestige, very fancy salaries, and in many cases apartments in Whitehall Palace. Moreover, the members of the royal household had many opportunities to beg from their master special privileges and monopolies, grants of land, forfeited estates, and the like. Sometimes the badgered monarch rebelled. It is related that once, when one of his favorites took advantage of a convivial occasion to whisper a request in the royal ear, Charles the Second replied, "You must ask that of your King!"[3]

Whitehall Palace swarmed with servants. At every main entrance to the rambling collection of old buildings were posted yeomen of the guard, carrying "gilt partizans"[4] and brilliant in their scarlet uniforms faced with black velvet and trimmed with silver and gilt spangles. The King was hampered at every turn by equally gaudy Gentlemen and

---

* For example, Lady Shrewsbury bought her second husband, George Bridges, a place as Groom of the Bedchamber for £4,500. At about the same time, Laurence Hyde paid £10,000 for a post as Secretary of State (HMC, *Rutland*, II, 52). Buckingham sold his place as Gentleman of the Bedchamber for £6,000, and his position as Master of the Horse for £6,000 plus an annuity of £1,500 (Burghclere, *Buckingham*, p. 302).

Grooms of the Bedchamber, Gentlemen and Grooms of the
Privy Chamber, Pages, Waiters, Carvers, Sewers, Cupbearers, Esquires of the Body, and Gentleman Ushers.
When he rose in the morning, the Groom of the Stole with
appropriate ceremonies handed him the royal shirt, the
Grooms and Esquires of the Body helped him wash and
dress, the Royal Barber shaved the royal chin, rubbed His
Majesty's cropped head with a linen bag filled with
"aromatized sweet powder,"[5] and adjusted the royal peri-
wig, and finally the Master of the Robes decorated the
product of the assembly line with orders and jewels. When
the King strode through the palace galleries or sauntered
in the Privy Garden, he was pursued by Grooms, Pages,
Sergeants, Messengers, Gentlemen Pensioners, and other
eager courtiers. When he dined in the Banqueting Hall
under the appraising eyes of the general public, he was
served by a long procession of Waiters, Carvers, Sewers,
and Cupbearers. When he ate in private, he was served by
his impatient Grooms, who were to have the leavings of
his table for their own meat. At night, a Gentleman of the
Bedchamber slept on a pallet bed in the royal bedchamber.
We are not told what arrangements were made when William Chiffinch, Page of the Bedchamber and Keeper of the
King's Privy Closet, introduced some pretty little actress
into the royal chamber.[6]

Four important officials held sway over the host of
"Servants in Ordinary." In order of rank, these were the
Lord Steward of the Household, the Lord Chamberlain,
the Master of the Horse, and the Vice Chamberlain. Each
had specific duties to perform, and a fairly well defined
area of authority. All were ex officio members of the King's
Privy Council. In "Dignity, State, and Honour," they
ranked only slightly below such political officers of the
crown as the Lord Chancellor, Lord Treasurer, Lord
President of the Council and Lord Privy Seal.

The post of Lord Steward (fee, £100 yearly "and Six-

teen Dishes each Meal, with Wine, Beer, etc.") was usually
given to a nobleman full of years and dignity. In 1710, it
devolved upon the once-rakish Earl of Mulgrave, who at
sixty-two had arrived at the age of discretion. As Lord
Steward he had authority over the entire Court, and was
empowered to judge of "all disorders, as Treasons,
Murders, Felonies, Bloodshed, committed in the Court, or
within the Verge"—*i.e.*, within a radius of twelve miles
from the center of Whitehall. Only London by charter was
exempted. For Mulgrave the position was the culmination
of a long career of service in Parliament and at Court.

Two of the Wits held consecutively the important post
of Lord Chamberlain (fee, £100 yearly "and Sixteen
Dishes each Meal"). Mulgrave was appointed by King
James in 1685; with the coming of William and Mary,
he gave way to the Earl of Dorset (then a prominent
Whig) who held the position for eight years. The duties
of the Lord Chamberlain were numerous and exacting,
and actually, if not technically, he was more powerful than
the Lord Steward. He had the supervision of most of the
officers of the King's Privy Chambers and the Wardrobe;
he was in charge also of all Court musicians, actors, messengers, artisans, heralds, physicians, surgeons, barbers,
and chaplains, and such odd patent-holders as two "oper-
ators for the teeth," a cormorant keeper, a perspective
maker, a comb maker, a peruke maker, a yeoman of the
leash, and a corn cutter. Through the office of the Master
of the Revels, the Lord Chamberlain had control over all
theatrical affairs, including the licensing of plays. Both
Mulgrave and Dorset, long-time patrons of the arts, were
actively interested in this phase of their duty.

The Lord Chamberlain was aided by a Vice Chamberlain, who acted as deputy to his superior and in the latter's
absence wielded full authority. The post was held from
1680 to 1687 by Henry Savile (at £600 a year). To judge
from Savile's letters during his years of service, he was kept

very busy swearing in servants, deciding petty disputes, and taking care of a thousand small affairs. Partly because of his office and partly because of his good nature he was much imposed on by all his friends at Court.

Salaries, fixed generations earlier, rarely changed, while the responsibilities of an office might be greatly increased or lessened with the passing of years. As a consequence, in the reign of Charles II there was very little correlation between the duties of a post and its remuneration. The Master of the Horse was an official of great dignity, few duties, and £666, 16s, 4d per annum. Technically he was in charge of the King's stables, horses, coaches, footmen, grooms, farriers, smiths, coachmen, and saddlers. Actually, the stables were run by under-officers, and the chief duty of the Master was "to ride next behind the King in any Solemn Cavalcade." In 1668, when the Duke of Buckingham was prime minister in everything but name (the term had not yet been invented) and needed a Court appointment with a title to give dignity to his power, he bought the place of Master of the Horse from the Duke of Albemarle for £20,000. He held it for six years, until he fell from office before the onslaught of the Commons in 1674.

Of all the numerous places at Court, those of Gentleman and Groom of the Bedchamber were most in demand. Ordinarily there were twelve of each rank, although for reasons of economy attempts were made from time to time to reduce the number.[7] The Gentlemen of the Bedchamber were all "of the Prime Nobility of England," and, following a well-worn law that to him who hath shall be given, they were paid at the rate of £1,000 a year. The Grooms of the Bedchamber were esquires, knights, and sons of the nobility; consonant with their lower rank at Court, they received lower pay, £500 a year. The duties of Gentlemen and Grooms were much the same: one of each group waited on the King for one week out of every quarter; they helped their master in the bedchamber and at the dinner table; and while a Gentleman spent the night sleeping at the King's feet, a Groom was on duty—and probably slumbering—in an outer chamber. This arrangement, designed to assure the King's privacy and safety, was not without its weaknesses. One February night at Windsor Castle, when that wildest of the Wits, Harry Killigrew, was on duty in an anteroom to the King's bedchamber, a mysterious brawl took place. Killigrew's man-servant was stabbed (" 'tis said he killed himself"), and the Duke of York, fearing for the King's safety, persuaded Charles to rise and return to Whitehall at once.[8]

Bedchamber servants were regularly sent abroad as special envoys or messengers. When an Italian duke died or a French prince married, King Charles dispatched a couple of his favorite retainers on errands of condolence or compliment. They were also used for lesser errands: to bear orders to lord lieutenants, governors, or ambassadors; to convoy important visitors to England; or to settle the King's private affairs at home or abroad. Finally, the bed-chamber servants were the King's personal companions. They were supposed never to absent themselves without leave.* They were expected to be on hand, even when they were not officially on duty, to dine with the King in private, to drink, hunt, walk, and talk with him, to go with him to Windsor or Newmarket, to a playhouse, to a Lord Mayor's banquet, or even to church.

The noble Wits—Buckingham, Dorset, Mulgrave, and Rochester—were appointed to bedchamber places without spending their apprenticeship in lesser positions. The com-moner Wits—Killigrew, Guy, Bulkeley, and Savile—started at the bottom, and by dint of perseverance, in-fluence, and courtship worked their way up. Henry Guy

---

* Unless, of course, a substitute was provided. So Buckingham once wrote to Rochester: "Beeing to goe a hunting tomorrow and not knowing whither I shall return time enoughf to doe my duty to his Majesty, I hope your Lordship will not refuse mee the honour to wayte for mee that day and ly in the bedchamber at night." (Prinz, *Rochester*, p. 278.)

began his Court career as Cupbearer to the Queen; it is probable that he held several intermediate posts; and by 1675 he was a Groom of the Bedchamber to the King. In 1661 Harry Killigrew was a mere Page of Honor to the King, at £120 a year; a year later he became a Groom of the Bedchamber to the Duke of York, at £300 per annum. In 1674 he was made a Groom to the King, and in 1694 he was created Court Jester by King William, with £300 a year additional pay. Henry Bulkeley rose slowly from ensign to captain in the King's Guards. In 1675 he stepped up to the job of Master of the Household (a kind of superior clerk and auditor), "His fee one hundred marks [about £140], and Seven Dishes Daily." In 1683 he was promoted to Groom of the Bedchamber. Harry Savile started out as a Groom to the Duke of York, and after many efforts finally (in 1673) achieved the post he wanted as Groom to the King. When he became Vice Chamberlain he sold his position in the bedchamber.

Of course the King's servants could hold more than one office concurrently, and often did so. Buckingham was a Gentleman of the Bedchamber from 1649 to 1674. During that period he held from time to time such diverse places as Secretary of State, General of the Eastern Division of England, Lord Lieutenant of Yorkshire, Master of the Horse, and Chancellor of Cambridge. The Earl of Rochester, at the time of his death in 1680, was holding the places of Gentleman of the Bedchamber, Gamekeeper for the County of Oxford, Deputy Lieutenant of Somersetshire, Ranger and Keeper of Woodstock Park, and Alderman of Taunton. Others of the Wits held military posts, ambassadorships, places on administrative committees, and memberships in the House of Commons, while they were bedchamber servants. Sometimes their collateral appointments were sinecures, but more often they demanded energy, attention to detail, and judgment on a fairly high level. And courtship was not the easiest way of making a living.

Once, in a letter to his wife, Rochester included a bit of impromptu verse, expressive of his disgust at the life he was obliged to lead:

> Is there a man yee gods, whome I doe hate
> Dependance and Attendance bee his fate
> Lett him bee busy still & in a crowde
> And very much a slave & very proude.[9]

And worthy Mr. Pepys said, "Upon the whole, I do find that it is a troublesome thing for a man of any condition at Court to carry himself even, and without contracting enemies or enviers; and that much discretion and dissimulation is necessary to do it."[10]

I I

POSITIONS in the military, diplomatic, and colonial services of the state went at a smaller premium than places at Court. They were more often acquired by gift from the King than by purchase. However, because of love of adventure, desire for glory, or hope of advancement, many of the Wits sought such employments, even though the pay was frequently small.

Henry Bulkeley was the only Wit who had been trained as a professional soldier. Wycherley and Rochester held captaincies for brief periods, and Sedley once had a commission in the Kentish militia, but it is doubtful if any of them ever exercised their troops. Lords Vaughan, Mulgrave, and Buckingham commanded regiments in times of war, but Vaughan and Buckingham never led theirs in battle, and Mulgrave only once carried out a halfhearted campaign in France.[11] In 1672 Buckingham was nominated as Lieutenant-general in command of the English armies, but he was quickly superseded by Count Schomberg. In the Civil Wars Buckingham had demonstrated his courage but not his wisdom, and King Charles was too shrewd to entrust a campaign to his headlong management. His ambition to be the conquering leader of European armies was never realized.[12]

The fighting spirit of the young Wits was better displayed at sea than on land; most of them took some part in the Dutch Wars of 1664-67 and 1672-74. In 1664, when it suddenly became fashionable to volunteer for sea duty, squads of gay young courtiers appeared on the rough decks of the English warships. Among them, Lord Buckhurst distinguished himself by writing a gay ballad, "To All You Ladies Now on Land," which made an immediate hit in London.[13] In the two following summers, Killigrew, Savile, Rochester, Wycherley, Mulgrave, Buckingham, and probably others of the Wits took their share of sea duty. Rochester was with Sir Thomas Teddiman at the Battle of Bergen in 1665, and saw two of his best friends killed at his side—an experience which added little to his liking for war. Nevertheless, he returned to the Fleet the following summer, and distinguished himself by his bravery in the Four Days Battle of the Channel.[14] Henry Savile (following the Duke of York, then admiral) was in almost every major engagement during the Second Dutch War, and in the Third, at the bloody battle of Solebay, he was falsely reported among the slain.[15] Mulgrave took a liking to seafaring life, and in 1672 he was given command of the *Royal Katherine*, the best "second-rate" in the English navy.[16] In the same year, Buckingham, denied command of a warship (for ministers were supposed to govern, not fight), defiantly hired a small sailing vessel and joined the fleet as admiral of his one-ship navy.[17] It is not recorded that he exposed his frail bulwarks to the Dutch guns.

As might be expected, the Wits were lighthearted in war. On December 1, 1664, when the Fleet was on its way to meet the enemy, Buckhurst wrote flippantly that the Dutch "in all likelihood sometime to morrow, or next day may do us the favour to fill the news books and empty our ship where at present the crowd is intollerable."[18] Sometime the following summer, Savile and Mulgrave were shipmates under the command of Prince Rupert. Seeing their admiral slip a loaded pistol in his pocket just before a battle, the two courtiers guessed that the old warrior meant to blow up the ship's magazine, if worst came to worst. "Therefore," wrote Mulgrave, "Mr. Savile and I, in a laughing way, most mutinously resolved to throw him overboard, in case we should ever catch him going down to the powder room." In 1680, Mulgrave was sent in command of an expedition to the relief of Tangiers. Since there had been some gossip about him and "some Ladies in whom the King was not unconcerned," he was given a leaky old ship which had been condemned as unfit for service. He literally pumped his way to Tangiers. However, the light-hearted Wit had his small revenge: not once during the three weeks' voyage was the King's health drunk at the commander's table. Mulgrave spent much of his time on the voyage in writing a long, dull poem, "The Vision," bewailing a lost love.[19] War, of course, was not a proper subject for poetry.

The rewards for diplomatic missions were much larger than those for military service, and the Wits were consequently more eager to serve their country in the salons and throne rooms of Europe—particularly in France. It was customary to heap gifts on visiting diplomats, and Louis XIV was a munificent monarch. In 1670 the Duke of Buckingham, Lord Buckhurst, and Sir Charles Sedley were sent to France with condolences on the death of the Duchess of Orleans. They were magnificently entertained. On their departure, the Duke was presented with a "rich sword and belt . . . valued at 40,000 crowns," and we may be sure that the lesser members of the embassy were not forgotten.[20] Buckhurst and Savile, sent to Paris in 1669 with compliments "upon the indisposition of the Dauphin," were presented with miniatures of King Louis, "set with diamonds, to the value of £600 sterling each."[21] Savile and Colonel James Hamilton, in 1670 dispatched to Florence to commiserate with the Grand Duke of that city-state on the death of his father, were lavishly entertained for a week, and surreptitiously ("so as to avoid making a precedent") loaded with gifts.[22] These, of course, were exceptional cases; however, there were rich rewards in diplomacy, and the only dangers were seasickness and bedbugs. It must be added that in spite of the dire predictions of gossips,* the Wits and their friends usually behaved themselves on their diplomatic travels and occasional pleasure trips abroad. They performed their missions acceptably, enjoyed their brief vacations, and came home without scandal.

Two of the Wits, Henry Savile, the letter writer, and Sir George Etherege, the dramatist, held posts as permanent ministers. Savile was Envoy Extraordinary to France from February, 1679, to March, 1682. Etherege was Envoy to the Diet at Ratisbon from August, 1685, to the Revolution in 1689. The labors of such posts were not particularly heavy; they consisted chiefly of writing newsletters to the secretaries of state in England, and conveying to the local governments diplomatic communications from Whitehall. Savile enjoyed himself thoroughly at Paris and left with a regret which was, however, sweetened by his newly acquired and more lucrative places as Vice Chamberlain and member of the Admiralty Commission.[23] In Germany, Etherege was less happy. It is likely that he accepted the post at Ratisbon only as a means of retrieving

* For example, in 1681, Anthony à Wood noted that the Earl of Dorset, Lord Vaughan, Sir Cyril Wyche, and Fleetwood Shepherd had gone to Paris to visit Harry Savile, "the English Embassador there—where at this time they were enjoying themselves, talking blasphemy and atheisme, drinking, and perhaps that which is worse." Two days later, he wrote smugly that Shepherd had been hanged or broken on the wheel at Paris "for some roguery that he had committed"—a report which was fortunately a baseless rumor. (Wood, *Life and Times*, II, 559, 560.)

his fallen fortunes. He took no joy in his work and
constantly bewailed his exile on the bleak Danube. He did
his duty, but he found the German princelings insufferable
and their wives hideous.[24]*

Only one of the Wits achieved the dignity of a colonial
governorship, Lord John Vaughan, who in his youth had
been called by Clarendon "a young, confident man . . . a
Person of as ill a Face as Fame, his looks and his Manners
both extreme bad," and by Pepys, "one of the lewdest fellows of the age, worse than Sir Charles Sedley."[25] In 1674,
this rake-hell (if we may accept the indignant language of
a political enemy and a gossip) was appointed Captain
General and Governor of the colony of Jamaica, a brawling, lusty infant, which had already wrecked the disposi-
tions of a succession of viceroys. Vaughan set forth early in
1675, full of high resolves and fine ideals. Even the sight
of the primitive Caribbean colony could not dampen his
enthusiasm. In May, two months after his arrival, he wrote
to his friend, George Legge,

> I do not a little please myself that the Island is like to receive
> in my government their first fixed and established laws. I do not
> find but the climate, air, and people are agreeable enough to me,
> but the government not so glorious as it was figured in England;
> however, I am resolved to serve his Majesty and the Island in
> what manner soever I serve myself.[26]

Apparently Vaughan did do his best, to the confusion of
his detractors in England. On the whole, he was a pretty
good governor. But his ways and those of the colonists were
leagues apart. Vaughan was a punctilious courtier, rigid in
his adherence to the letter of the law; Jamaica was a

---

* Probably, too, he was disappointed in the pay he received. His salary
as an envoy was fixed at three pounds per day, paid quarterly (Etherege,
Letterbook, p. 16). Savile, on earlier missions as temporary envoy to
France, was paid at the rate of five pounds per day (*CSPD*, 1672-73,
October, 1672, p. 107), and presumably was paid the same amount during
his residence as permanent envoy. Probably the embassy to France was
regarded as much more important than that to the Empire.

John Vaughan, Earl of Carbery. About 1710
By Sir Godfrey Kneller. Courtesy of the National Portrait Gallery

Charles Sackville, Earl of Dorset. About 1685
By Sir Godfrey Kneller. Courtesy of the National Portrait Gallery

frontier colony, and the colonists were easygoing individu-
alists. From the beginning, Vaughan had trouble with his
vice-governor, the romantic privateer, Sir Henry Morgan;
with the Spaniards, who were forever breaking the peace
and seizing English vessels; with French and English
pirates and the colonists who were leagued with them, with
Negro uprisings, with the climate, and with his superiors in
England who failed to support his hand. The combination
finally defeated him. In January, 1678, he was succeeded
by Charles, Earl of Carlisle, and returned to England with
his health and his fortune much impaired. Thereafter,
Vaughan limited his public life to membership in Parliament and two brief turns of duty on the Admiralty Commission. There was no permanence in diplomatic appointments.

Vaughan's reputation as governor has suffered from the
wild claims of one Ralph Palmer, who wrote at the time of
Vaughan's death in 1713,

> He had redeemed his estate and amassed wealth by the govern-
> ment of Jamaica, where he carried many shauntelmen of Wales
> with him, and sold 'em there for slaves, as he did his chaplain, to
> a blacksmith. . . .[27]

There is absolutely no evidence for these accusations, yet
they have been all too frequently accepted by modern
historians.[28] On the contrary, Vaughan's administration
seems to have been distinguished among colonial governor-
ships for honesty and fair dealing.

III

ONLY a few steps south of Whitehall was the ancient
palace and hall of Westminster, a sprawling mass of
buildings, close to the stately pile of Westminster Abbey.
In the hall, the Courts of Justice fought for space with
hucksters and sempstresses in a brawling confusion. Else-

where in the palace, Parliament held its sessions (with almost as much confusion), opening daily (except Sunday) at nine o'clock, and usually closing promptly at noon. The exclusive House of Lords sat in an ancient, vaulted chamber at the south end of the palace (the very chamber which Guy Fawkes tried to blow up), while the teeming House of Commons, with five hundred and thirteen members, was jammed into narrow St. Stephen's Chapel.[29] In both houses quite a few of the Wits appeared from time to time, sitting as lawmakers for the nation.

When the newly elected House of Commons convened on May 8, 1661, it was destined to be the most tenacious, quarrelsome, and turbulent, as well as the longest, of the reign of Charles II. It was called variously the "Pensionary Parliament," because so many of its members drew incomes from the crown, the "Pump Parliament," because it had to be primed with bribes before it would deliver, and the "Drunken Parliament," because so many of its members found inspiration in bottles.[30] There were, of course, honest and selfless men among the cynics and bribe-takers; and there were many pensioners who could be high-minded on occasion. Most of the Wits were pensioners; sometimes they were public-spirited.

In the House of Commons at its first session were Charles, Lord Buckhurst, from East Grinstead, and John (later "Lord") Vaughan, from Caermarthen. Both were very young; Buckhurst was only seventeen. As the eldest son of a peer, he was accorded the ancient privilege of a seat on the backless, green-covered benches at the right of the Speaker's chair, where the Privy Councillors sat in aged dignity. Properly, neither he nor twenty-year-old Vaughan had a right to be in the House, but the laws against minors had long been unenforced.*

* Christopher Monck, Earl of Torrington (son of the Duke of Albemarle), was elected from Devon in January, 1667, when he was only thirteen! He was seated without question. (See E. F. Ward, *Christopher Monck, Duke of Albemarle*, London, 1915, p. 23.)

As time went on and by-elections were called, more of the Wits found seats in the House. In 1668, Sir Charles Sedley appeared, representing New Romney. In 1670, Henry Guy was elected from Heydon. In 1673, jovial Harry Savile won an election at Newark, but had to await the decision of a Parliamentary committee before taking his seat. In 1679, Henry Bulkeley was elected from Anglesey; in later Parliaments he represented Beaumaris. There were many other courtiers in Parliament from time to time, rakes and near-wits, men like Charles Cornwallis, Bab May, Sir Robert Howard, Sidney Godolphin, Silas Titus, and Richard Newport. There were also, as Elder Statesmen, two famous poets, Andrew Marvell and Edmund Waller.

The House of Lords had its quota of Wits also. The Duke of Buckingham ("Dux Bucks" in the euphonious term of the *House of Lords Journal*) had long been a forceful member of the upper chamber. His younger and less vocal associates among the Wits were the Earls of Rochester and Mulgrave, both of whom were summoned in 1667, before either was of age, and the Earl of Middlesex and Dorset (Buckhurst), who was boosted upstairs when he became a peer in 1675.

Unless one inherited or acquired a peerage and became automatically a member of the House of Lords, it was difficult and expensive to enter Parliament. So great was the demand for seats in the House of Commons that boroughs and counties often sold their favors for considerable sums, properly disguised, of course.[31] Harry Savile, complaining of the great cost of his re-election at Newark in 1677, wrote bitterly that, in the words of Francis I, "Tout est perdue hors l'honneur."[32] His was a universal complaint; unless the aspiring politician's family or friends "owned" a borough, his seat was likely to cost him anywhere from twenty-five to a thousand pounds. Furthermore, members received no salaries; not even their traveling expenses were paid by their constituencies.

There were some rewards. A Member of Parliament had the privilege of franking his mail, no small saving. Better still, from forty days before a session opened until forty days after it closed, his person, his servants, and his land and goods were inviolable. He was not safe from the consequences of treason, felony, or breach of peace, but neither he nor his servants could be arrested for debt.*[33] Furthermore, the ambitious young man who, to win a seat in Parliament, bought gallons of ale for the voters of a borough or offered money for church improvements (Mr. Pepys offered fifty pounds for such a purpose to the town of Castle Rising, and refused to pay when he failed of election)[34] might find himself in time a sinecure in the Custom House, the Navy Office, or at Court.

On the other hand, the courtier found that membership in the House of Commons was part of his duty as the King's servant. "In places of members who died," wrote Clarendon, "great pains were taken to have some of the King's menial servants chosen; so that there was a very great number of men in all situations in the Court, as well below stairs as above, who were members of the House of Commons."[35] Justifying his expenses at Newark, Savile wrote to his brother, Halifax, "our measures at Court are so taken that it is essentiall to a man's succeeding there to be of the parl^{mt}."[36] The long-suffering electorate was well aware of the political situation. Pepys records the flat rejection of Mr. (later, Secretary) Williamson at Morpeth, where the rallying cry of the voters was "No Courtier!" and of Bab May at Winchelsea, where the righteous citi-

---

* In 1672, Sir Charles Sedley, arrested for debt, complained to the House of Commons, and had the satisfaction of seeing the constable who had arrested him imprisoned, fined, and reprimanded for daring to lay hands on a Member while Parliament was in session. See Pinto, *Sedley*, pp. 131-2.

zens declared that "they would have no Court pimp to be their burgesse."[37]

The Court Wits who were members of the House of Commons almost invariably voted according to the King's desires. When they failed to toe the mark (because of some personal grudge, or, perhaps, public spirit) they were punished. In 1678, for example, when the Duke of Lauderdale, the brutal High Commissioner of Scotland, was under fire in the House, Charles sent orders to all his servants to attend the sessions, warning that those who failed to attend, or who "voted not according to their duty," would be turned out of their places. Two courtiers, Sir William Lowther and Henry Savile, high-mindedly voted against Lauderdale, and promptly lost their places in the Custom House and the Bedchamber respectively. Charles was in a towering passion. However, in Savile's case the dismissal was only temporary.[38]

It is hardly to be wondered that the Wits failed to distinguish themselves in the Restoration House of Commons. For the most part, Buckhurst, Savile, Guy and Bulkeley were content to keep their seats and obey orders. Vaughan, obeying orders,[39] took an active part in the fight against Chancellor Clarendon in the House of Commons in 1667, but thereafter did nothing either in that House or in the House of Lords, to which he ascended in 1686 as the Earl of Carbery. Even Sedley, who held no Court appointments, seems to have followed the party line during the reign of Charles II. In the Parliaments from 1690 to his death in 1701, however, Sedley was an influential member who spoke often and with eloquence and wit. His leanings were decidedly Whiggish, but he was never a conventional party man.[40]

In the House of Lords, too, the Wits (with one famous exception) did little but attend sessions and vote with the Court party. In their younger days, Rochester and Mulgrave even scorned attendance. The records of the House of Lords, which listed every attending *Epus, Dux, Comes, Vice-Comes,* and *D* (for *Dominus*), show that from October 10, 1667, to February 24, 1674 (over four hundred meetings), *Comes* Rochester attended eighty meetings, and *Comes* Mulgrave one hundred. Of course, courtship, poetry, duels, war, and love distracted them from their legislative duties. After 1674 their attendance was more regular, and it is interesting to note that during the troubled sessions of 1678 and 1679, when the King needed all the support he could get, the Wits were almost constantly present. Mulgrave, in particular, distinguished himself by his assiduity, if not by his leadership. In succeeding reigns, he became an important Tory politician, and from 1702 to 1705 he served as Lord Privy Seal.

Of all the Wits, the Duke of Buckingham was the most active politician. Dryden's "blest mad-man" was not only poet, playwright, chemist, fiddler, buffoon, soldier, manufacturer and lover; in his own opinion at least he was an outstanding diplomat and politician. He saw himself in his father's shoes, a king-maker, and arbiter of the fate of nations. As headlong in politics as in love and war, he lacked the patience and the laborious attention to details that mark the truly successful politician. Yet he could court "all the Members in towne, the debauchees by drinking with them, the sober by grave and serious discourses, the pious by receiving the sacrament."[41] He could be all things to all men, but his fundamental instability of character made it impossible for him to be anything for long. As a result his political career was a progress of peaks and valleys, of temporary alliances, violent friendships, and more violent hatreds. His love of intrigue and offensive warfare made him better in opposition than in power, when he had to be on the defensive. His failures were numerous, and the final stage of his career, when he was broken in power and wealth, was ignominious.

Yet an impartial observer, surveying Buckingham's hectic life, must admit that, in the main at least, he acted as he thought best for the good of England. Often he erred in judgment because of his impetuosity or stubbornness; sometimes he was brilliantly right. His friends at Court loved him, supported him when they could, came to his rescue when he was in trouble with the King, and refused to take him seriously. He was too enthusiastic for most of the Wits; he had convictions. Accepting monarchy, he saw the values of republicanism. Accepting Protestantism (for he was no atheist), he distinguished himself for all time by upholding and working for religious toleration of nonconformists at a time when Anglican bigotry was in the saddle. It is almost certain that the short-lived Declaration of Indulgence of 1672 was the direct result of the duke's influence, and his calm admission of the fact before the Commons in 1674 had much to do with his fall from power.[42] Yet even with that warning, when he was in opposition Buckingham returned again and again to the attack. One of his most eloquent speeches was made in 1675, when he asked leave of the House of Lords to bring in a new bill for liberty of conscience.[43] Let his untiring efforts for toleration stand to the credit of the Restoration Wit, playboy, and buffoon. Yet let it be noted also that he hated the "papists" bitterly, and sought no toleration for the Roman Catholic religion. He was ahead of his time, but not *that* far ahead.

Only little Sir Carr Scroope, who died young, seems to have sought no public office or Court position. Captain William Wycherley might have made a considerable Court career, but he tossed away the first post offered him—as tutor to the King's bastard son, the Earl of Richmond—to marry the Countess Drogheda.[44] Thereafter he succumbed to misfortune. All the rest of the Wits served the state in some capacity or other, and even Fleetwood Shepherd, the Earl of Dorset's faithful follower, was Gentle-

man of the Black Rod from 1694 to 1697, while Dorset
was Lord Chamberlain.

The Wits' offices were often troublesome and servile;
sometimes they were gilded by the fancies of men, and
labeled with resounding titles; sometimes they were gilded
also by the guinea's stamp. But Court and political affairs
were pursued with difficulty, payment was slow, and pensions were often many months in arrears. There were even
some physical dangers in holding office, especially during
the troubled times of the Popish Plot, when, as Rochester
wrote ironically, "things are now reduc'd to that extremity
on all sides that a man dares nott turne his back for feare
of being hang'd, an ill accident to be avoyded by all prudent
persons."[45]

It should be apparent that the conventional picture of
the Court Wits as elegant idlers, "occupied in such pleasures as the period of Charles II has made familiar to us:
horseracing at Newmarket, gambling at Whitehall, and
above all the pursuit of women"[46] is one-sided, and therefore not true. It is also not quite fair for a writer to call
them "idle and debauched young scamps," even though
he adds correctly that they were "also men of real culture
who preserved much of that love of elegance and grace
which had descended to them from the courtiers of the
Renaissance...."[47] Whatever else they may have been, what
with courtship, diplomacy, politics, and literature, they
were certainly not idlers. They were very busy men, who
crowded a world of zestful experience into their lives, and
succeeded in a surprising variety of enterprises. Most important of all were their achievements as literary men, as
writers of familiar letters, lyrics, satires, plays and criticisms.

Letters of Wit and Friendship

LET us imagine the Earl of Rochester seated in his study in the High Lodge, Woodstock Park, catching up on his correspondence. For some time he had been occupied with business letters: instructions to lawyers, underkeepers, the bailiff of his wife's estates in Somersetshire, and the like; now for more personal matters. A letter from Harry Savile had gone unanswered for over a week, and Harry was always complaining about his friend's dilatoriness. Rochester took up a fresh sheet of paper, folded it to make four pages, and thought for a moment, seeking a gambit. At last he dipped his quill and began.

"Whether Love, Wine, or Wisdome (wch. rule you by turnes) have the present ascendant, I cannott pretend to determine att this distance . . ."

Wisdom and fat Harry Savile! Wine, for a simple guess. The rascal was forever drunk and forever purging. Godfry the apothecary saw him as often as the drawers at Locket's.

". . . but good Nature, wch. waites about you with more diligence than Godfry himselfe, is my security that you are not unmindfull of yr. Absent freinds . . ."

Rochester's pen scrawled on; now and then he paused for a word, or scribbled through a phrase before rewriting it. He was confident that Savile showed his letters about the Court—only among the Wits, of course—and he had a reputation to maintain.

"I have seriously considered one thinge, that of the three buisnisses of this Age, Woemen, Polliticks & drinking, the last is the only exercise att wch. you & I have nott prouv'd our selves Errant fumblers, if you have the vanity to thinke otherwise, when wee meete lett us appeale—"

Rochester frowned at his last sentence. The clash of "meete lett" annoyed him. He inserted a caret, and above the line, "next."

"—when wee meete next lett us appeale to freinds of both sexes & as they shall determine, live & dye sheere drunkards, or intire lovers; for as wee order the matter—"

"Order?" A foolish word; scratch it out.

"—for as wee mingle the matter, it is hard to say wch. is the most tiresome creature, the loving drunkard, or the drunken lover."

A few more words of raillery; Savile's "fatt Buttocks" made an irresistible target for the pen. Then the date and the customary "your obedient humble Servant." With a flourish, the young earl signed "Rochester" (the word bristled like a broken-toothed comb), folded the letter into a small rectangle, sealed it with a blob of wax, and on the blank side wrote, "For Mr. Henry Savile." There was no need for further superscription. The letter could go out in the morning when Morgan, the footman, went up to London.

Rochester chose another sheet of paper, folded it once and dipped his pen. Now for his kinsman, the Earl of Lichfield. No labor to this; Ned Lee was no wit, nor a judge of witty letters. A simple note of compliment would do for him. "My deare Lord," wrote Rochester, and proceeded to the obvious.[1]

In an age when travel was slow and difficult, and newspapers were few, the unfortunate dwellers in the hinterlands of England had to depend upon friends in the large cities for their contacts with the world of affairs—for the latest news, gossip, fashions, doings at Court, prices current, and practically everything else. Professional journalists like Henry Muddiman made a fair living by sending periodic newsletters to country subscribers.[2] Town dwellers and courtiers were bombarded with letters from friends in the country and overseas begging for news, scandal, anything to relieve the tedium of life spent in exile from glorious London.

Countless thousands of letters were written by Restoration gentry, and thousands were saved and carefully stored away. Out of the musty libraries and archives of England have come stacks and bales of newsletters, business and political letters, and personal letters, some so intimate and private that the modern reader is abashed. Quantities of letters (for the dead have no privacy) have been printed and edited by modern scholars and learned societies. The letters of such writers as Dryden, Rochester, Otway, Wycherley, and Etherege are, of course, valuable for their biographical content. Letters such as those of Sir Joseph Williamson, the Earl of Essex, the Hatton family, and the Verney family, are valuable for the light they throw on historical events, on political affairs, and even on the development of the English language. From the philosophical correspondence of Anne, Viscountess Conway, with Henry More, the sentimental letters of Dorothy Osborne to Sir William Temple, the gossipy letters of Rachel, Lady Russell, and Dorothy, Dowager Countess of Sunderland (Waller's "Sacharissa"), comes a deal of information on the thought, manners, and customs of genteel society. The labors of the Royal Commission on Historical Manuscripts have resulted in the discovery and printing of innumerable letters of almost every conceivable variety and on almost every possible subject.[3]

Apart from their informative value, Restoration letters are sometimes literature, the familiar essays of a self-conscious generation, brought up in a tradition of letter writing which is now long dead. Gentlemen who attended either of the universities were taught to read and imitate the chatty letters of Cicero, the little moral essays of Seneca, and the familiar epistles of Pliny. In the immediate

English tradition were such models of correct and often witty correspondence as Roger Ascham, Gabriel Harvey, Joseph Hall, John Donne, and the famous *Epistolae Ho-Elianae* of James Howell. There were French models of polish and refinement in epistolary style: De Sales, Malherbe, d'Urfé, Balzac, and Voiture. The would-be writer of elegant letters could follow any of fifty earlier masters, or, if he chose, learn by precept and example from such elaborate manuals as *The Academy of Complements* (1640), *The New Academy of Complements* (1671), or *The Young Secretary's Guide* (1687).[4]

Men of dignity and learning wrote formal and elegant letters; those of lesser learning (including, alas, most of the ladies) wrote according to the conventions, but they were ignorant of the simplest skills. In an age of loose grammar, theirs was licentious; in an age of bad spelling, theirs was atrocious. The Countess of Lichfield (Charlotte Fitzroy, one of the King's illegitimate sprouts) wrote the following to the Earl of Danby:

> My Lord. I have receaved your Lordshipes the wich gives me a great deale of joy to see that you dont beleave those malitous reportes wich have bin spred of me, for I have all waise had a very great eistame for your lordshipe and I wiche that it weare in my poure to doue you any sarvis that you mit have reasone to beleave that as I am reallay am your Lordshipes most fafull sarvant ever to command.—C. Lichfield.[5]

The Countess is not quite typical; some great ladies were literate. Between her artlessness and the formal art of the men of learning there were many levels of epistolary skill. But whatever the skills, the results were usually only letters of news, business, or compliment, valuable only historically. In the great mass of correspondence, however, there are some hundreds which are true familiar letters. Of these, a good many were written by or to members of the circle of Court Wits.

Unfortunately, all too few of the Wits' own letters have

survived. Not being conventional people, they had no filing systems and kept no copies. Of the many letters which Rochester must have written to his friend Savile only nineteen are extant, and we have only fourteen of Savile's replies. A few personal letters by Buckingham, Dorset, and Sedley, and some by Rochester to other correspondents, have been found and edited by biographers. We have a few business letters by Henry Guy, one personal letter by Bulkeley, one by Shepherd, one personal letter by Mulgrave and a couple of moral and literary effusions written by him in his old age, none by Killigrew or Scroope. Only two personal letters by young William Wycherley have been rescued from oblivion, but his senescent letters to Pope were edited and published by that poet. The largest collections of Wits' letters are those to and from Etherege in his exile abroad (many of them are merely informative), and the personal and political correspondence of Henry Savile. The gaps are tantalizing; nevertheless, there are enough extant letters of wit and friendship to give a fair picture of the Wits as epistolarians.

I

USUALLY, when the Court Wits wrote to correspondents outside their little circle, they wrote only to inform or compliment, and they wrote in the conventional style. But when they wrote to each other, they wrote to entertain, to delight by brilliance of phrase and deft turn of thought. They were conscious craftsmen, and their letters are as sophisticated, as polished (and sometimes as bawdy) as their lyrics. They never defined their standards; they followed no formal rules, but they knew what they were doing.

They set a high value on letters of wit. Once Rochester wrote to Henry Savile, thanking him for "a fine Letter from Mr. Savile, which never wants Wit and Good Na-

ture, two Qualities able to transport my Heart with Joy,
tho' it were breaking!" Again he commented to Savile, of
one of the lesser libertines, "Mr. Shepheard is a Man of
a fluent Stile and coherent Thought; if, as I suspect, he
writ your Postscript."[6] Muddiman, the journalist, in a
letter to Rochester in the country, praised Henry Killigrew's "talent" for "description," and denied that he
could add anything to that worthy's previous letter.[7] Etherege, exiled at Ratisbon and doomed to write diplomatic
reports, complained to the Earl of Dorset that he had "lost
for want of exercise the use of fancy and imagination,"
and wrote to the Earl of Sunderland that he was beginning
to be "more vain of making a good dispatch than of writing
a witty letter."[8]

Even those on the periphery of the circle felt the pressure to be entertaining when writing to one of the Wits.
Dryden's letters, for example, justify Scott's remark that
they are, "with a few exceptions, singularly uninteresting."
Yet the one extant letter he wrote to Rochester, in spite
of its air of enforced levity, is polished, well phrased, and
not lacking in wit. He even closed it in the right vein: "I
dare almost promise to entertain you with a thousand baga-
telles every week; and not to be serious in any part of my
letter." With Etherege also he could sustain the note.
"Pardon [he wrote] a poor creature who is your image, &
whom no gratitude, no consideration of friendship no letters tho' never so elegantly written can oblige to take up
the penn, tho' it be to manage it half an hour."[9] ·

When the Wits wrote personal letters they tended to
follow a simple formula. Usually they opened with a fan-
tastic or jovial salutation and continued with a compliment
or two, often written with tongue in cheek. Then came a
comment on the writer's own condition or situation, followed by a bit of superficial philosophy or mock moralizing. News (when there was any) was delivered with all
the whimsey and irony of a modern newspaper columnist.

The writer concluded the letter with a graceful flourish and begged to remain his correspondent's most faithful (or humble, affectionate, or obedient) servant.

Occasionally the Wits wrote letters in the other harmony of verse, following a popular and long-established fashion. Rochester's elaborate "An Epistolary Essay from M. G. to O. B. upon their Mutual Poems," addressed to the Earl of Mulgrave, is an informal critical essay.[10] His "Letter from Artemisia, in the Town to Cloe, in the Country" is a satiric picture of the follies of the day. The more usual form of the verse letter—such a squib as "A Letter from Mr. Shadwell to Mr. Wicherley" or "The Answer," by Wycherley[11]—is simply a Rabelaisian letter written in rough Hudibrastic verse, with the usual epistolary devices of flippant comments on persons and events, a few sallies of wit, and a flourish at the conclusion. Two letters from "B[uckhurst] to Mr. E[therege]" with their replies from "Mr. E[therege]" either were written in the spirit of bawdy jest or indicate a remarkable preoccupation with bawds and cyprians, especially with one Mistress Cuffley,

> . . . Cuffley, that Whore Paramount!
> Cuffley! whose Beauty warmes the Age,
> And fills our Youth, with Love, and Rage. . . .[12]

Etherege seems to have been fond of this kind of correspondence. Years later he wrote two verse letters to Lord Middleton, in much the same vein as his earlier answers to Buckhurst. (Etherege was forever trying to recapture the delights of his youth.) Apparently Middleton, who was no poet, showed the verses to Dryden, and the great laureate unbent long enough to write Etherege a verse reply in the same flippant (if less Rabelaisian) spirit.[13]

Though the epistolary style of the Wits was always elegant, their vocabulary was often visceral. This, however, would not have shocked a Restoration lady or gentleman. The King himself, the model of a cultured Court, wrote some charming personal letters to his sister, the Duchess of Orleans, yet he occasionally interjected a homely phrase which startles the modern reader.[14] Rochester, in his letters to his wife as well as in those to Savile, used the Anglo-Saxon monosyllables freely. "Wife," he wrote (from "his tub at Mrs. Fourcard's"), "our gut has already been griped and we are now in bed."[15] Wycherley's epistolary vocabulary was no coarser than that of his comedies. In 1677 he wrote to Lord Middleton, "This Town is now as empty, as if your Army were marching over the Bridge; and the whores are as p——x'd, as if the French had possess'd the Town 3 days."[16] Any writer of familiar letters speaks in the idiom of his age, and the idiom of the Restoration was frank and vigorous.

I I

WITH the familiar style of the rakes goes inevitably their flippant attitude toward the phenomena of life. On such diverse subjects as politics, courtship and courtiers, religion and clergymen, and sex and marriage, they wrote with cynicism and irreverence. The comic spirit (handmaid of Reason) had touched their trembling ears; life was devilishly diverting. "Never," wrote Sir Charles Sedley, "Never was any age so comicale as this, and a Laugher where ever he turns himself will have occation to hold his sides."

It was the incongruities in the world of politics which tickled Sir Charles. He was writing to Lord Chesterfield (a rather weary old rake) in 1682, during the political calm following the stormy winds of the Popish Plot. The Town was empty of good acquaintance, he wrote, and "besides, the distinction of Whigg and Tory doth much add to the present desolation, they are in my opinion . . . much of the same stuff at bottom, since they are so easily converted one to another." "Self interest" was the only motive of all politicians. Ministers won their way by flattering titled prostitutes, and lost all by telling the truth. People of quality introduced new fashions to hide their own deformities, and covered up "their want of sence and conversation with extravagant play." A new lady had come to Court, Madame de Soissons; perhaps she should be called "Madame de Soyxante," she was so ancient. "But whether our Court will have her a beauty, a Mis [prostitute], a Wit or a pollitition, is not yet known."[17]

The Earl of Rochester was a courtier by necessity, and he had no illusions about the courtly life. Wine sharpened his senses and released his wild spirit from the bondage of ceremony. To Savile he wrote,

> Oh that second bottle Harry is the sincerest, wisest, & most impartiall downright freind wee have, tells us truth of our selves, & forces us to speak truths of others, banishes flattery from our tongues, and distrust from our Hearts, setts us above the meane Pollicy of Court prudence, wch. makes us lye to one another all day, for feare of being betray'd by each other att night.[18]

The Wits were not to be overawed by mere rank and title. Even the King could be referred to flippantly as "Charlemayne,"[19] and in the next reign Fleetwood Shepherd, writing that Dowager Queen Catherine had made a long, tortuous compliment to the Earl of Dorset, added caustically, "no rat or weasel ever crept into so many holes as she did yesterday."[20] Etherege wrote to the Earl of Dover, newly made Commissioner of the Treasury, "However honourable your title is, you are no other than one of the first cash-keepers in the nation."[21] Wycherley, in a letter to Mulgrave, bantered the Earl of Middleton on his professed laziness:

> I suppose He rides properly like a Foot-Officer, to avoid the Fatigue of pulling on his Boots, and lies rough rather than take Pains to unbutton himself; and upon a March has always the Place of Honour in bringing up the Rear: And if the whole Army

were routed, would be kill'd, not to be at the Trouble of running away.[22]

And Rochester, who revered nobody, wrote at the time of the Prince of Orange's marriage to the Princess Anne a mocking proposal that the Prince should be required to take back to Holland a whole set of worn-out courtiers and courtesans. He added,

A Foreign Prince ought to behave himself like a Kite, who is allow'd to take one Royal Chick for his Reward; but then 'tis expected, before he leaves the Country, his Flock shall clear the whole Parish of all the Garbage and Carrion many Miles about. The King had never such an opportunity; for the Dutch are very foul Feeders, and what they leave he must never hope to be rid of, unless he set up an Intrigue with the Tartars or Cossacks.[23]

Outwardly good Anglicans, the Wits were circumspect with God, but they were often flippant about the forms and ceremonies of the Church and scornful toward its ministers. Sent by the King to act as godfather to Rochester's newborn son, Lord Buckhurst wrote cheerfully to the father,

his Majesty is graciously pleased to make mee his Leiutenant General against the world the flesh and the devil a thursday I shall begin my march, and in the mean time am resolved to behave myself so discreetly, that the Enemy as vigilant as hee is shall have no suspicion of the quarrell, I must confess 'tis with some unwillingness: I begin a war against a prince I have so long served under but since (pax queritur bello) and this short dispute is like to purchase a firmer peace hereafter I will obey my King.[24]

During his residency at Paris, Savile made a policy of regular attendance at the Protestant church of Charenton. Rochester, much amused, suggested that his friend should be rewarded "with the Title of that place, by way of Earldom or Dukedom, as his Majesty shall think most proper to give, or you accept."[25] Savile was in no mood to be rallied; he had heard from England that he would be forced to keep a chaplain. He was indignant at the idea that he needed a personal parson and whimsically aghast at the increased expense, "for my house must be bigger, and my Sunday's dinner must be a new and great expense to me, besides the extraordinarys that every clergyman living will put the family he lives in to."[26]

Although policy required that King and courtiers attend church and appear attentive to sermons, the appearance was commonly deceptive. King Charles wrote to his sister in France,

> We have the same disease of Sermons that you complaine of there, but I hope you have the same convenience that the rest of the family has, of sleeping out most of the time, which is a great ease to those who are bound to heare them.[27]

The Wits' scorn for clergymen sometimes passed beyond the bounds of flippancy. Etherege, deploring the kind of life he led as Envoy, wrote to his friend William Jephson,

> There is but one [life] I like worse, which is that of a clergyman. The mischief they daily do in the world makes me have no better an opinion of them than Lucian had of the ancient philosophers; their pride, their passion, and their covetousness makes them endeavour to destroy the government they were instituted to support, and, instead of taking care of the quietness of our souls, they are industrious to make us cut one another's throats.[28]

The fashion of thumbing noses at the matrimonial state was long established, not only on the stage and in the sophisticated songs of the day, but in life itself. In the fourth year of his reign, King Charles wrote to his sister, "I finde the passion Love is very much out of fasion in this country, and that a handsome face without mony has but few galants, upon the score of marriage."[29] So it is not surprising to find Etherege writing gleefully upon the occasion of Mulgrave's marriage, "Numps is now in the stocks in earnest," and again, to young Lord Arran who had recently married,

It is one of the boldest actions of a man's life to marry. Whoever passes that Rubicon has need of the fortune of Caesar to make him happy. . . . But to be less serious with your Lordship, I have had the honour of your confidence and you have told me of mighty deeds you have performed. I should be glad to be satisfied whether you are as great a hero now you fight in a good cause as when you drew your sword in a querelle d'allemande; the truth is that sort of courage is a little too violent for the present purpose. The business you have now on your hands is to be spun out at length and not to be ended at once.[30]

On the other hand, it is surprising to find now and then a Wit writing to his wife in terms of sincere affection. Etherege's one extant letter to Dame Etherege is a bitterly sarcastic formal note,[31] but several letters from Dorset to his first wife, Mary Bagot, Countess of Falmouth, are couched in terms of "the most sincere, violent, and yet humble passion that the heart of man was ever capable of."[32] Some of Rochester's letters to Lady Rochester are even more passionate; for example, this:

I kiss my deare wife a thousand times, as farr as imagination & wish will give mee leave, thinke upon mee as long as it is pleasant and convenient to you to doe soe, and afterwards forgett mee, for though I would faine make you the Author & foundation of my happiness yet would I not bee the cause of your constraint or disturbance, for I love not my selfe soe much as I doe you, neither doe I value my owne satisfaction equally as I doe yours.[33]

Few love letters from the Wits to ladies *not* their wives have been preserved. Some by Rochester, allegedly to Mrs. Barry, the actress, and one by the Duke of Buckingham to an unknown lady,[34] have an elaborately artificial tone, as if they were written as literary exercises. Some show that a Wit could be flippant in love. "Dear Madam," Rochester wrote to an unknown mistress, "You are stark Mad, and therefore the fitter for me to love; and that is the Reason, I think, I can never leave to be your Humble Servant."[35] A letter from Dorset to a mistress (possibly the notorious Moll Hinton) who had done him a very ill turn, is more ironic than flippant:

Madam

I had obeyed your comands exactly; but that i was ashamed to send you so inconsiderable a summ immediately after receiving a greater favour then any of your Sex have bestowed on mee this five yeare; the best return i can make you is good councell; for i doubt not, considering your youth and strong constitution, but a Little advice and a great deale of Physick may in time restore you to that health i wish you had enioyed a Sunday night instead of

your humble suffring

Servant.[36]

On the subject of their amorous exploits the Wits were invariably flippant, and often boastful. Although they rarely named their conquests (unless the victims were actresses or others of low degree) they sometimes threw out broad hints. Etherege referred to his German actress (whose name was *not* Julia, as some biographers have claimed[37]) as "no less handsome and no less kind than Mrs. Johnson was in England," and again as "something handsomer, and as much a jilt, as Mrs. Barry."[38] The inference is that the two English actresses had enjoyed his favors in the past. Although Savile was usually discreet with the name of his mistress, Lady Scroope, he wrote about her to his friends (in letters which have not been preserved) so wittily and so obviously that everyone knew whom he meant. Halifax warned him: "You are so happy in your writing talent that things are repeated and whisper'd for secrets to so many that they will cease to be so at last."[39] Buckingham made no mention of a specific lady in a letter to Dorset, but his hint must have been an obvious clue: "I can truly assure your Lordship . . . that I have not contaminated my body with any person below my quality since I saw you."[40]

An amour was not to be discussed seriously, in prospect

or in retrospect. Savile was at least half jocular when he
tempted his friend Rochester to come to London with
sugary reports of a French comedienne, pretty Françoise
Pitel,

> . . . a young wench of fifteen, who has more beauty and sweet-
> nesse then ever was seen upon the stage since a friend of ours
> [Nell Gwyn] left it . . . it were a shame to the nation shee should
> carry away a maydenhead shee pretends to have brought, and that
> noe body heer has either witt or addresse or money enough to goe
> to the price of.[41]

Mulgrave's levity over a past escapade with an unknown
"Lady in the Garret" is only slightly marred by a bit of
smug moralizing. He wrote to Etherege,

> For the last memorandum I thank you with all my heart; the
> remembrance of her being very sweet, both as a pleasure enjoyed
> and a danger escaped. I am not so young now but I can chew
> the cud of lechery with some sort of satisfaction; you who are so
> amorous and vigorous may have your mind wholly taken up with
> the present but we grave, decayed people, alas, are glad to steal
> a thought sometimes towards the past, and then are to ask God
> forgiveness for it too.[42]

Mulgrave was only thirty-nine, and still engaged in the
pursuit of mistresses. Etherege was forty-three.

Much of the Wits' epistolary jollity was a pose *à la
mode*: one must be clever in all circumstances. But the
Wits wrote seriously when occasion demanded, and sometimes the sober note was struck in the midst of drollery.
The Earl of Rochester, who could banter even in the face
of death, once broke off after a bit of whimsey with, "But
it is a most miraculous thing . . . when a Man, half in the
Grave, cannot leave off playing the Fool, and the Buffoon."[43]

I I I

WITHIN the Court circles, Henry Savile was considered the master writer of familiar letters. He wrote constantly, to friends and relatives, secretaries and diplomats, on business, to tell the news or make reports from abroad, and sometimes, apparently, for the sheer joy of writing. Dorothy, Dowager Countess of Sunderland, once wrote acidly, "Mr. Savile does show what is very probable, that he has no business, by his writing so many witty letters that nobody could do if anything else were in his head."[44] Perhaps she was jealous, for she too had an eloquent pen. Certainly she was unfair, for Savile, in spite of his claim to be "the lazyest man alive"[45] was really a very industrious person. He was constantly traveling; he held numerous employments; he was always engaged in running errands or doing small kindnesses for friends. Yet he found time to write thousands of entertaining letters, of which nearly two hundred have been preserved.

Savile was flippant, of course, but there was more than ordinary irony mingled with his levity. He wrote dryly, after a naval battle, "We have lost nobody worth hanging." He excused his lack of news from Paris on the ground that "all the world has been so devout here the last week [Lent] that they are not yet returned to sinning enough to make any news." He wrote to his brother (the Marquis of Halifax) for money, warning him that a bill of exchange was on its way, "my method in those cases being but a word and a blow."[46] He wrote that an army was to be disbanded, to the grief of the gentry who had bought commissions, and so "layd out summes which will inconvenience them; soe that if suffering bee part of the businesse of a souldier, diverse of them have made a notable progresse."[47]

An excellent ambassador, he acted according to the forms of ceremony, but he belittled them in his private letters.

He found it hard to "give in to the true and decent gravity of a minister."[48] The jingoism and magniloquence of Louis XIV, "His Most Christian Majesty," were constant causes of amusement to him. From Paris, Savile wrote that the Algerines had "declared warr against this King for detaining theire subjects in his gallyes; perhaps as Christian a ground of quarrell as *pour ma gloire*."[49] He had little respect for people of rank, from the King of France to the famous Duke of Pastrana, "a person that at Madrid is called the terror of husbands, being there what the Earl of Mulgrave would willingly be thought in London."[50]

It is never easy to be sure how much of Savile's levity was assumed. His desire to be entertaining cropped out even in his dispatches from abroad, and he once ended a formal report to a Secretary of State with, "Till I can find more and better entertainment for you, you must please to content yourselfe with the assurances of my beeing . . . your most faithfull and most humble servant." His dispatches were read aloud before the Committee on Foreign Affairs, and Halifax often commented on the applause that greeted them. Even in times of crisis, Savile hid his concern beneath his flippancy. In 1679, when Charles II was reported ill, when the struggle for the succession had begun and it was a question of supporting York or Monmouth, Savile wrote from France complaining that he knew so little of conditions in England "that I am reduced to the truest part of wisdom, which is silence, and upon that foundation must I build my reputation here; in a word, I am fain to nibble in my discourses of England like the asse mumbling thistles; and, whatever good guess I could give, I know not from those I intend to showte with whether I was to cry a Y[ork] or a M[onmouth]."[51]

Beneath his levity was much sober sense. He understood himself and he knew his world. He was ambitious, but no egotist. "What would you have?" he wrote once to Rochester. "The lease of my house lasts above two yeares longer, and the steame of Guy's wisdome dos soe fly into my head, that I cannot but attempt notable undertakings and wanting ballast to sayle steadily upon the least foule weather, I am apt to oversett."[52]

But it was not his lack of bottom that made fat Henry capsize so often; it was his blunt honesty. In a time-serving age he was cursed with more integrity than is good for a politician. Once he gave the Duke of York a piece of his mind, and was banished from the Court. Once in Parliament he spoke and voted against Lauderdale, the King's tyrannical ruler for Scotland—and was dismissed from his post in the bedchamber. Airily he wrote to Rochester that he had been "sacrificed to that filthy dogg Lauderdale."[53] Within the month he was back in service again.

Of no particular religion himself, he did all in his power for the unfortunate Huguenots during his ministry in France. His brother was pleased and somewhat amused. Commenting on Savile's zeal for the Protestant cause and his constant attendance at church, Halifax wrote: "Heaven reward you for giving such countenance to the Gospel! Sure when you come home and find my Lady Scroope [a Catholic] return'd from hearing 4 masses in a morning at Nostre Dame you are both very merry; for I take it to be an equal laughing match between you about your respective devotions." Yet Savile was a humanitarian, and pleaded eloquently for a naturalization bill to give English sanctuary to Protestant refugees. His letter drew from Secretary Jenkins the comment, "What you write of the poor Protestants of that side is great sense and a noble compassion."[54]

Like all the Wits, Savile was a study in contradictions. He was given to wine and revelry, and his reckless disposition often got him into trouble; yet he worked hard for his country, with all the grumbling individualism of the true-born Englishman. He was careless, cynical and profane; yet he was an honest man, a good friend, and, in his way, an artist. His was no organ voice, but his tones were often forceful and ringing.

As Savile grew older his excesses became fewer and his vivacity of expression less. In his forties his letters had lost much of their ingenuity; yet the old fire smoldered, lacking only the wind of repartee to fan it to flame. Once a breezy letter came from that wild Wit, Harry Killigrew, and Savile replied from the depths of a long illness:

Noble Henry,—Sweet namesake of mine, happy-humoured Killigrew, soul of mirth and all delight! the very sight of your letter gave me a kind of Joy that I thought had been at such a distance with me, that she and I were never more to meet. For, since I have been at St. Alban's, heaven and earth were nearer one another than Joy and Fermyn, for here, some half a mile out of town, absent from all my friends, in the fear of being forgot by 'em, I pass my wearisome time in a little melancholly wood, as fit for a restless mind to complain of his sad condition as I am unfit to relate my sufferances to one so happy as your blessed humour makes you; therefore as freely I quit you of hearing what I could say on this subject. Also, allow me the liberty of not answering in your own style; yet, dear Harry, write still the same way. Once I could drink, talk strangely, and be as mad as the best of you, my boys: who knows but what I may come to it again? Comfort me: 'tis well I can stay thus long upon the matter; after the life I have led it is more than I did believe it was possible for me to do; therefore do not abandon me yet; try two or three letters more; there is great hopes of me, and, if that does not do the business, send me to my wood again, and allow me noe other correspondent but pert and dull Mast. . .s, a punishment great enough for a great offender; for in this my misery he plays the devil with me, surpasses himself by much. Prithee, Killigrew, allay his tongue with two or three sharp things, as you and I used to say of you know who, for I lost mine; and so farewell.

H. Savile.[55]

But the fuel was too nearly consumed; there were no more letters of wit and friendship from Henry Savile. A few months later he died, in his forty-fifth year.

Love Songs to Phyllis

THE Court Wits were urban and civilized gentlemen, who wrote poetry according to long-established traditions. They drew their themes and forms from classical ancients or from certain of their immediate poetic ancestors. They had no interest in nature and the language of flowers; for them the countryside was no more than a place of hideous banishment. Religious contemplation and the concept of the Sublime they left to such out-of-fashion poets as Cotton, Flatman, and Wanley. Their chief lyric product was the song of sophisticated love, addressed to a mistress whose identity was concealed by a fanciful name. They wrote to Phyllis or Chloris, or to Amidea, Aurelia, Celia, Corinna, Daphne, Lucinda, Mariana, Olinda, Panthea, Sylvia, Urania, and many more.

For this characteristic use of pastoral names, the Court Wits had many models. Catullus wrote love songs to Lesbia, who was his mistress, Clodia, wife of a Roman politician. Tibullus's Delia was a beautiful courtesan, whose real name was Plania. Cynthia was the pseudonym of Propertius's sweetheart, Hostia of Tibur. Horace's Lydia, Lalage, and Pyrrha were only names.[1] Habington wrote songs to Castara, who in life was the Honorable Lucy Herbert. Lovelace's Lucasta has not been positively identified.[2] Waller's Sacharissa was Lady Dorothy Sidney. Herrick's Julia, Perilla, and Anthea were probably figments of that poet's imagination.

Unfortunately, the love songs of the Wits are deficient in autobiographical evidence. They wrote with half-ironical sentiment, and dealt more with persiflage than with per-

sonalities. They were playful poets, singers of light loves.
As a result, attempts at the identification of Phyllis (or
Chloris, Chloe, or Dorinda) with some real light of love
are rarely fruitful. Two songs by Buckingham may have
been written to the Countess of Shrewsbury.[3] One song by
Sedley was perhaps written to the actress, Mrs. Knip, and
two others may have been written to his permanent mistress, Ann Ayscough.[4] Four songs by Dorset were probably
aimed at Katherine Sedley, but they were hardly amorous.[5]
Some three or four songs by Rochester may have been written to his legitimate lady, perhaps while she was still Elizabeth Malet.[6] These are guesses; no one can be sure.

Like Ovid's elegiac sweetheart, Corinna, who was all his
loves rolled into one, the Restoration Phyllis was one
woman and every woman. The Wits did not even follow
the classical principle that the poetical pseudonym should
be the metrical equivalent of the real name: Phyllis could
stand for Anne, Mary, or Elizabeth. She could also represent an abstraction, a fashionable composite picture of
obdurate or complaisant womanhood. In the Restoration,
amor winked at *omnia*.

Of course, the Wits were not the only Restoration poets
who wrote songs to Phyllis—or to Chloris, who was run-
ner-up in poetic popularity. Every courtier with any pretensions to wit, every professional dramatist or song writer,
every small-wit of the Town poured out amorous verses,
and the names of Phyllis and Chloris were famous throughout the land. Even the King, enamored of Mistress Frances
Stewart, tried his hand at a song, and addressed it to Phyllis.[7] In humorous disgust at the monotony of the cognomi-
nal fashion, young Dorset, in 1671, wrote a famous protest:

> Methinks the poor town has been troubled too long,
> With Phillis and Chloris in every song;
> By fools, who at once can both love and despair,
> And will never leave calling 'em cruel and fair;
> Which justly provokes me in rhime to express
> The truth that I know of bonny black Bess.

The stanzas which follow are all in praise of black (that is, brunette) Bess Morris, who was no pastoral fantasy but a notorious prostitute. The Court and Town were not shocked; they were merely amused. The spate of love songs to Phyllis continued unabated.

Most of the Wits' songs are simply changes rung upon various themes of love and sex, with an occasional paper of verses in praise of drinking. They were written as exercises in lyric skill, or to please the friend or protégé in whose play they were designed to be sung. They were sent with tender billets-doux to soften Phyllis's hard heart; they were read aloud at coffeehouses or taverns for male entertainment only. They were songs written to amuse, with no thought of profundity or moral instruction.

Like their master, King Charles, the Wits were a tuneful lot, pleased by better forms of music as well as by the bawdy songs which (says Pepys) the fiddlers of Thetford were made to play before His Majesty.[8] Magnificent Buckingham kept his own band of musicians, and was himself not only chemist, statesman, and buffoon, but fiddler also.[9] Rochester patronized the composer Paisible, and sent him to Court where Charles heard "with very great delight" his new compositions.[10] Lonely Etherege at Ratisbon wrote to a friend in England,

I have three in my little family [his servants] who now and then give me a little music; they play very well and at sight. We have all the operas, and I have a correspondent at Paris who sends me what is new there.[11]

Even Harry Savile, whose tastes were more for drinking songs, could look forward with pleasure to "a moments titillation by Mr. Staggins who is come over [from France] with great credit and many new aires."[12] It was only natural that the Wits should write their verses with an eye to musical notation.

It was a fruitful age for songs, for little lyrics composed for the harpsichord, violin, bass viol, or theorbo lute. Be-

tween 1660 and 1700, more than one hundred and fifty
song-books were published, with such hopeful titles as
Choice Songs and Ayres (1673), *The Banquet of Musick*
(1688), *Deliciae Musicae* (1695), and *Orpheus Britan-
nicus* (1698). To these, and to others of their kind, the
Wits made a notable contribution; at least fifty of their
songs were set to tunes by such competent composers as
Grabu, Playford, Purcell, Staggins, Turner, and Dama-
scene. Some songs were set by more than one composer;
Rochester's famous "All my past life is mine no more,"
was sung to airs composed variously by Blow, Bowman, and
Reggio. Some of the Wits' songs were reprinted in song-
book after song-book, and a few were still popular until
the middle of the next century.[13]

Among these, as among those lyrics not designed to be
sung, one looks almost in vain for expressions of tender
emotion. The Wits were, in the main, enemies to sentiment; in the Age of Reason, the profession of sincere love
was out-of-fashion stuff. Rochester, the strangest and wildest genius of the period, occasionally used the standard poetic devices of his age for the expression of true emotion.
A few of his songs are unique—two in particular, "Absent
from thee I languish still" and "My dear mistress has a
heart," neither of which, by the way, was ever set to music.
The second of these songs is worth presenting in full, partly
for its own sake, as one of the best lyrics of the century,
and partly because it is so unlike the typical Restoration
song to Phyllis.

> My dear Mistress has a Heart
>   Soft as those kind Looks she gave me;
> When with Love's resistless Art,
>   And her Eyes, she did enslave me.
> But her Constancy's so weak,
>   She's so wild, and apt to wander;
> That my jealous Heart wou'd break,
>   Should we live one Day asunder.

Melting Joys about her move,
    Killing Pleasures, wounding Blisses;
She can dress her Eyes in Love,
    And her Lips can arm with Kisses.
Angels listen when she speaks,
    She's my Delight, all Mankinds Wonder:
But my jealous Heart would break,
    Should we live one Day asunder.

I

THE Wits liked to think of themselves as the poetic
    sons of Horace, and to their putative parent they paid
their filial respects, imitating and translating his odes and
satires, and giving due heed to his instructions as set forth
in *The Art of Poetry*. But as lyricists the Wits were closer
to Anacreon, Catullus, and Ovid among the classic poets.
Anacreon's Ode xv comes close to expressing the lyric mood
of the Court Wits, especially in such a passage as this:

All my care is to prepare
Fragrant unguents for my hair;
Roses for a coronet;
All my care is for today;
For tomorrow who can say?
Come then, let us drink and dice,
And to Bacchus sacrifice,
Ere death come and take us off,
Crying Hold! thou's drunk enough.[14]

Instead of preparing unguents, the Wits combed their
periwigs; but, like the Anacreontic ideal, they drank, diced,
and gave little thought to death. With equal zest they
sang the praises of love and of drinking. It is not without
significance that Rochester imitated two of Anacreon's most
famous songs, Ode xviii, "On a Silver Drinking-Cup,"
and Ode xx, "On the Need for Drinking."[15]
    The Wits held that sensual love was one of the chief
joys of life, and they cared nothing for the reproofs of

grave fops and reverend graybeards. Catullus, whose lyrics they admired and imitated, expressed their attitude as well as his own:

> Come, Lesbia, let us live and love,
> Nor give a damn what sour old men say.[16]

Perhaps the Wits' songs are harder and more brutal than their Catullan models, but there are similarities of theme and form.

Ovid's influence, of course, is apparent throughout the whole stream of seventeenth century love poetry. The Court Wits felt a strong kinship with the Augustan courtier and man-about-town. They were attracted by "the lasciviousness of his *Elegies*, and his *Art of Love* . . . no man," wrote Dryden, "has ever treated the passion of love with so much delicacy of thought, and of expression, or searched into the nature of it more philosophically than he."[17] In Dryden's *Ovid's Epistles: with his Amours* (1680), Epistles i and xv were translated by Scroope and Mulgrave respectively, while Elegies I, viii, II, v, and III, iv, were translated by Sedley, and Elegy II, ix, by Rochester. And there are echoes of Ovid in many of the Wits' songs.

Whatever kinship the Wits had with the classic poets, they were still Englishmen, and their poetic themes were woven on English looms. Like any generation of poets, they thought themselves superior to their ignorant and unskilled ancestors; the greatest English poets (in their eyes) were their older contemporaries: Cowley, Waller, and Denham. Shakespeare they loved and read, deploring his crudities and ineptness. Jonson they admired, patronizingly, as the pattern of correctness in a barbaric age. Milton was quite a fellow (for a Republican), but not to be mentioned in the same breath with Cowley. Spenser was all right for "the enthusiastic parts of poetry," but he lacked the advantages of modern conversation. (Only Dryden ad-

mitted Spenser as a master.) As for the rest, one looks almost in vain for comment on the famous Jacobean and
Caroline poets, although the Wits must have known (and
perhaps felt some kinship with) Donne, Herrick, Carewe,
Lovelace, Suckling, and Marvell. Perhaps Dryden, who
was something of a Boswell to the Wits, expressed something of their attitude toward their immediate poetic ancestors, when he said of John Donne,

> He affects the metaphysics, not only in his satires, but in his
> amorous verses, where nature only should reign; and perplexes
> the minds of the fair sex with nice speculations of philosophy, when
> he should engage their hearts and entertain them with the soft-
> nesses of love.[18]

The "metaphysics" of Donne and his followers was too
complex and roundabout for the direct minds of the Wits;
they might toy with an idea, but they would never carry it
out "with nice speculations of philosophy." By the time of
the Restoration, the metaphysical school of poetry had
worn itself out with farfetched conceits and strained antitheses. Only religious poets found the style still suited to
their mystical concepts.

One other great tradition of seventeenth century poetry,
Spenserian courtly love, was also wearing out. The Spenserian style was too verbose and elaborate to suit well with
the Wits' impatience, and the wave of Elizabethan enthusiasm had dashed itself to spray on the hard rocks of Restoration cynicism. In style and theme, the Wits were more
akin to the pagan sons of Jonson: Brome, Randolph, and
Suckling.

The Restoration Wits carried on the seventeenth century war against Elizabethan romance. The Elizabethans
had exalted their stony-hearted ladies in luscious lines;
the Wits called their mistresses bad names. The Elizabethans had emphasized the religious nature of love, the
superiority of mind (or soul) over body, and they had

wallowed in the grief of unrequited love.[19] The Court Wits
dwelt on carnal love, on the superiority of body over mind
(souls they refused to meddle with), and their attitude
toward unrequited love is well expressed by a poem of
Etherege's which is sharply reminiscent of Suckling's
"Why so pale and wan, fond lover?"

> If she be not as kind as fair,
>   But peevish and unhandy,
> Leave her, she's only worth the care
>   Of some spruce Jack-a-dandy.
> I would not have thee such an ass,
>   Hadst thou ne'er so much leisure,
> To sigh and whine for such a lass,
>   Whose pride's above her pleasure.
> Make much of ev'ry buxom girl,
>   Which needs but little courting;
> Her value is above the pearl,
>   That takes delight in sporting.[20]

There is nothing new in this attitude of rebellion against
the power of woman; it is the natural and almost automatic
reaction against chivalric love, and it is found even in
those periods in which courtly love was dominant. The
Court Wits were the inheritors of a highly complex lyric
tradition, from which they took those elements most suited
to their skeptical minds. However, they did not completely ignore courtly love; a few of their poems still
echoed faintly the themes of Provençal and Petrarch. The
makers of modern anthologies have used some of these
songs as the substance for their pictures of the Restoration,
to the exclusion of more typical representatives of the age.
The most popular single poem has been Sedley's over-
praised (for its initial figure),

> Love still has something of the Sea,
>   From whence his Mother rose;
> No time his Slaves from Doubt can free,
>   Nor give their Thoughts repose:

Like a ship at sea, the lover is alternately "becalm'd" when his mistress smiles, or "in Tempests lost" when she frowns. He suffers from "Disdain and Pride," endures "Rivals and Falshood," and comes so slowly to any degree of joy that he hardly finds pleasure in it. All this in the conventional Petrarchan strain. Then (perhaps with Marvell's winged chariot hurrying near) Sedley ends on a different note, and we realize that all the pretty nonsense which went before was no more than a build-up for the commonest of Restoration appeals:

> 'Tis cruel to prolong a Pain,
>   And to defer a Joy;
> Believe me, gentle Celemene
>   Offends the winged Boy.
>
> An hundred thousand Oaths your Fears
>   Perhaps would not remove;
> And if I gaz'd a thousand Years
>   I could no deeper love.

In "Love's Slavery" the Earl of Mulgrave rejoiced that he was bound in Celia's chains. In "I Cannot change, as others do," Rochester insisted that, in spite of Phyllis's obduracy, he would still love on, break his heart, and die. In Sir Carr Scroope's "One Night when all the village slept," a disconsolate shepherd, Myrtillo, sang his love's-complaint to the woods and died.[21] Sedley, in "Fear not, my Dear, a Flame can never dye," claimed to prefer his mistress's mind over her body and swore eternal constancy in love. Buckingham, in "To his Mistress," labored to prove the soul superior to the body. Mulgrave asserted that he cherished the pain of absence from his mistress; perhaps he wrote "Since from my dear Astrea's sight" on his voyage to Tangier.

These poems and a few more like them were all the Wits had to offer on the altar of the dying chivalric tradition—a cooling altar which was barely kept warm by such romantic poetasters as Wolseley, Ayloffe, Duke, Behn, and Tate. With the Wits, the reaction against chivalric love, which had been working spasmodically since the very Provençal originators themselves, may be said to have reached its climax. But no new altar was raised: in matters of love the Wits were atheists. Influenced by Horace, Catullus and Ovid, by such mechanistic philosophers as Hobbes and Lucretius, and by the scientific spirit of the century with its emphasis on right reason (the test of the senses) as the true guide to man's conduct, the Wits concluded that chivalric love was irrational madness. As Wycherley phrased it (in "A Song. To one, who thought to get His Mistress by Scribling to Her"),

> Since Nonsense is the Proof of Love,
> Reason in Love, wou'd Folly prove.

To the intellect, love was folly; to the senses, it was delightful. Love was lust—no more; a matter to be considered apart from all questions of morality, religion, or the code of the gentleman. It followed that the Wits' ideal beloved was the woman who was "kind," and the word had a very special, carnal meaning.

As they gave up the Elizabethan love tradition, the Wits gave up also the Elizabethan prosody, with its expanded figures of speech, its lengthy similes, metaphors, and conceits. Hailing Waller as their master and their leader in the revolt against the elaborate straining after effect which had characterized so much of earlier English verse, they wrote in the easy language of "refined" society, using only such simple figures and allusions as the moderately well-read courtier could easily understand. Their commonest verse forms were the ballad stanza of four lines and the tetrameter couplet. Their rhymes were short and obvious. Their aim was to turn a neat phrase or to polish a couplet. Their notion of the perfect love song was much like that of Ambrose Philips; it should have

. . . an exact purity of style, with the most easy and flowing numbers; an elegant and unaffected turn of wit, with one uniform
and simple design. A song is, as it were, a little image in enamel,
that requires all the nice touches of the pencil, a gloss and a smoothness, with those delicate finishing strokes, which would be super-
fluous thrown away upon larger figures, where the strength and
boldness of a masterly hand gives all the grace.[22]

It should be added that the "uniform and simple design" often came to a point, much like the "nub" of an
anecdote. Sometimes, one suspects, the lyric was constructed solely to surprise the reader with the neat twist
at the end. The wit lay partly in the design of the poem,
partly in its polished turn of phrase, and partly in the quip
with which it ended—a smart antithesis, an epigram, or a
play on words. Simplicity, clarity, smoothness, and brevity
—with a clever twist at the end—these were the poetic
aims of the Court Wits.

The *vers de société* which the Wits produced is all so
similar in form and theme that it is difficult to differentiate
their styles. Rochester was sometimes rough in his meter
and rhymes; "easy" Etherege was usually graceful and
polished; Sedley was likely to be a bit long-winded; Mulgrave was often colorless; Dorset was inclined to be humorous; Buckingham was usually slipshod in his versification;
and Wycherley was often turgid. Nevertheless, attempts at
identifying the author of an anonymous song are usually
fruitless. No doubt, the fact that every Wit wrote primarily
for the applause of his fellows had much to do with the
similarity of lyric style within the group. Wycherley once
wrote a well-meant reproof "To Sir George Etheridge,
on his shewing his Verses imperfect":

> Be wise, and ne'er to publick View produce
> Thy undrest Mistress, or unfinisht Muse;
> Since either, by that Dishabilé, seem
> To hurt their Beauties in our good Esteem;
> And easier far we kind Impressions make,

Than we can rooted Prejudices shake.
From Nature learn, which Embrio's does conceal,
Thine, till they're perfect, never to reveal.

I I

MOST of the Wits' love-songs are dominated by
rationalism, the eternal enemy of romance. When
Phyllis refused to be kind (i.e., complaisant) and made it
clear that she preferred romance and wedding bells, her
lover wasted no words on flattery or cajolery; instead he
sought to beat down her defenses with the cudgel of argument. Many a Phyllis must have proved coy, for the commonest theme of Restoration verse is what Thomas Carewe
called (and exemplified) "Persuasions to Enjoy." The
postulate of the argument was that Phyllis was chaste
because of foolish timidity, stupid pride, or mistaken
honour (which Rochester labeled "mean, mistrustful
shame"). The poet's task was to overcome these silly attitudes by sophistry. So, to pick a few examples, we find
Phyllis urged to be kind to the poet:

Because "Valour's a Vice, if not with Honour joyn'd, Beauty a
raging Plague, if never kind." (Sedley, "To Celia")
Because "age shall come" and with age Phyllis's beauty will be
gone. (Buckingham, "Phyllis, though your all-powerful
charms")[23]
Because lovers have only a "few short moments snatch'd by love,
From many tedious days." (Dorset, "Phyllis, for shame")
Because moderns "live in an age that's more civil and wise, Than
to follow the rules of romances," and, anyway, "all maids
are mortal at fourteen." (Dorset, "Ah! Chloris, 'tis time")
Because to give of one's favors freely is true honor, while to marry
would be to "scandalize our love." Moreover, the woman
who marries "grows by the Church a licenc'd Whore."
(Wycherley, "The Conscientious Mistress")
Because Phyllis can hope for no mercy from heaven unless she
relieves "poor mortals in despair." (Rochester, "Fling this
useless Book away")[24]

Because, if Phyllis is peevishly coy, her reputation will suffer anyway, and she will "die with the Scandal of a Whore, And never know the Joy." (Rochester, "Phyllis, be gentler, I advise")

So with arguments and threats the Wits wooed their mistresses, offering in exchange for capitulation nothing but mutual pleasure. With logical consistency, they did not promise constancy. On the contrary, like Rochester (in "Love and Life. A Song") they warned Phyllis,

> If I, by Miracle, can be
> This live-long Minute true to thee,
> 'Tis all that Heav'n allows.

Or with Sedley (in "Phillis, let's shun the common Fate") they proposed an amicable settlement,

> When we begin to want Discourse,
> And Kindness seems to taste of Force,
> As freely as we met, we'll part,
> Each one possest of their own Heart.

Etherege even managed to twist the question of constancy into a new "Persuasion to Love," when he wrote "To a Lady, asking him how long he would love her":

> It is not, Celia, in our power
> To say how long our love will last;
> It may be we within this hour
> May lose those joys we now do taste;
> The blessed, that immortal be,
> From change in love are only free.
> Then, since we mortal lovers are,
> Ask not how long our love will last;
> But while it does, let us take care
> Each minute be with pleasure pass'd.
> Were it not madness to deny
> To live because we're sure to die?

This is all very reasonable, no doubt, but one wonders what effect it had on the cruel fair. Wooing by disputation seems

more than a bit dry and unromantic; but for sighing and
whining and much mooning about, the Wits had no use.
Wycherley wrote to his romantic-minded mistress (in
"For Fruition"),

> Fantastic Phillis! cease to please,
> Or else consent to give me Ease;
> Pox! of your dull Platonic Schemes;
> 'Tis wasting Life in idle Dreams,
> And quitting solid Joys, to prove
> What crowns the Fairy Land of Love.

The Wits preferred the direct approach. A fool might
sigh and whine before the feminine fortress, but the man
of reason was supposed (poetically, at least) to take it *vi et
armis*. So we have quite a few songs of advice to lovers, including these outspoken instructions by the Earl of Dorset
(in "The Advice"),

> Wou'd you in Love succeed, be Brisk, be Gay,
> Cast all dull Thoughts, and serious Looks away;
> Think not with down cast Eyes, and mournful Air,
> To move to pity, the Relentless Fair,
> Or draw from her bright Eyes a Christal Tear.
> This Method, Foreign is to your Affair,
> Too formal for the Frolick you prepare:
> Thus, when you think she yields to Loves advance,
> You'll find 'tis no Consent, but Complaisance.
> Whilst he who boldly rifles all her Charms,
> Kisses and Ravishes her in his Arms,
> Seizes the favour, stays not for a Grant,
> Alarms her Blood, and makes her sigh and pant;
> Gives her no time to speak, or think't a Crime,
> Enjoys his Wish, and well imploys his time.[25]

Perhaps this is not to be taken literally as a prescript
for rape—or even seduction. It may simply represent the
extreme of the reaction to the "Slave of Love" theme so
popular in earlier poetry, and still playing a major role in
Restoration heroic drama. The Wits had to compete with
the romantic lushness of Scudéry's *Le Grand Cyrus*, to be

found on every lady's toilette table, and with the great lovers of *The Indian Queen* and *The Conquest of Granada*, at the Covent Garden Theatre.

In addition to arguments, promises of inconstancy, and threats of force, the Wits had another weapon in their arsenal of blandishments. When, perhaps, all other devices had failed to break the unholy deadlock, the Wits, with low cunning, wrote little erotic stories in verse to remind Phyllis of the delights of love, and to tempt her from her joyless chastity. In Rochester's opinion (in "An Allusion to Horace"), it was his companion Sedley who was most successful with such weapons—Sedley, who

> . . . has that prevailing, gentle Art,
> That can with a resistless Charm impart
> The loosest Wishes to the chastest Heart.
> Raise such a Conflict, kindle such a Fire
> Betwixt declining Vertue and Desire;
> 'Till the poor vanquish'd [maid] dissolves away,
> In Dreames all Night, in Sighs and Tears all Day.

Such verse-tales fall into two classes: the mock-pastoral episode and the pornographic narrative. The first of these is well represented by Sedley's "Smooth was the Water, calm the Air," in which Strephon and his nymph are introduced at the Strawberry Garden, whither they had gone "to quench their mutual flames." The waiter brings them strawberries and cream. In the following lines, Sedley makes use of a simple device—disappointment of the reader's erotic expectations:

> The amorous Strephon ask'd the Maid,
>   What's whiter than this Cream?
> She blush'd, and could not tell, she said:
>   Thy Teeth, my pretty Lamb.
>
> What's redder than these Berries are?
>   I know not, she reply'd.
> Those lips, which I'll no longer spare,
>   The burning Shepherd cry'd.

> And strait began to hug her:
> > This Kiss, my Dear,
> > Is sweeter far
> > > Than Strawberries, Cream and Sugar.

In another, more obvious example, Sedley begins:

> Young Coridon and Phillis
> Sat in a lovely Grove,
> Contriving Crowns of Lillies,
> Repeating toys of Love,
> And something else, but what I dare not name; [26]

The phrase "and something else" is repeated frequently in the balance of the poem, with an obvious intention. A similar aim is apparent in an erotic mock-pastoral by Rochester, which begins

> In a dark, silent, shady Grove,
> Fit for the Delights of Love,

and uses the oft-repeated "Et Cetera" as the equivalent for "and something else."

These are comparatively mild; others are downright, impudently pornographic. Of this species, those written in the mock-pastoral form—like Rochester's "As Chloris full of harmless Thoughts Beneath a Willow lay," and "Fair Chloris in a Pig-Sty lay"—are perhaps least offensive. The use of the absurd conventions of Italian pastoralism for base purposes gives to such trifling verses a touch of burlesque which tends to save them from blatant vulgarity. On the other hand, the non-pastoral forms—remote imitations of the lusciousness of Carewe's "A Rapture" or Randolph's "A Pastoral Courtship"—are frankly lascivious. Mulgrave's "The happy Night"[27] and Wycherley's "Chloris enjoy'd in her Sleep" are two examples of this type. Such poems as Etherege's "The Imperfect Enjoyment" and one by Rochester under the same title (beginning "Naked she lay,") were apparently written in imitation of Ovid's "Imperfect Enjoyment" (*Amores*,

III, vii), and are superficially pornographic. Actually they are frank studies of impotence written from the depths of spiritual revulsion.

One final device must be mentioned in connection with the almost universal attempt to impart loose wishes to chaste feminine hearts—the frequent play on the verbs "to die" and "to expire." In apparently innocuous little verse episodes, or in conventionally phrased lyrics, either of these verbs is likely to be used (without warning) as a euphemism for the consummation of passion. Such word play was not new in English verse,* but it was probably more often used in the Restoration, and with more twists and variants than ever before. Consider for example the following by Rochester:

> While on those lovely Looks I gaze,
>   To see a Wretch pursuing,
> In Raptures of a blest Amaze,
>   His pleasing happy Ruin.
> 'Tis not for pity that I move;
>   His Fate is too aspiring,
> Whose heart, broke with a Load of Love,
>   Dies wishing and admiring.
>
> But if this Murder you'd forego,
>   Your Slave from Death removing;
> Let me your Art of Charming know,
>   Or learn you mine of Loving.
> But whether Life, or Death, betide,
>   In Love 'tis equal measure,
> The Victor lives with empty Pride;
>   The Vanquish'd die with Pleasure.

The nub is in the last two lines. The victor (the woman who remains chaste) has only her empty pride as her reward, while the vanquished (the "kind" Phyllis and her lover) "die" in the ecstasy of fulfillment.

---

* Donne made considerable use of this pun. See, for examples, "The Canonization," "Sweetest love I do not go," "The Damp," and "The Prohibition."

There is nothing very subtle or clever about this device,
yet a surprising number of minor poets were fascinated by
it, and the great John Dryden himself made very obvious
use of it in one of his most infamous songs, "Whil'st Alexis
lay prest," *not* to be found in ordinary anthologies. For
further examples see Rochester's "My Goddess Lydia,
heav'nly Fair," Mulgrave's "From all uneasy Passions
free," and Sedley's "None, but a Muse in Love, can tell."[28]

Phyllis has left us no record of her reaction to these
various attempts at seduction by erotic songs. We can be
sure only that she saw or heard them; many of them were
sung on the stage, and there is no evidence that Phyllis left
the theatre in an agony of outraged modesty. All of the
songs were printed in various song-books or poetical miscellanies, and no feminine proscription of the volumes is
recorded. In fact, if we can believe the cynical poet, Evelyn,
the lover who visited his mistress betimes of a morning was
sure to find some "Lewd song on table," for, after all (said
Evelyn) women are

> Vain, foolish, fond, proud, whimsical,
> Dissembling, hypocritical.[29]

Apparently erotic songs were not necessarily vulgar to
the Restoration reader. They were "mannerly obscene,"
and since they were "mannerly" they were permissible.
The bookseller's preface to Rochester's collected poems of
1691 tells us with the utmost gravity that the publisher

> . . . has been diligent out of Measure, and has taken exceeding
> Care that every Block of Offence shou'd be removed. So that this
> Book is a Collection of such Pieces only, as may be received in a
> vertuous Court, and not unbecome the Cabinet of the Severest
> Matron.

But despite this elaborate precaution, the volume contains
most of the noble poet's erotic verse; the poems omitted
(they appeared in the scandalous "Antwerp" edition of
1680) were obscene without being mannerly.[30]

When all poetic arguments and seductions failed, the Wits used their last weapon, vituperation. Their satiric songs must have truly distressed Phyllis and her pastoral colleagues, not because they are more obscene than the wooing songs, but because they are sharply anti-love and anti-woman in theme. With them the Wits not only dragged Phyllis from her Petrarchan pedestal, they threw her in the gutter. Perhaps in the revulsion of sexual satiety, perhaps in resentment at their own libidinous weakness (or failure), perhaps in the ancient masculine convention that women are basically evil, the Wits belabored Phyllis with foul words strung on the lyric frame. Little satires rather than true songs, their anti-woman poems are sometimes clever, sometimes merely nasty.

Among the cleverest of the lot are Dorset's songs on Dorinda (otherwise Sylvia), who has been identified as Sir Charles Sedley's daughter Katherine. Eventually ennobled as Countess of Dorchester, Katherine had the doubtful honor of being a recognized mistress of James II. Against her, Dorset (perhaps he had been a rejected suitor) made a decidedly unpleasant use of his poetic license. See, for examples, "Proud with the spoils of royal cully," "Dorinda's sparkling wit, and eyes," "Sylvia, methinks you are unfit," and this vicious attack:

> Tell me, Dorinda, why so gay,
>   Why such embroid'ry, fringe, and lace?
> Can any dresses find a way,
> To stop th' approaches of decay,
>   And mend a ruin'd face?
>
> Wilt thou still sparkle in the box,
>   Still ogle in the ring?
> Canst thou forget thy age and pox?
> Can all that shines on shells and rocks
>   Make thee a fine young thing?
>
> So have I seen in larder dark,
>   Of veal a lucid loin;

> Replete with many a brilliant spark,
> As wise philosophers remark,
>   At once both stink and shine.

To this group of satiric lyrics belong several more by Dorset, notably "Methinks the poor town," and "Phillis, the fairest of love's foes." Add also Etherege's "If she be not as kind as fair," and Sedley's "Drink about till the Day find us"—anti-feminine songs only in the sense that they maintain women are hardly worth the wooing.

The anti-woman theme was carried to its bitterest extreme by the Earl of Rochester, who was by turns the Restoration's most famous amorist and its most cynical misogynist. It must have been in a mood of savage disgust with all women that he wrote the scabrous "Against the Charms our Passions have," which exists in two versions, one bowdlerized and one frankly scatological. Similarly bitter moods must have produced such songs as "I Wench as well as others do," in which Phyllis is called a downright whore; " 'Tis not that I am weary grown," in which Phyllis is advised to fulfill her destiny—to be the mistress of all mankind; and "How now, brave Swain, why art thou thus cast down?" with its contention that all women are creatures "so mean, so senseless, and so common; That Nature blusht when first she made the Sex." Much milder in tone, but typical in theme, is this:

> Love a woman! you're an Ass,
>   'Tis a most insipid Passion
> To chuse out for your Happiness
>   The silliest Part of God's Creation.
>
> Let the Porter, and the Groom,
>   Things design'd for dirty Slaves,
> Drudge in fair Aurelia's Womb
>   To get Supplies for Age and Graves.
>
> Farewel, Woman, I intend,
>   Henceforth, ev'ry night to sit
> With my lewd well-natur'd Friend,
>   Drinking to engender Wit.

As far as Rochester was concerned, chivalric love was dead. He buried it, and sang his bawdy songs at its funeral.

The lyric vein of the Court Wits breathed itself out in songs to Phyllis, coaxing, threatening, tempting, or vilifying the symbolic Restoration mistress. Even some of their drinking songs have an amatory twist, as if (according to Etherege in "The Libertine")

> Wine and women only can
> Cherish the drooping heart of man.

Poets of the objective, they rarely looked into their own minds for subject matter or inspiration. They had little desire to deal with generalities, to rehash the eternal verities, or to discover new truths. Perhaps most of them died too young; youth is for love, age for contemplation. It is interesting to note that in his dotage William Wycherley wrote some tedious poetical disquisitions upon such subjects as "In Vindication of Simplicity, and Good Nature," "Upon Jealousie," "Upon the Tyranny of Custom," and "Upon Life, and Death"; also that the Earl of Mulgrave, who lived a long life, in his later years turned out some passable odes, one an "Ode on the Death of Henry Purcell," another "On the Loss of an only Son, Robert Marquis of Normanby," and, surprisingly, a pious ode "On the Deity," in which the aging rake professed to envy the

> Thrice happy Angels in their high Degree;
> Created worthy of extolling thee!

III

IT is difficult to determine what influence the Wits may have had upon their own and succeeding generations, but there can be no doubt of their popularity as lyric poets. They were quoted, cited as authorities or examples, envied, admired and flattered—alive or dead. Part of their fame, of course, was due to their rank. Noble authors alive had pelf and preferment to bestow; dead, they bequeathed to their songs the prestige of their own quality.

So (to list a variety of instances) we find Prior writing:

> Sedley, indeed, and Rochester might write
> For their own Credit, and their Friends Delight,
> Shewing how far they cou'd the rest outdo,
> As in their Fortunes, in their Writings too.[31]

So, with less envy and more flattery, Captain William Ayloffe praised Mulgrave, Dorset, Rochester and Sedley by claiming for them the "gallant easy Wit of Horace."[32] To Dryden, Sedley was a modern Tibullus.[33] To Aphra Behn, Rochester was the "young Lucretius" of his time, one who in love and verse had outdone Ovid.[34] Dorset was not only the Maecenas of his age, but, in the opinion of many critics (Dryden among them), he was the Horace as well.[35]

If parody is a proof of popularity, Sir Carr Scroope's little song, "As Amoret with Phyllis sat,"[36] must have been widely known and liked. It had the doubtful honor of being parodied by one Alexander Radcliffe (a very minor poet), in verses beginning "As Tom and I well warmed with wine."[37] Probably other parodies of the Wits' songs were written, but no more have survived.

By at least one contemporary the lyric style of the Wits was thought to be worthy of emulation. Aphra Behn, defending her own "unstudied and undesigned way of writing," cited as models the poems of "the late Lord Rochester and the present Lord Mulgrave" and "those little chance things of Sir Carr Scroope," all of which "so infinitely exceeded the flights and Industry" of the professional poets. She had the grace to elevate John Dryden from the ranks of the professionals, and to place him side by side with the Wits.[38]

Of all the Wits, Rochester was the poet most quoted and most admired by his own and following generations. Some of his fame, no doubt, was due to his reputation as the

Mall Kirke

By Sir Peter Lely. Courtesy of the British Museum

Mary, Countess of Falmouth
Courtesy of the British Museum

Wicked Earl; but to some extent it was the result of his
genius as a poet. When he died in 1680, all Parnassus
lamented his death, and wondered who could succeed him.
John Oldham had no doubts. He wrote:

> If I am reckon'd not unblest in Song,
> 'Tis what I owe to thy all teaching Tongue:
> Some of thy Art, some of thy tuneful Breath,
> Thou didst by Will to worthless Me bequeath:
> Others thy Flocks, thy Lands, thy Riches have,
> To me thou didst thy Pipe, and Skill vouchsafe.[39]

It is possible, too, that the content of his verses, rather
than their metrical excellence, had something to do with
Rochester's poetical longevity. Samuel Pepys owned a copy
of the 1680 edition of Rochester's works, which he kept in
a drawer, apart from his other books. His comment on the
dead poet (in 1680) was: "as he is past writing any more
so bad in one sense, so I despair of any man surviving him
to write so good in another."[40] Perhaps it was to such
readers as Pepys that the anonymous author of "Reformation of Manners, A Satyr" (*ca.* 1695) was referring when
he wrote indignantly,

> Let this describe the nation's character,
> One man reads Milton, forty Rochester.
> This lost his taste, they say, when h'lost his sight;
> Milton had thought, but Rochester had wit.
> The case is plain, the temper of the time,
> One wrote the lewd, and t'other the sublime.[41]

The anonymous reformer was guilty of exaggeration,
no doubt, yet there is something in his complaint. The
noble and sublime in poetry has its universal appeal and
always will have, yet in any age there is an unregenerate
portion of mankind which recognizes itself as of the earth,
earthy, and which takes delight in that which the moral reformer calls lewd. The lyrics of the Restoration Wits have
been condemned for their lewdness by the critics and ped-

agogues of the last two centuries; only recently have they been formally rediscovered and discussed as if they were something more than a stench in the nostrils. Perhaps this rediscovery is merely a passing fad, a phase of a momentarily frank and easy generation.

The Wits, fortunately for their ghosts, wrote with utter indifference to the judgments of posterity. They wrote to please each other; they wrote little because they had no need to write, and they had not much to say. As they dressed their persons with the utmost concern for appearance, yet strove to give a gentlemanly impression of carelessness in dress, so they wrote their songs. It was the fashion to pretend that a painstakingly polished lyric had been dashed off in haste. Their lyrics were reflections of a fashionable attitude toward the phenomena of sex relationship; yet so deeply ingrained did the fashion become that pose often turned into reality, and their lyrics became personal reactions expressed with all the limited skill at their command. The lesser lyricists among the Court Wits —Scroope, Buckingham, Mulgrave and Wycherley—like the numerous "Town-Wits" and semi-professionals— Behn, Ayloffe, Duke, Sprat, Wolsely and their ilk—were derivative and imitative. But Dorset, Etherege, Sedley and Rochester were true poets in whose hands the merely fashionable themes and forms were new molded into verses of enduring worth.

Libels and Satires

ACCORDING to Bishop Burnet, the Earl of Rochester regularly hired a footman, equipped him "with a red coat and a musket as a centinel, and kept him all the winter long every night at the doors of such ladies [at Whitehall] as he believed might be in intrigues." By this device (so the story went) the poet acquired a deal of scandal, and, "when he was well furnished with materials, he used to retire into the country for a month or two to write libels."[1] When Burnet scolded the dying sinner for his many malicious verses, Rochester insisted that "there were some people who could not be kept in Order or admonished but in this way." The bishop was not convinced; he read his lordship a severe lecture on the sin of libeling "out of spite," mixing "Lyes with Truth," or writing "to Gratifie Revenge." "The most malicious things," warned Burnet, "if wittily expressed, might stick to and blemish the best man in the World, and the malice of a Libel could hardly consist with the charity of an Admonition."[2] The bishop was right, of course, but his scoldings were futile. In the Restoration, satire was rampant, malice was wanton, and misbegotten lies were innumerable.

The terms satire and libel (or lampoon) were used very loosely by the Restoration poets. In an attempt to order the confusion, John Dryden described the true satirist as one who sought "to correct the vices and follies of his time, and to give the rules of a happy and virtuous life." As examples of such laudable work he offered among the ancients the writings of Horace, Juvenal and Persius, and, among the moderns, Butler's *Hudibras* and (modestly) his own *Absalom and Achitophel* and *Mac Flecknoe*. Libels and lampoons he consigned to a lower level; they were dangerous weapons "and for the most part unlawful." For the penning of libels he saw two permissible reasons: the first, for revenge, "when we have been affronted in the same nature, or have been any ways notoriously abused"; the second, in rebuke, when the subject of the libel is "a public nuisance," for (he wrote), " 'Tis an action of virtue to make examples of vicious men." Throughout his discussion runs the argument that there should be truth and wit in satire—elements obviously lacking in the libels of the age. For the last, Dryden had reason to complain; he said with truth "more Libels have been written against me, than almost any man now living."[3]

Few among the so-called "satires" preserved in manuscript collections, commonplace books, miscellanies, the various "Works" of the poets, or such anthologies as the *Poems on Affairs of State*, conform to Dryden's hopeful definition. Few have any particular merit of thought or phrase. To the uninitiated they are often as pointless as yesterday's topical jokes. They were written for a small audience which was close to the people attacked and the events discussed. They are chiefly assaults on ladies of dubious honor, on poets, politicians and pedants, on kings, commoners and coxcombs, on anyone, in short, who ever engaged in a quarrel or achieved such notoriety as to become to some poetaster "a public nuisance." Many of the libels are understandably anonymous, and attributions by copyists or printers must be taken with caution. Such libels reached the public through devious channels. Many were presented at the coffeehouses (particularly at Will's) where they were seized upon, copied, and vended by such scandalmongers as "Captain" Robert Julian, "Secretary to the Muses," who made a disreputable living with his pockets full of libels for sale.[4] Libels which fell into the hands of booksellers were printed either as broadside sheets or in miscellanies, ascribed sometimes to a known poet, sometimes to "A Person of Quality" or "A Gentleman of Honour." Eventually many such verses appeared in "The Works of"—almost any poet, dead or alive. The result is a bibliographical nightmare.

A considerable number of extant libels and satires are attributed to the Court Wits. Whether those gentry were indeed the authors, or whether their reputations attracted poems into their canon it is impossible to say. Certainly they were famed and feared as satirists in their own day. Andrew Marvell, a first-rate muckraker himself, said that Rochester was "the only man in England that had the true vein of satire."[5] Dryden, in an effusive dedication to Dorset, claimed to have formed his own satires on Dorset's "as the most perfect model."[6] Tom Brown praised Rochester, Dorset, and Oldham (a protégé of the Wits) as the three "Greatest Satirists of the English."[7] Buckingham was so well known as a libeler that it was sometimes a toss-up whether a "new Treasonable lampoon" was to be charged to him or to Rochester.[8] Etherege was once described as that "Sir George" who "always of women Writes, and always Rails."[9] Mulgrave was often censured as one who wrote libels yet was himself a fit subject for invective. Even the lesser Wits, who wrote nothing of importance, tried their hands at scandalous squibs, most of which are lost.

The lost libels of the Wits must have been as numerous as those which have survived. What, for example, became of the "numberless ballads" which Grammont said were written by Rochester, Dorset, Sedley, and Etherege against Lord Chesterfield, when he selfishly took his amorous wife into the country? And what of the lampoon by Rochester against Miss Price, of which the perfidious Hobart made such deadly use? Or the "letter in verse, which my Lord Rochester had written some time before, upon the

intrigues of the two courts"?[10] Grammont, of course, is
unreliable, but to turn to other informants, what became of
Buckingham's attempt to "Rehearse" in couplets the "lewd
crimes" of Mrs. Jenny Middleton,[11] and of Fleetwood
Shepherd's lost "Songs on the Duke of Monmouth with
his Oration-Consolatory on my Lady Dorset's death, and
a Politick Dissertation between my Lady Powis and Capt.
Dangerfield"?[12] Or what of Sir Carr Scroope's lampoon on
Katherine Sedley, daughter of Sir Charles Sedley, which
charged that she was "as mad as her mother and as vicious
as her father"? Or the dainty poetic essay on Sir Carr's
pox and his mistress' pregnancy which "she [Katherine]
repay'd him with"?[13] We are informed that many of
Rochester's "immoral writings" were burned at his death,
among them "a history of the intrigues of the court of
Charles II in a series of letters to his friend Henry Se-
ville."[14] Henry Killigrew was famous for his railing
tongue; did he never set pen to paper? And surely Henry
Bulkeley must have written libels, for we find an anonymous prophet saying,

> When Buckley the Cynic leaves being Satirick,
> And of his Wife's Vertue writes a large panegyrick,
> Then his manners shall fight for his good natures merit,
> And popery out of the nation shall run.[15]

The libels we have are often witty, but rarely edifying.
Yet Rochester's claim of a didactic purpose in his libels
cannot be lightly dismissed, and most of the Wits would
have made similar claims for their own verses. Dorset (in
"A Faithful Catalogue") professed himself to be fighting
in the cause of the Gods, and called upon his muse to

> proclaim
> The vicious lives, and long detested fame,
> Of scoundrel lords, and their lewd wives, amours,
> Pimp statesmen, canting-priests, court bawds and whores:

Sir Carr Scroope, in "A Satyr upon the Follies of the Men
of the Age," asserted that

Nothing helps more than Satyr, to amend
Ill manners, or is trulier Virtues Friend.[16]

And, in "An Essay on Satire," the Earl of Mulgrave commended satire as

the boldest way, perhaps the best,
To shew Men freely all their foulest Faults;
To laugh at their vain Deeds, and vainer Thoughts.

If it was the intention of the Wits to rebuke vice, they
were certainly well-qualified: they knew all about it. The
fact that they themselves were not virtuous was immaterial.
Their own departures from convention were rationalized
and therefore permissible; "right Reason" gave them
license to live freely according to their senses without re-
gard to respectability. But the victims of their libels were
(in their eyes) people whose sins went beyond reason; they
were fools, blockheads, hypocrites, and sycophants, mon-
sters of rascality, cupidity and lust. Moreover it was easy—
and very human—to elevate a personal enemy to the rank
of a "public nuisance" and then destroy him in righteous
anger. There was much malice and ill-nature in the Wits'
libels, but sometimes there was honest indignation and real
concern for the nation's good.

I

THE Wits admired and imitated Horace but rarely
approached that urbane satirist. Of them all, Dorset
was perhaps the only one to achieve something of the
Horatian polish and finesse. The others battered their
victims to a pulp where Horace (or Dryden, his famous
follower) would have skewered them with rapier thrusts.
The Wits were frequently witty in invention—especially
of opprobrious epithets—but they lacked restraining judgment. Their libelous character sketches are occasionally
hysterical and often vulgar. Their mildest epithets were

"rogue," "pimp," "bawd," and "whore." Sometimes they aimed their libels at a bold leading coxcomb of the town, or a lewd lady of high rank and low tastes. Sometimes they stigmatized whole categories of fops and jillflirts in one long poem. Form had no apparent relation to subject; the poem could be long or short, in ballad meter or heroic couplets, rough or smooth. Force was the one indispensable element.

Since we can never have complete knowledge of the circumstances under which a given poem was written, it is always difficult to be sure of the poet's motives. But personal enmity and sheer malice were the most obvious incitements, especially with so ferocious a libeler as the Earl of Rochester. For example, there is his famous quarrel with Sir Carr Scroope.

Sometime in the winter of 1675-76, Rochester was writing a critical satire in verse—an imitation of Horace's Tenth Satire—directed chiefly against John Dryden. Horace had sniped at a minor critic and poetaster, "that bug Pantilius," "a wretch obscene," who had dared to find fault with his verses. Seeking a modern counterpart for Pantilius, Rochester bethought him of Sir Carr Scroope, a fellow Oxonian and a lesser member of the motley Wits. The two young poets had been friendly, but it could have been as well said of Rochester as it was of Buckingham that "he would rather lose his friend (nay, his King) than his jest."[17] Perhaps, too, Scroope had dared to criticize Rochester's verses. So the earl wrote

> Should I be troubled when the Pur-blind Knight,
> Who squints more in his Judgement than his Sight,
> Picks silly faults, and censures what I write?

Sir Carr, who was painfully nearsighted, recognized himself as "the Pur-blind Knight." Furious at the sneer, he set himself the task of retaliating in kind. Within a few months, a lengthy lampoon from his pen was in circulation among the coffeehouses. Variously titled "In Defense of Satire" and "A Satyr upon the Follies of the Men of the Age," it too was modeled, appropriately enough, upon a Horatian satire. In part it was a defense of Scroope's God-given right to scribble libels; more particularly it was a sharp attack on Rochester and some others of the Court circle. Scroope's best weapon was a withering allusion to the affair at Epsom (in June, 1676) when Rochester had betrayed Captain Downes into "a fatal Mid-night quarrel" and then run away, "leaving him to be murdered in the street."

It was a well-aimed broadside, catching Rochester be-twixt wind and water, but Scroope lived to regret it. Rochester's "On the Supposed Author of a Late Poem in Defence of Satyr" was an iambic howl of rage. Scroope was pictured as a perfect parody on man, "a lump deform'd," "hideous to the sight," "an Ugly Beau-Garçon, Spit at, and shun'd by ev'ry Girl in Town," a dreadful "Scare-Crow" to frighten maids from love. Finally Rochester summed him up,

> Half-witty, and half-mad, and scarce half-brave,
> Half-honest (which is very much a Knave.)
> Made up of all these halfs, thou canst not pass,
> For anything intirely, but an Ass.

To this torrent of insults, Scroope replied in a short epi-gram, entitled simply "The Answer,"

> Rail on, poor feeble Scribler, speak of me,
> In as bad Terms, as the World speaks of thee.
> Sit swelling in thy Hole, like a vext Toad,
> And full of Pox and Malice, spit abroad.
> Thou can'st hurt no Mans fame with thy ill word,
> Thy Pen, is full as harmless as thy sword.[18]

With this genteel rejoinder, Scroope rested his case. But Rochester was by no means finished; thereafter he never missed a chance for an insulting reference to Scroope,

who became a leading figure in the earl's running dunciad
of Court fools and rogues. It was Rochester's peculiar gift
in satire to hit upon and popularize the single descriptive
epithet. As he had earlier dubbed John Dryden "Poet
Squab," a name by which he was to be known for a generation, so now he succeeded in labeling Scroope the "ugly
Beau-Garçon."* Moreover, Rochester led an army of
lesser libelers, who now fell on the luckless baronet with
glee. In a variety of lampoons, Sir Carr was described as
blind, foolish, whimsical, mad, proud, vain and nauseous.
Linked with foppish Sir George ("Beau") Hewitt and
raised to the rank of a "public nuisance," he became fair
game for any poetaster.[19]

One poem in the chorus of attacks on Sir Carr is worth
a brief examination because it so well illustrates the libelers'
common trick of misrepresenting facts. "A Familiar Epistle
to Julian" by the Duke of Buckingham (*ca.* 1677)[20] was
devoted to an analysis of Scroope as a rhymester upon
whom Julian, the Muses' Secretary, could depend for
salable scandalous verses. After the usual name-calling plus
a description of Scroope ("Strephon") as the knight "of
the hard-favour'd Face," Buckingham went into a sarcastic
discussion of Sir Carr's poetic activities. Finally he concluded,

> Strephon's a very Dragon at his Pen,
> His Brother Murder'd, and his Mother Whor'd,
> His Mistress lost, and yet his Pen's his Sword.

It is true that Scroope's younger brother had been killed
by Sir Thomas Armstrong in a duel at the Duke's Theatre
in August, 1675. But the killing was not a murder, and
the provocation seems to have come from the younger

---

* In 1678, Scroope laid siege to Nell Gwyn, hoping she might consent to
"put the dog where the deer should lie." For a while she seems to have
enjoyed the game, but finally (as she wrote in a letter to Laurence Hyde)
Scroope "begune to be a littel uncivil, which I could not sufer from an
uglye Baux garscon" (*Camden Miscellany*, V, 25).

Scroope. Armstrong was found guilty of technical manslaughter and promptly pardoned.[21] Scroope's young and
witty mother had indeed lived an unconventional life. An
attractive widow, she had been mistress at one time to the
Earl of Arlington, and in 1677 she was living happily in
sin with Harry Savile.[22] But Scroope was no Hamlet, to
curb and woo for leave to do his mother good; Hamlet at
the Restoration Court would have been ridiculous. Finally,
Scroope had lost the lady to whom he had been paying his
addresses (Cary Frazier, daughter of the King's physician,
Sir Alexander Frazier), but through no fault of his own:
he discovered that she had been secretly married to
Charles, Viscount Mordaunt, since 1675. Although the
marriage was not officially announced until 1680, it had
been common knowledge for at least a year.[23]

Rochester's feud with Sir Carr Scroope is by no means
the only one in which he was involved. His gift for the
telling nickname is further illustrated in his verbal campaign against the Earl of Mulgrave. The two young
nobles had been good friends until November, 1669, when
a quarrel was bred of an airy word, and a duel averted only
by the fact that Rochester—on the field of honor—was too
sick to fight. According to Mulgrave, Rochester's disease
was cowardice, and his version of the encounter was told
and credited throughout the Town, "which being never in
the least either contradicted or resented by the Lord Rochester, intirely ruined his reputation as to Courage."[24]

Rochester bided his time, and it was probably at the
climax of Mulgrave's ridiculous affair over Mall Kirke in
1675 that he wrote "A very Heroical Epistle from My
Lord All-Pride to Doll-Common."[25] This gave the Town
a new nickname for the proud earl who wore the "Blazing
Star" of the Garter so haughtily. He is represented as
bored with the unhappy woman whom he has loved and
ruined, and, in the concluding lines, he addresses a "happy
Sultan" in envy because

> Thou fear'st no Kinsman's threat'ning Blade,
> Nor Midnight Ambushes by Rivals laid.*

Mulgrave had his revenge in November, 1679, when "An Essay on Satyr," his attack on a number of Court figures, was passed about in manuscript. Rochester sent Savile a copy with the mild comment, "my own share is not the least."[26] Mulgrave had raked him fore and aft, claiming to despise him "for's want of Wit," to find him a very devil for mischief, false in words, cringing, mean, lewd, and, above all, cowardly. He concluded,

> A Life so infamous is better quitting,
> Spent in base injuring, and low submitting.

It was for the "Essay on Satyr," at the time attributed to him, that John Dryden was attacked and beaten by a gang of ruffians in Rose Alley on the night of December 18, 1679. The instigator of the attack was long thought to have been Rochester,[27] although it was more probably the Duchess of Portsmouth (who was badly treated in the poem) and the actual attacker may have been her brother-in-law, the murderous Earl of Pembroke. Rochester played the game according to the rules, and he very well knew who was the author of the "Essay." He was not long in retaliating. His *Epigram upon my Lord All-Pride* was printed with the date 1679 and must have been written soon after Mulgrave's libel appeared.[28]

In this, one of the most vicious of Rochester's attacks, Mulgrave is a "loath'd Impostume," a "lewd Scribler" who writes "with as much force to Nature as he fights," a "baffled Fop," with a fancy so weak that he is "compelled to take Among the Excrements of others wit." He has

> a red Nose, Splay Foot, and Goggle Eye,
> A Plough Mans looby Meen, Face all awry,
> With stinking Breath. . . .

---

* That is, Mulgrave's duel with Percy Kirke, and the ambush set for him by the Duke of Monmouth, his rival. See Chapter 11 for details.

And

> Go where he will, he never finds a Friend,
> Shame and derision all his steps attend;
> Alike at home, abroad, i' th' Camp and Court,
> This Knight o' th' Burning Pestle makes us sport.

Perhaps both libelers gave some measure of the truth. Certainly Mulgrave had some disagreeable characteristics, chief among them the overweening vanity which stands out in every line of his "Memoirs."* "Lord All-Pride" he was to remain for years, and for variety "King John" or "Bajazet" after the proud king in Marlowe's *Tamburlaine.* In 1682, when it became known that Mulgrave had lost his places at Court for daring to aspire to the affections of the Princess Anne, the libelers had a field day. Most effective of the verses celebrating this affair was Aphra Behn's "Bajazet to Gloriana," which was merely her "Ovid to Julia" retitled to serve a topical function.[29] (According to tradition, Ovid was banished from Rome for daring to make love to Julia, daughter of the Emperor Augustus.) Fortunately for Mulgrave, none of the Court Wits took advantage of the opportunity for a libel; he was no longer a member of the circle, and their derisive name for him was "numps," i.e., fool.[30]

I I

COMPARATIVELY few of the Wits' libels resulted from bickering within their own circle. Most were attacks on people with whom they may have had no personal quarrels: certain ladies of the Court, various politicians, fops and fools, and the King himself.

---

* In *Pope's Own Miscellany* (ed. Norman Ault, 1935, p. 117) is an illuminating quatrain entitled "Written by the Earl of Mulgrave to be put under his own Picture,"

> Here a Poet you behold,
>   Who with disadvantage wrote;
> For, of Authors new or old,
>   I would never steal a thought.

The custom of libeling Court ladies was by no means restricted to the Wits. It seems to have come into vogue early in the Restoration, and until the end of the century the scandalous lives of Whitehall ladies were chronicled, either in short libels devoted to a single victim or in long shotgun lampoons by which any number of titled trulls and their noble or ignoble lovers were brought down at a blast. Arranged chronologically, anonymous pieces such as "Cullen with his Flock of Misses," "Satyr on the Court Ladies," "The Town Life," "Essay of Scandal," "Utile Dulce," "The Ladies' March," "Satyr on the Ladies of Honour," "The Lovers' Session," or "The Session of Ladies," to name a few, give a colorful (and probably exaggerated) picture of intrigue, adultery, incest, and sodomy at the Restoration Court.

Most frequently attacked by the Court Wits were the three chief mistresses of the King: the Duchess of Portsmouth, the Duchess of Cleveland, and Nell Gwyn. With these, in shotgun lampoons, appeared the names of such ladies as Hortense Mancini, Duchess of Mazarine; Frances Stuart, Duchess of Richmond; Anne Carnegie, Lady Southesk; Anne Lennard, Lady Sussex; Cary Frazier, Betty Felton, Mall Howard, Jane Middleton, and such small-fry cyprians as Mall Hinton and Sue Willis. It is likely that, with the exception of Frances Stuart, these ladies deserved their poetical chastizing; in an age of open immorality their sins were scandalous.

The fact that the Court Wits were apparently on friendly terms with the ladies constituted no bar to the writing of libels about them, although at times the intimacy of relationship casts doubt on the authorship of a libel. Mulgrave, for example, was once one of Cleveland's lovers, and to her he was said to owe his proudly worn Order of the Garter—an appropriate decoration.[31] Yet in his "Essay on Satyr" he described her as one of the "beastly Brace" of "Royal Mistresses," and (with Portsmouth) "False, foolish, old, ill-natur'd and ill-bred."[32] Equally ungracious are the Wits' libels on Nell Gwyn, who had once been mistress to Dorset (perhaps to Rochester also) and in 1677 was clearly a member of "the Merry Gang," as Marvell called the Wits.[33] In June, 1678, Savile wrote to Rochester warning him of a new intrigue at Court designed to "bring Mrs. Jenny Middleton into play" as a royal mistress, to the disadvantage of Nelly, "who is soe much your friend." Rochester's reply was sound common sense; he urged "the Lady you wot of" to be at peace with the King and all the world, to contribute to his pleasure in every way possible, and to "Make Sport when you can, at other times help it." Evidently he had Nell's interests at heart.[34] Yet in "Signior Dildoe" (1673),[35] he listed her as "The Countess of the Cockpit," among the Court ladies given to licentious practices. In "A Satyr which the King took out of his Pocket" (ca. 1675) he described her as a "Bitch" whose very sight was maddening to "the People." "A Panegyrick on Nelly" (ca. 1679), which may not have been Rochester's, gave her whole history from cinder bed to royal bed, labeling her ironically "a Virtuous Countess, an Imperial Whore," "the darling Strumpet of the Crowd," and "the incomparable Madam Gwyn."* Etherege, too, for no apparent reason, attacked Nell in two long and very nasty libels: "Madame Nelly's Complaint" (ca. 1682) and "The Lady of Pleaure, a Satyr" (ca. 1687) written presumably after Mistress Gwyn's death.[36]

The same misogyny which gave birth to such poems as Rochester's "Woman's Usurpation" and Etherege's "If she be not kind as fair" may have accounted for the libels against Nell Gwyn. More probably, however, the Wits,

* The so-called *A Genuine Letter from the Earl of Rochester to Nell Gwyn* (Dyce Collection, Victoria and Albert Museum) is a fairly obvious example of an eighteenth century forgery. It was presumably copied "from an original manuscript in the French King's Library," a manuscript which existed only in the bawdy mind of the hack who wrote the dull and stupid doggerel.

friendly enough toward Nell as a person, saw her as a "public nuisance" in her capacity as mistress to the King, and it became an "action of virtue" to make an example of a politically dangerous woman. Moreover, in striking through the mistress they hit the Royal Keeper, a fair and open target. In nearly every libel against Nell there is a strong undercurrent of reproach directed against her "Charles the Third."

Certainly, it must have been as public nuisances that the unpopular Duchesses of Cleveland and Portsmouth were pilloried in so many libels. Much less amiable than Nell, they were much more expensive to the public purse. Outwardly the Wits were friendly toward the two ladies— even subservient, for both were mighty with the King— but secretly they joined in the national chorus of execration. Mulgrave struck at both in his "Essay on Satyr." Rochester celebrated the insatiable lechery of Cleveland (his cousin, by the way) in "Lais Senior: a Pindarick," in which he listed by name six of her more recent "Stallions," all of whom were tiring rapidly. He developed the same theme more briefly in "A Satyr which the King took out of his Pocket," summarizing with this elegant couplet,

> Full Forty Men a Day provided for this Whore,
> Yet, Like a Bitch she waggs her Tail for more.

The Duchess of Portsmouth, French and Catholic, was "The Damned, Dirty Duchess" to hundreds of angry rhymesters; she was blamed for everything, from high taxes to lost battles. So in "The Royal-Buss" Rochester attributed to her all those ills of the nation which might have been cured by Parliament in 1673, except that

> Portsm[ou]th, the incestuous Punk
> Made our most gracious Sov'raign drunk.
> And drunk she made him give that Buss
> That all the Kingdom's bound to curse,
> And so red hot with Wine and Whore,
> He kickt the Commons out of door.

Nell Gwyn. About 1670
By Sir Peter Lely. Courtesy of the National Portrait Gallery

Barbara Palmer, Duchess of Cleveland. About 1675
By Sir Peter Lely. Courtesy of the National Portrait Gallery

"Portsmouth's Looking Glass" (*ca.* 1679), also by Rochester, is a more general attack on "Madam Carwell" as the real ruler of the state—a common, but mistaken, belief. This vulgar libel must have hit the Duchess in a tender spot; she was growing old and coming to depend more and more on "Powders, Trimmings, and curl'd Wigs." Each morning she found it necessary to "varnish and smooth o'er those Graces" which had rubbed off during the night. But in spite of her fading charms, it was she (said Rochester) who governed every council meeting, gave commands to Charles, her "Royal Cully," and steered the ship of state while the King sat at the helm and slept.

As late as 1683, when Cleveland had lost most of her power over the King and Portsmouth had settled into fubsy middle age, Dorset reiterated the old theme in "A Faithful catalogue of our most Eminent Ninnies." The two royal strumpets were, he wrote,

> A brace of cherubs, of as vile a breed,
> As ever were produc'd of human seed.
> To all but thee [Charles], the punks were ever kind,
> Free as loose air, and gen'rous as the wind.
> Both steered thy ———, and the nations helm;
> And both betray'd thy ———, and the realm.

But Barbara, Duchess of Cleveland, was singled out for "everlasting shame," because of her insatiable lust, which no "num'rous host" of lovers could ever satisfy.

In addition to the royal mistresses, various other ladies were libeled by the Wits for reasons which are rarely clear. In his "Signior Dildoe" Rochester spat at Ladies Southesk, Suffolk, Falmouth, Northumberland and Modena, at Mistresses Howard, Sheldon, Temple, Killigrew and Knight, as well as at the Duchess of Cleveland and Nell Gwyn. For some reason Portsmouth was not mentioned. In 1678, Buckingham wrote "A Character of an Ugly Woman," a vulgar prose libel against the Mother of the Maids in the service of the Duchess of York—possibly a Mrs. Lucy

Wise. In the course of his attack on Nell in "Madame Nelly's Complaint" Etherege belabored also Madam Knight, a famous singer.[37] Dorset wrote a series of four ironic lyrics against Katherine Sedley, Countess of Dorchester, possibly because she too was a royal mistress—in this case to the Duke of York. Another libel by Dorset, "The Antiquated Coquet,"[38] was said to be directed against a well-known Court lady, Anne, Dowager Countess Clanbrassil, who had evidently set her cap for him. She was described as too eager and too old. The same lady was briefly mentioned in Rochester's short pasquil "On the Women about Town" (together with other "Irish Whores," the two Coots, and one Mrs. Fox), and may have been the subject of "Upon an Old Affected Court Lady" by Dorset's follower, Fleetwood Shepherd.[39] In "A Faithful Catalogue" Dorset smeared a long list of frail creatures, among them the Duchesses of Portsmouth, Cleveland and Grafton, Ladies Bellasis, Oxford and Vernon (Mall Kirke, Mulgrave's old flame), and such notable doxies as Jenny Cromwell, Jenny Middleton, and Mall Hinton. In various shorter squibs he attacked Phyllises of lesser rank, among them Dolly Chamberlain, a seamstress in the New Exchange, whom he threatened with a dire punishment involving some surgical sewing. Wycherley wrote a number of lengthy, confused libels on ladies who cannot be identified; we can be sure of only two of his victims. "An Heroic Epistle. To the Most Honourable Matchmaker, a Bawd, call'd J.C." is obviously on Jenny Cromwell, and "To the Sappho of the Age, suppos'd to Ly-In of a Love-Distemper, or a Play" is an attack on the playwright Aphra Behn. Only Sedley among the literary Wits was gentleman enough to write no libels against ladies, but it is quite possible that some of the scurrilous epigrams which he translated or adapted from Martial were meant to have a local application to a name.

I I I

SOME of the Wits' libels against their male contemporaries, like many of those against the great ladies,
were motivated by political hate. The boiling fury of Restoration politics brewed bitter enmities, and sometimes the
sword decided the issues of the ballot-box. Until about
1680, when Whigs and Tories set up their standards, there
were no clear-cut parties or policies; every man sought
power, and every man's hand was against his rivals. De-
famatory verses were weapons of offense to be dreaded by
any group or cabal.

Several of the Wits took no sides, and contented themselves with an occasional jibe at politicians of every persuasion. The political views of Etherege, Sedley and Wycherley were expressed conventionally in the plays they
wrote to please an aristocratic audience, and cannot be
taken too seriously. In his violent youth, Rochester, as a
member of the opposition party, had written a libel "On
the Lord Chancellor Hyde" to celebrate Clarendon's fall
from power. But in his later years, Rochester joined with
Dorset in sneering with superior impartiality at King and
Parliament, Whig and Tory. In "Satire, by the Lord R."
and "A Satyr. By the same Hand" (both about 1679), he
lashed at the whole political system; for, no matter what
the philosophy of politicians,

> Some do for Pimping, some for Treach'ry rise,
> But none's made Great for being Good and Wise.
> Deserve a Dungeon if you would be great,
> Rogues always are our Ministers of State.[40]

Similarly, Dorset wrote an "Opinion of the Whigs and
Tories" condemning the followers of Monmouth and of
York alike, and concluding,

> Had I this soft Son, and this Dangerous Brother,
> I'd hang up the one, and I'd piss upon t'other,

I'd make this the long and the short of the Story,
The Fools might be Whigs, none but Knaves shou'd be Toryes.[41]

The Duke of Buckingham, chief politician of the Wits
and the object of numerous satiric attacks, probably wrote
many more libels than he has been credited with. One
acknowledged to be his is a bawdy piece of doggerel in the
style of the "Directions to a Painter" poems, made famous
by Denham and Marvell.[42] "Advice to a Painter to draw
my L[ord] A[rling]ton: Grand Minister of State" (*ca.*
1671) was written when Buckingham was moving successfully to bring Arlington into discredit and replace him as
chief minister to the King. "Upon the Installment of Sir
[Thomas] Os[bor]n and the Late Duke of New-castle"
(1677) was written in revenge against one of Buckingham's own creatures, Sir Thomas Osborne (later Earl of
Danby), who had deserted the Duke to achieve his own
aims. Nothing was so transitory as a friendship based on
politics. In 1679, when Danby was impeached and lan-
guishing in the Tower, Buckingham wrote and circulated
a triumphant ballad which urged that the former treasurer
be hanged, for

> I never heard of Subject tell,
>   Nor can one in this land be,
> Deserves a Halter half so well
>   As Thomas Earl of Danby.[43]

The Wits had no compunctions about kicking a man
when he was down, or even clubbing his corpse. When the
Duke of Grafton (natural son of Charles II), who had
Tory leanings, was killed at the siege of Cork in 1690,
Fleetwood Shepherd wrote a Whiggish mock epitaph for
the dead hero. The point of his very poor jest was that
Grafton had never feared "Shot made of Lead, or Cannon
Ball,"

> Yet a Bullet of Cork
> Soon did his Work:
> Unhappy Pellet,

With Grief I tell it,
It has undone
Great Cesar's Son!
G—— rot him
That shot him;
A Son of a Whore,
I say no more.[44]

The Earl of Mulgrave, a strong Tory in 1679, devoted
a good part of his "Essay on Satyr" to four opposed politicians: Buckingham, "the merriest man alive"; Shaftesbury, "our little Machiavel," leader of the Country, or
Whig Party; Halifax, "the new Earl," the famous Trim-
mer, or fence-straddler; and Heneage Finch, "Tropos,"
the Lord Chancellor.[45] For Finch, a mighty orator, Mulgrave seems to have had a grudge which inspired him to a
neat bit of satiric characterization.

So odd a Mixture no Man else affords;
Such Scarcity of Sense, such Choice of Words!
At Bar abusive, on the Bench unable,
Knave on the Wool-sack, Fop at Council Table!

While there can be no doubt that in such verses as these
the poets were venting their spleen and hoping to further
their own ambitions, a few of their political libels seem to
be honest convictions expressed with sincere wrath. An excellent example is "Advice to a Painter to draw the Duke
by," written by Henry Savile sometime in 1673, after he
had left the Duke of York's service. There had long been
animosity between the Duke and his ex-Groom of the Bedchamber, but Savile's attack was on patriotic rather than
personal grounds, motivated by York's disclosure of his
adherence to the Catholic faith. In the spirit of a true-born
(Protestant) Englishman, a hater of Popery and tyranny,
Savile depicted the Duke as plotting to Romanize England with the aid of several Catholic courtiers. His attack
was adequately violent, and his conclusion was Britannia
made vocal:

Old England on its strong foundations stands,
Defying all their heads and all their hands.
Its steady Basis never could bee shooke,
When wiser men its ruine undertooke:
And can her Guardian Angell lett her stoope
At last to fools and mad men and the Pope?
Noe, Painter, noe; close up the peice and see
This band of traytors hang'd in Effigie.[46]

In the small category of the sincere we must place also
Rochester's libels against Charles II. It is not easy to picture the skeptical earl as a patriot, but it is difficult to ex-
plain his attacks against sacred majesty on any other ground
than righteous indignation that so intelligent a king should
waste his time and his kingdom in trivialities. Probably
Rochester never understood Charles and the complicated
trickery by which that royal prestidigitator ruled his realm.
In four libels, ranging from about 1675 to 1679, Rochester
rang the changes on a simple theme: that Charles, an easy
prince, kindly and well-disposed, was so much a slave of his
passions that he was only a titular king, ruled by his mistresses. In "A Satyr on King Charles II For Which He
Was Banished the Court," Rochester wrote,

Restless he rolls about from Whore to Whore,
A Merry Monarch, Scandalous and Poor.

In "A Satyr Which the King took out of his Pocket" the
theme was repeated.

Was ever Prince's Soul so meanly Poor,
To be a Slave to every little Whore?

In "The Restauration, or the History of Insipids" the concept was enlarged. All the adverse affairs of several past
years—the prorogations of Parliament, the mistakes on
land and sea in the Dutch wars, the government's errors in
diplomacy, even the stopping of the exchequer—all were
blamed on the King's fatal weakness for women. The series
ended about 1679 with "The Royal Angler," still in the

same vein. Old Rowley, the King, an ardent fisherman, was himself easily caught by "every Kingfisher of State,"

> So well, alas! the fatal Bait is known,
> Which Rowley does so greedily take down;
> And howe'er weak and slender be the String,
> Bait it with Whore, and it will hold a King.

This is not exactly a case of the pot calling the kettle black. Rochester was a private gentleman, whose sins, unlike the King's, did not affect the nation.

Buckingham also was angered by Charles' apparent incompetence, but his one sharp libel against the King may have been motivated in part by jealousy. George Villiers fancied himself as an administrator. In the squib which he called "The Cabbin-Boy," he alluded to the King's fondness for the sea.

> Nay, he could sail a Yatcht both nigh and large,
> Knew how to trim a boat, and steer a Barge:
> Cou'd say his Compass, to the Nations Joy,
> And swear as well as any Cabbin-Boy.
> But not one Lesson of the Ruling Art,
> Cou'd this dull Block head ever get by heart.
> Look over all the Universal Frame,
> There's not a thing the Will of Man can name,
> In which this Ugly, perjur'd Rogue delights,
> But Ducks, and loytering, butter'd Buns and whites.*

Such libels verged on treason, of course, but the Wits were reckless—Rochester most of all. In "A Satyr . . . For Which He was Banished the Court" he gave vent to his hatred of all kings, "from the Hector of France, to the Cully of Britain," and in "The Restauration, or the History of Insipids" he drew a daring parallel between the misrule of Charles II and the tyranny of Louis XIV of France. However, the Wits knew their master's temper,

---

* Charles was fond of walking, which he called "sauntering." He loved to feed the ducks in St. James's Park. For *butter'd buns* read *prostitutes*; for *whites, silver money.*

for "as he had an extraordinary share of wit himself, so he loved it in others even when pointed against his own Faults and Mismanagements."[47] A well-known story—which has many variants—illustrates the easy-going nature of the King. Either in a spirit of malice, or at the King's request, or as a notice to be posted on the door of a bedroom where Charles lay with a Maid of Honor (take your choice), Rochester wrote a ditty of which this is one version,

> We have a pretty witty King,
> Whose word no man relies on,
> Who never said a foolish thing,
> Nor ever did a wise one.

The King was amused. His words, he said, were his own; his acts were those of his ministers.[48]

I V

OF all the Court Wits, Rochester was most fitted for satire in Dryden's sense of one who tried "to correct the vices and follies of his time." Cursed with more intelligence than his fellows, and with a clearer sight for the evils both within himself and about him, as he matured he developed a true misanthropy. In his thirties, man delighted not him "no, nor woman neither." He was roused to anger by the contrast between man's promise and his performance and was brutal in exposing man's follies. Pathetically unaware of the immemorial futility of satire (for knaves and fools never read it), he made war on mankind at large.

Rochester's initial attack was comparatively mild. "Timon, a Satyr" (*ca.* 1673) is a narrative piece which is almost jovial in tone. Timon (Rochester, of course) is tricked into dining with a bore on the promise of Sedley, Savile and Buckhurst as his companions. Instead, he finds four hectors, "Halfwit and Huffe, Kickum and Dingboy." His hostess, an antiquated coquette, presides over the banquet, which consists of a huge piece of beef, a dish of carrots, "Pig, Goose, and Capon," and gallons of wine and small beer. The conversation is as vulgar and indigestible as the meal; the host brags of his service to the King in the late times; his lady whines of the decay of love and poetry; the other guests roar out their comments on recent plays, argue over foreign affairs, and finally fall to fisticuffs, while Timon flees, vowing nevermore to eat and drink in such dreadful company. Rochester's attitude is that of the refined courtier sneering at the crude ways of his social inferiors.

His second attempt at social satire was a long conversation piece called "A Letter from Artemisia in the Town, to Chloe, in the Country" (ca. 1674). In the main it is a sharp attack on the follies and vices of womankind. Rochester presents as one speaker Artemisia, a would-be poetess, who is enduring a visit from the second speaker, a ridiculous country lady, newly come to Town. Through the monologues of the two women, the baneful folly of womankind is revealed. For male readers the satire contains a warning: these modern females, who have substituted carnality for true passion, are dangerous; they are capable of cozening any male and destroying him. See, for example, how Corinna, a woman of the Town, having tried "all th' several ways of being undone," looks about her and finds no cully but a raw young country squire. She captures the "o'er-grown School-Boy," bubbles him of a house, plate and jewels, uses up his physical and financial substance, and finally poisons him. He dies, leaving "her Bastard Heir to his Estate." The moral is clear; poor, weak, silly woman is capable of incredible monstrosities. Only the man of wit can escape her ravenings.

This is the longest and mildest of Rochester's satires against women. In his last years, something—perhaps age, perhaps venereal disaster—turned the poet into a raging

anti-feminist. He became almost pathological in his hatred
of the sex; having loved too often in haste, he denounced
at leisure. In such general libels as "On the Women about
Town," "On a False Mistress," "A Satyr against Marriage," "Women's Usurpation," and "The Nature of
Women," he shrilled his anger at the folly, cruelty, carnality, and general nastiness of Everywoman, who

> . . . is a Snare, a Shamble and a Stews.
> Her Meat and Sawce she does for Letch'ry chuse
> And does in Laziness delight the more,
> Because by that, she is provok'd to Whore.
> Her Beauty and her Tongue, serve both one end—
> Some to ensnare, and then betray her Friend;
> She may defer the Punishment she gives
> But ne'er forget the Injury she receives:
> Ingrateful, Treacherous, enviously Enclin'd—
> Wild Beasts are Tam'd, flouds easier far confined,
> Than is her stubborn and rebellious Mind.[49]

Still in his twenties when he was writing most of his
longer satires, Rochester's pessimism deepened poem by
poem. "Tunbridge-Wells" (subtitle, "June 30, 1675")
came third in his series of extended attacks on the human
animal. The poem has a personal note which may be valid;
Rochester's health had begun to fail sometime in 1671,
and the waters of Tunbridge and Epsom were universally
prescribed as cures for rheumatism, gout, fevers, strangury,
pleurisy, cancer, impotence, barrenness and upset stomachs.

The poet describes a typical morning at the famous spa.
At the entrance to the wells he meets a ridiculous "Bawling
Fop" with a train of silly companions. In the lower walk
it is his bad luck to meet a ceremonious coxcomb, equally to
be avoided. In the upper walk he runs headlong into a
tribe of curates and priests gathered around Archdeacon
Parker, recently the loser in an acid controversy with Andrew Marvell. Seeking to avoid the babbling clerics and a
"fulsom Irish Crew" that next heaves into sight, Rochester

hides himself among the crowd. There he is forced to over-
hear two conversations, first between a formal would-be
wit and a conceited jillflirt, second between two wives who
have come to the Wells because of the famed power of the
waters to quicken unwilling wombs. Seeing two brawny
bullies bearing up to the ladies, the poet comments that
through the deeds of such potent rascals the "waters got
their Reputation" for curing barrenness. Turning from
this medley of fools and gossips, he sees and avoids a bois-
terous lot of "war-like Men," younger sons of the gentry,
"damn'd to the stint of Thirty Pounds a Year," with commissions in the army. In leaving, Rochester soliloquizes
over the whole motley crew of beaux, clerics, upstarts, silly
women and stupid hectors,

> Bless me! thought I, what Thing is Man, that thus,
> In all his Shapes, is so ridiculous?
> Ourselves with Noise of Reason we do please
> In vain, Humanity's our worst Disease;
> Thrice happy Beasts are, who, because they be
> Of Reason void, are so of Foppery.
> Faith, I was so asham'd, that with Remorse,
> I us'd the Insolence to mount my Horse;
> For he, doing only Things fit for his Nature,
> Did seem to me by much the wiser Creature.[50]

This is a preview of Gulliver, with a Yahoo astride a
Houyhnhnm; and indeed the ascetic Dean Swift went little further in his condemnation of mankind than the libertine Earl. So far, however, in all Rochester's satires there
was still some humor, some lightness of touch that marked
him as one of the Court Wits, to whom seriousness was a
sin.

Some time in the gloom of the winter of 1675-76,
when Rochester was at Woodstock, sick in mind and body,
in disgrace at Court, and fighting off claimants for his posts
and properties, he wrote *A Satyr against Mankind*.[51] The
essentially philosophic bias of his mind, which is apparent

even in his most flippant and lecherous poems, for once held full sway. The result—whether it came from moral indignation, personal disappointment or indigestion—is a flaming indictment of humanity.

The poem opens with a quick jibe. Were Rochester a spirit, free to pick his fleshly housing, he would choose to be

> . . . a Dog, a Monkey or a Bear,
> Or any thing, but that vain Animal,
> Who is so proud of being rational.

Then follows a scornful attack on rationalism, false reason, that "*ignis fatuus* of the Mind, Which leaves the Light of Nature, Sense, behind." Rochester's false "Reason" is the metaphysical speculation of the schoolmen and divines, the endless argument on points of doctrine and dogma, the building of pyramids of conjecture on foundations of wild surmise. It is this kind of speculative reason which drives foolish man into "Doubt's boundless Sea," where he tries to swim with inflated "Bladders of Philosophy."

In answer to this diatribe, a clergyman (a "formal Band and Beard") is allowed to defend reason and praise man,

> Blest glorious Man, to whom alone kind Heav'n
> An everlasting Soul hath freely giv'n;

whom God has made in His own image and endowed with reason to raise him above the beasts,

> Reason, by whose aspiring Influence,
> We take a flight beyond material Sense,
> Dive into Mysteries, then soaring pierce
> The flaming limits of the Universe,
> Search Heav'n and Hell, find out what's acted there,
> And give the World true grounds of hope and fear.

Rochester is not impressed; this is old stuff to him. His reply is a eulogy of "right Reason," the "material Sense" beyond which the clergyman would go. Wise men know that they are limited by their senses. Only fools lose them-

selves in "Nonsense and Impossibilities," in speculative
thought in a vacuum. The power to think was given to
man for one purpose only: to govern his actions. Therefore,

> Where Action ceases, Thought's impertinent.
> Our Sphere of Action is Life's happiness,
> And he that thinks beyond, thinks like an Ass.

This is the pragmatist speaking, the practical man who
believes that pleasure is the sole end of life, and who de-
fends right reason—i.e., common sense—because it is an aid
to enjoyment. "My Reason is my Friend," cries the poet,
but (to the speculative coxcombs) "yours is a Cheat":

> Your Reason hinders; mine helps to enjoy
> Renewing Appetites, yours would destroy . . .
> Hunger calls out, my Reason bids me eat;
> Perversly yours, your Appetite does mock;
> This asks for food, that answers, what's a Clock.

Formal rules may satisfy a flatulent mind, but they are no
food for lean stomachs. So "true Reason" is justified.

But man himself cannot be defended on any grounds. In
spite of all his pride and his "Philosophy," he is inferior
to the beasts. The animal is more efficient than man; he is
more moral, just and good. Animals prey on other animals
only for food, "But savage Man alone, does Man betray,"
to no other end but sheer wantonness. Man is motivated in
all things by wretched fear,

> For Fear he arms, and is of Arms afraid:
> From Fear, to Fear, successively betray'd.

The best passions of man, his boasted honor, his desire for
fame and power, all the good he does, all the ill he endures,

> 'Tis all from Fear, to make himself secure.
> Meerly for safety, after Fame they thirst;
> For all Men would be Cowards if they durst:
> And Honesty's against all common sense—

In the evil world of knaves, sharpers and villains, there is no use trying to be honest, for "the knaves will all agree to call you Knave."

> Wrong'd shall he live, insulted o're, opprest,
> Who dares be less a Villain than the rest.
> Thus here you see what Human Nature craves,
> Most Men are Cowards, all Men shou'd be Knaves.
> The Difference lies, as far as I can see,
> Not in the thing it self, but the degree;
> And all the subject matter of Debate,
> Is only who's a Knave of the first Rate.

A Satyr against Mankind is not completely original. It belongs to a long series of writings in which comparable attitudes are expressed,* and it had an immediate model in the Eighth Satire of Boileau. But the vigor of phrase and the savagery of denunciation are entirely Rochester's.[52] The notion of man versus animal had developed in the poet's mind over a long period. The inception of the theme may be traced to about 1669, when the earl had his portrait painted (by Wissing or Huysmans[53]) crowning a monkey with a wreath of bays, while the eager simian offers its master a leaf torn from a volume—possibly intended to represent the work of a contemporary poet. The theme was given its first poetic expression in "A Letter from Artemisia" when that lady's affected visitor embraced her hostess's pet monkey with the cry,

> Kiss me, thou curious Miniature of Man;
> How odd thou art, how pretty, how japan:
> Oh! I could live and die with thee . . .

---

* In his dotage Wycherley, too, dealt with much the same thing in a complex poetical dissertation entitled "Upon the Impertinence of Knowledge, the Unreasonableness of Reason, and the Brutality of Humanity; proving the Animal Life the most Reasonable Life, since the most Natural, and most Innocent." In several lines he seems to be echoing Rochester; for example,

> They, who on others prey, their Kind will spare;
> Whilst Man, does Man more for his Reason feare;

The conclusion to "Tunbridge-Wells" substituted a horse for a monkey as the symbol of the superior world of animals, while in *A Satyr against Mankind* three animals, dog, monkey and bear, were preferred. These may have been chosen for their manlike qualities, or simply because they were familiarly known in the Restoration world. But the monkey comparison was a theme which Rochester never wearied of pursuing. In June, 1678, he wrote in a letter to Savile, apropos of the follies of mankind, "But most human Affairs [are] carried on at the same nonsensical rate, which makes me (who am now grown Superstitious) think it a Fault to laugh at the Monkey we have here [at Woodstock], when I compare his Condition with Mankind."[54]

From the doctrine of animalism to that of nihilism is an easy step. If man is no more than a monkey, plucking at metaphysical fleas, then the cosmos is topsy-turvy, a vast, chaotic Nothing. Though there is no way of proving that Rochester wrote "Upon Nothing" after 1676, its maturity of style and detached irony stamp it as the product of the last years of his life. It is not (as one of his critics claims[55]) a "merely witty effusion"; it is a grim parody on a famous theme in Genesis—the Creation.

> Nothing! thou elder Brother ev'n to Shade,
> Thou hadst a being e're the World was made,
> And (well fixt) art alone, of ending not afraid.

In the beginning, there was only *Nothing*, eternal and formless. *Nothing* begat *Something* (Rochester's ironic name for God or Spirit, "the gen'ral Attribute of all"). *Something* overcame the power of *Nothing*, and from its void "snatch'd Men, Beasts, Birds, Fire, Air, and Land." Aided by *Something*, wicked Matter escaped from the embrace of *Nothing* and formed a league with Form, Time, and Place to pillage and destroy the peaceful world of *Nothing*.

So the world of Matter was created, while "Rebel Light

obscured" the "reverend dusky Face" of *Nothing*. Yet in time, the material world inevitably returns to *Nothing*. Meanwhile, all truth and wisdom reside solely in *Nothing*; its "Mysteries are barr'd from Laick Eyes," and philosophers and statesmen vainly strive to pierce the bosom of the "Great Negative," where the vast designs of Fate are safely hidden.

Moreover, powerful *Something* is losing control of the world of Matter. Monarchs sit at council with "Persons highly thought, at best, for nothing fit." *Something* has departed "from Princes Coffers, and from Statesmen's Brains," where now stately *Nothing* holds full sway. *Nothing* dwells with fools in lawn sleeves (the clergy), in furs (the merchants), and in gowns (the lawyers and scholars), and the men of power and learning look as wise as *Nothing*. The praise of *Nothing* ends with two quiet, devastating triplets,

> French Truth, Dutch Prowess, Brittish Policy,
> Hibernian Learning, Scotch Civility,
> Spaniards Dispatch, Danes Wit, are mainly seen in thee.
>
> The great Man's Gratitude to his best Friend,
> King's Promises, Whores Vows, tow'rds thee they bend,
> Flow swiftly into thee, and in thee ever end.

So God's mighty effort to create order out of disorder comes to an inglorious end; omnipotent *Nothing* has quietly reestablished its rule, while self-deluded mankind goes on babbling its twaddle, arguing about *Something*, and certain that it is going *Somewhere*.

This was Rochester's final blast at rationalism; thereafter he seems to have given up his search for order and meaning in the world. The briefer verses which he wrote in his last two years of life are clouded by the pain of disease and despair.

John Wilmot, Earl of Rochester. About 1669
By Jacob Huysmans. Courtesy of the National Portrait Gallery

V

IN contemporary plays, poems, and letters, especially between the years 1670 and 1680, there are many overt references to the vogue for satire among the Wits and their protégés. Pretending to write as an inmate of Bedlam, one minor poet said,

> Bucks both and Rochester, unless they mend,
> Hither the King designs forthwith to 'end:
> Shepherd and Dreyden too, must on 'em wait;
> For he's resolv'd at once to rid the state,
> Of this Poetick, Wanton, Mad-like Tribe,
> Whose Rampant Muse does Court and City Gibe.[56]

But there is no way of measuring the effect of the Wits' libels and satires on their victims. Certainly they must have stirred up and perpetuated many enmities. Rochester, supreme libeler and satirist, was a much hated man, but he had chiefly himself to blame. We can only pity him when he writes to his friend Savile (in 1677), "I ever thought you an extraordinary Man, and must now think you such a Friend, who, being a Courtier, as you are, can love a Man whom it is the great Mode to hate. Catch Sir G[eorge] H[ewitt] or Sir Carr [Scroope], at such an ill-bred Proceeding, and I am mistaken."[57] Rochester spared no one; he could hardly hope to be spared in his turn.

There is no record of any bawd reforming or prostitute turning penitent because of libels against her. It is possible that the Court ladies rather enjoyed the distinction of being libeled, and the woman "who miss'd her Name in a Lampoon" grieved "to find herself decay'd so soon."[58] That Restoration ladies were sensitively aware of libels is indicated by the many dramatic references to such verses, indicating such opposite attitudes as that of Wycherley's Alithea, who cried in defense of her virtue, "Why, pray, who boasts of any intrigue with me? What lampoon has made my name notorious?" and that of Congreve's Lady Wishfort, for whom Mirabel "got a friend to put her into a lampoon, and compliment her with the imputation of an affair with a young fellow."[59] Perhaps some real-life Lady Wishfort was frightened into virtue by the dread of scandalous libels, but the real-life Clevelands, Portsmouths and Gwyns went on sinning in apparent serenity. It should be noted, however, that whenever the publisher or author of a libel against a royal mistress was discovered, the direst penalties were invoked against him. The hide of the sinner was thick, but it was not impenetrable.

Political libels, more vigorous and unrestrained than modern editorials, were probably more effective also. Buckingham once quoted a minor politician as being "angry against Lampoons," and, like his superiors the "Grand Politicians," "as much affrayed of them."[60] Rabble-rousing is the same in any generation, and verse libels appealing to prejudice were probably as fruitful as the rank stump oratory of later times. Buckingham and Mulgrave lambasted their opponents, and were lambasted in return. The voters tended to follow the side with the strongest adjectives. It was only the stubbornness of Charles II which saved Danby from attainder and probable execution in 1679, for such ballads as Buckingham's savage appeal for a lynching had put Parliament into a frenzy. But Danby lived to prosper as the Duke of Leeds in the reign of Queen Anne.

Of Rochester's longer poems only the *Satyr against Mankind* seems to have caused much stir in its own day. As one might expect, it made the clergymen furious, and two of them climbed down from their pulpits to meet the famous Wit on his own ground and with his own weapons —heroic couplets. "An answer to the L——d Rochester's Satyr against man, by Tho: Lesly of Waddam Coll: Oxon:" exists only in manuscript. It is a dull, long-winded

attack on the follies and sins of the tavern gallants and
rakes of the day, written in an aggrieved tone, as if the
author were hurt that Rochester, a graduate of Wadham
College, had turned Hobbist. *An Answer to the Satyr
against Mankind*, by the Reverend Mr. Griffith, was published in 1679 shortly after Rochester's poem was first
printed. Probably both answers were written much earlier
than 1679. Griffith's reply is a clever attempt to reconcile
"Sense" and "Reason," and it must be admitted that although he was a worse poet than Rochester he was a better
logician.[61]

But we may be sure that more people than logicians and
divines were troubled by the famous satire. Two years after
Rochester's death, his witty friend Alexander Radcliffe
immortalized the earl among the damned as

> A Lord who was in Metre wont
> To call a Privy Member—
> Whose Verse, by Women termed lewd,
> Is still preserv'd, not understood.
> But that which made 'em curse and ban,
> Was for his Satyr against Man.[62]

A generation later, Rochester's verses were still being
read, with amusement or anger according to the reader's
convictions. Tom Brown distilled the judgment of his day
into careful phrases: "My lord Rochester was always witty,
and always very ill-natur'd . . . His wit was often profane,
and he neither spar'd Prince nor God."[63] He might have
added that Rochester fulfilled one part of Dryden's
definition of a satirist; he sought to "correct the vice and
follies of his time." But of all the Wits, only one attempted
to carry out the second part and "give the rules of a happy
and virtuous life." Sir Charles Sedley wrote a long poem
called *The Happy Pair: or, a Poem on Matrimony* (1702).
It is drearily didactic.

Patterns for the Stage

THE Restoration stage was owned and dominated by the Restoration Court. During the greater part of the reign of Charles II, there were only two theatrical companies; from 1682 to 1695 there was only one. The managers of the theatres—two courtiers—were the King's officers; the actors and actresses were the King's servants. Plays could be presented only with the approval of the Master of the Revels, and appeals from his authority were carried to Charles himself. The presence of His Majesty at a play usually meant a large audience and a good profit, while command performances at White-hall brought round sums from the Privy Purse. The King was the great patron of the stage. He settled disputes between actors and managers, encouraged playwrights, and suggested themes and plots for plays. He gave Court costumes to the actors and Court places to deserving play-wrights.

The theatres were the literary and social centers of London. Plays were presented at about three o'clock in the afternoon. They were attended by idle courtiers, officials, members of Parliament, bureaucrats, aspiring tradesmen, country gentlemen, ladies, prostitutes, and Mr. Pepys. (Republicans, Puritans, most "citizens," and all godly people stayed away.) The audiences were restless and noisy. Many came only to show off their august persons to the mob; some to make an assignation with a vizard mask; and a few to demonstrate their own wit at the tops of their voices. Anyone who disliked the play was privileged to cry out, "Damn me, Jack, 'tis a confounded Play, let's to a Whore and spend our time better."[1]

A new play was a social event, and admission prices were doubled for the first day. The King and Queen and perhaps the Duke and Duchess of York, with various Maids of Honor and Gentlemen in waiting, were likely to appear in the royal boxes, especially if the author had Court connections. If the play was a hit, it was presented several times in succession; it is probable that after half a dozen performances every habitual playgoer had seen it at least twice. The author received the profits from the third performance; if he was lucky and his friends were faithful, his reward might be as much as fifty pounds.[2] Although demand for new plays was great, the number of competent poets was small, and only five to fifteen new plays were presented each year. Between productions the theatres fell back on revivals of old plays, particularly those by Shakespeare, Jonson, and Beaumont and Fletcher.

No matter what the play was, it took a bored and cynical audience into the realm of make-believe. Here was no question of realism; here were dreams come true—dreams of prowess on the battlefield or in the boudoir. Under the soft glow of wax candles, the periwigged actors were all handsome, heroic and witty, and the painted actresses, with their white shoulders and bosoms and their rich, full-skirted gowns, were brightly seductive. They spoke in singing tones; gestured according to studied patterns; walked in graceful, almost dancing, measures. When a play gave opportunity, the actresses donned male attire—long laced coats, tight-fitting breeches and silk hose,—making the most of well-rounded limbs. In the colorful stage picture, red, green, gold and silver were favorites, and feathers were used lavishly for decorations and headdresses. All varieties of taste were catered to, and any play might include instrumental music, poetry, songs, dances, topical allusions, erotic situations, and bawdy jokes. The small, tightly-packed audience, half surrounding the apron stage, could feel itself an intimate part of the performance. The fops and beaux in the pit were an arm's-length from the actors; the ladies in the galleries were only a stage whisper farther away. It was all very cozy. Under the spell of a good play, it was easy to forget the cold, the damp (when it rained in at the clerestory), and the effluvium of the un-washed audience.

In the seventeenth century, "poet" was an inclusive term for one who wrote songs or epics, essays or plays, "scene individable or poem unlimited." Any "poet" could write a song or drudge out a compliment in rough pindaric verse, but not every writer had the patience to labor at the making of a five-act play. In the kingdom of literature, the dramatic poet wore the plumes; hence there were many wits who aspired to success upon the gilded stage, without thought of cash rewards. Of some sixty-six poets who had one or more plays produced in London between 1660 and 1685, at least twenty can be classed as "Persons of Honour" and amateurs. Two of them were dukes, four were earls, one was a viscount, and the others were knights and es-quires. No wonder that Shadwell, a professional poet, complained in his first play about the "Gentlemen of £5,000 a year" who wrote plays and so staked their reputa-tions for no gain "as poets venture their reputations against a sum of money."[3] The amateurs were bad for business.

Of all genteel dilettantes, the Court Wits were the most important as patrons and the most successful as play-wrights. They wrote nine comedies, one burlesque, one tragedy, one translation, and four alterations (one of which was not acted). Most of their plays were highly successful, either because of dramatic merit or because of the prestige of the authors. Moreover, their influence upon the stage was far out of proportion to their dramatic pro-ductivity. They were constant playgoers, whose critical judgments were humbly deferred to by lesser men. They were friendly with the actors,* and intimate with the actresses. In addition, they patronized most of the professional dramatists who carried the real burden of the stage, admitted them occasionally to evenings of brilliant conversation, and instructed them in the fine art of dramaturgy. The professionals not only listened and learned; they even submitted their manuscripts for revision and correction, and in the dedications to their printed plays they made much of the assistance they had received. Shadwell, in his dedication of *A True Widow*, claimed that his comedy had had the benefit of Sedley's corrections and the honor of his approval.† Nathaniel Lee, in his dedication of *The Rival Queens*, wrote that the Earl of Mulgrave had been "pleas'd" to read the play over, act by act, and by his praises had lifted Lee from his "natural Melancholy and Diffidence," and assured him of success. Dryden, dedicating *Marriage-à-la-Mode*, humbly offered Rochester the "poem" of which he had been "pleased to appear an early patron before it was acted on the stage." Almost timidly, the dramatist added, "I may yet go farther, with your permission, and say, that it received amendment from your noble hands ere it was fit to be presented."⁴

From such statements we get an impression of the obsequious professional dramatist waiting, hat in hand, while the godlike patron reads the labored manuscript, deigns to nod, and seems to shake the playhouse. The picture is

---

* See, for example, a letter from Nell Gwyn, written in June, 1678: "My lord of Dorscit apiers wonse in thre munthe, for he drinkes aile with Shadwell the dramatist and Mr. Haris [Henry Harris, actor] at the Dukes house all day long." (*Camden Miscellany*, V, 25-26)

† Dryden, in *Mac Flecknoe*, gibed at Shadwell for accepting assistance from Sedley:

> But let no alien Sedley interpose
> To lard with wit thy hungry Epsom prose.

Rochester was less specific in *Timon*:

> Insipid as the praise of Pious Queens,
> Or Shadwell's unassisted former scenes.

hardly overdrawn; the opinions of the Court Wits weighed heavily with writers, actors and audience—they were not only "Persons of Honour," but intimates and favorites of the King. Years after the Restoration, John Dennis asserted frequently that the Wits were the best critics of the period of Charles II, and that drama (particularly comedy) was superior then because "a considerable part of the audience were qualified to judge for themselves, and that they who were not qualified, were influenced by the authority of those who were."[5]

Occasionally, the Court Wits bestirred themselves and contributed prologues, epilogues or songs to the productions of their friends and protégés. For example, Sir Carr Scroope wrote a prologue and a song for his friend Etherege's *The Man of Mode*, a prologue for Lee's *The Rival Queens*, and a song for that playwright's *Mithridates*. Sedley contributed a prologue to Shadwell's *Epsom Wells*. Etherege wrote a prologue for the opening of the Duke's new Playhouse; the first play presented was a revival of Dryden's *Sir Martin Mar-all*. Rochester wrote an epilogue for Sir Francis Fane's *Love in the Dark*, and in return Sir Francis dedicated the play to the earl in fulsome terms. Dorset contributed an epilogue for a revival of Jonson's *Every Man in His Humour*, and another for Medbourne's translation of *Tartuffe*. Both Mulgrave and Rochester wrote prologues for Settle's *The Empress of Morocco* when it was presented at Court. These were no small gifts. A good prologue could turn a mediocre play into a success, "and good plays prove the better by the help of good epilogues"; while a clever song, well rendered, was often the high point of a performance. The Wits' occasional contributions were uniformly clever.

It would be too much to say that the Restoration professional playwrights wrote only to please the Court; but they knew which side their bread was buttered on. To please the King and the Wits was to be assured of a successful production and much prestige, perhaps a gift of money, a minor Court appointment, or an invitation to spend a fortnight in a luxurious country house. There was also the lash of fear: for the Wits had bitter tongues and their pens drew blood. Buckingham's *Rehearsal* did not kill the heroic play, but it minced the hides of a dozen dramatists. And, in 1676, after the professionals had been quarreling among themselves for several years, the Wits (led by Rochester) pulverized them all with "A Session of the Poets." Placated, the Wits were good patrons; annoyed, they were wicked censors of the stage.

In their own opinion (and in that of most Englishmen), the Wits were immeasurably above the "Clapping Fools" in the audience and the "vain mistaken" professional poets.[6] They patronized according to whim, and smote the poetaster who plumed himself too much. Rochester is said to have patronized in turn Dryden, Settle, Crowne, Otway, and Lee; like an animal trainer he alternately patted heads and lashed rumps. Only one poet ever dared retort. Smarting under the sting of Rochester's *Allusion to Horace*, Dryden replied viciously in his preface to *All For Love*. Even so, he protected himself against *scandalum magnatum* by pretending that Rochester's satire had been written by an anonymous poetaster wrapped in the lion's skin. Dryden was a commoner; Rochester was a peer.

However, in spite of their usual affectation of scorn for the judgments of the motley multitude, the Wits courted audience favor in the prologues to their plays. Probably their conciliatory attitude was for the sake of their friends, the players, whose profits were at stake. It is quite likely that the Wits themselves turned up their noses at the returns of the third day. We have little evidence for this theory, but it is hard to imagine, for example, lordly Buckingham (one of the wealthiest men in the kingdom) accepting his puny profits from *The Chances* or *The Rehearsal*. And perhaps it is significant that Wycherley, who spent nearly four years in debtors prison, made no known effort to write his way out. A gentleman could accept money from a woman or from the King (and James II paid five hundred pounds on Wycherley's debts), but he could not earn money as a "Trader in Wit."[7]

The Wits wrote their plays for fun, for prestige, and for the praises of the King and their companions. Perhaps, too, like old Sir John Denham, they wrote because they "had nothing else to do."[8] They were condescending enough to write patterns for the stage, but they had no intention of keeping it supplied. In his epilogue to *The Chances*, Buckingham begged the audience not to tempt him by their praises, and so encourage him to "write, and write again,"

> For he knows ways enough to be undone,
> Without the help of poetry for one.

None of the Wits wrote with any consistency; their plays were few and far apart in time. Rochester gently scolded "slow Wycherley" for his lack of productivity, and rebuked Etherege because,

> . . . in th' crying sin, idleness, he was so hardn'd,
> That his long seven years silence was not to be pardon'd.[9]

From 1663 through 1687 (ignoring Mulgrave's belated effort of *circa* 1710) the Wits produced only fifteen plays.

Their first play was an exercise in gentlemanly scholarship. In the early years of the Restoration, the thundering periods and set heroic speeches of Corneille were much in vogue among the literati of the Court. Sometime in 1662, "Certain Persons of Honour" took on the task of preparing Corneille's *Mort de Pompée* for the English stage. The translators have been generally identified as Edmund Waller, who seems to have been leader of the project and writer of Act I; Sir Edward Filmer, a rhyming nonentity (Act II); Sir Charles Sedley, already famous for the episode at the Cock Tavern (Act III); Lord Buckhurst (Dorset), a new favorite at Court (Act IV); and Sidney Godolphin, recently appointed Page to the King (Act v).[10]

Evidently the young courtiers boasted of their design; at any rate, rumor of the project reached the poetess Katherine Philips in Dublin, sometime in August, 1662. Katherine (known to her Platonic circle as "the Matchless Orinda") was upset; she was already at work on a translation of the play. She feared the other play might come out first; she feared her own work would not compare with that of the elegant Wits. For six months she was on tenterhooks; but she finished her play first and produced it successfully in Dublin, about February 10, 1663. Two months later it was printed, and a copy was presented to the King.

Apparently the Wits paid no attention to Katherine's play. In their dilatory fashion they went on with their own work, and in December, 1663, their *Pompey the Great* was produced at the Duke's Theatre. It was moderately successful, and, as one might expect, it was soon presented at Court. For the time at least, Orinda's work was completely overshadowed.[11]

Corneille's play is more a declamation than a drama.[12] Mrs. Philips' version is more accurate as a translation but less poetic than that of the Wits; but neither is a good play. The Wits bragged of their achievement in prologue and epilogue and made plans for the future. They were practicing, they declared, to "improve their Muse" so she would be better able to "Adorn the Stage."

Three months after the production of *Pompey*, a new member was admitted into the Wits' circle. George Etherege, a tall, fair young man of twenty-nine, with a gift for neat phrasing, emerged from the obscurity of the law courts with his first play, *The Comical Revenge, or, Love in a Tub*, produced at the Duke's Theatre in Lincoln's Inn Fields. Gentle George had no fortune, no patrons, and no post at Court, but he was undeniably a gentleman. *The Comical Revenge*, as its author implied in his dedication to Lord Buckhurst, was the means of making Etherege known to the Wits. Evidently they accepted him at once, for thenceforth he was established as a courtier.

The first three years of the Restoration had produced little more than a dozen new plays, half of them comedies written in the old "humours" style of Ben Jonson. Dryden had tried a new way of wit in his first play, *The Wild Gallant*, with little success. The most popular of the new comedies had been the amazingly involved (and amazingly dull) *Adventure of Five Hours*, by Sir Samuel Tuke, over which Pepys had regularly gone into ecstasies. There had been humor in the early comedies, but little gaiety. Perhaps Etherege's first claim to fame is that he brought merriment back on the stage.

"*Love in a Tub*," wrote Pepys, "is very merry, but only so by gesture, not wit at all."[13] Unless levity be the soul of wit, Pepys is quite right. The play is an *olla-podrida* of plots, humours, escapades, and merry, bawdy songs. There is a serious "love and honour" plot (done in heroic couplets) which is built on a conventional, almost algebraic pattern. A loves B, B loves A; C also loves A, and D loves C. With much hocus-pocus, fine sentiment, and honor debates, the letters are jumbled about until the author comes up triumphantly with AB and CD. Multiplication, of course, is expected to follow. There is a madcap comic plot, involving the love affair of a rake and a rich widow. For no discernible reason, these two back and fill, quarrel and make up through five acts, to marry at last. There is a gulling plot, involving a French valet, rotten with disease, a couple of waiting maids, and a tub. Restoration audiences had strong stomachs.

Confusing as the play sounds, it was theatrically effective, very successful, and the making of George Etherege. He fell happily into the riotous life of Whitehall; he was under no compulsion to write more plays, and for four long years he was content to do nothing. We are not told what profit he received from his play, if any; but the Duke's Company in a month's time gained from it a thousand pounds.[14] No doubt Etherege was taken care of by his Royal Master; in 1668, for example, he was made a gentleman of the Privy Chamber in ordinary, and sent off to Turkey with the new ambassador to that country.[15]

Sometime in '64 or '65, perhaps soon after the production of *The Comical Revenge*, the Duke of Buckingham, who strove to excel in all fields, began to write a burlesque on the windy rant and pompous rhetoric of Davenant, Killigrew, Sir Robert Howard and their fellow writers of heroic plays. Tradition has it that *The Rehearsal* was ready for production when the plague closed the theatres in June, 1665. When the playhouses reopened more than a year later (November 29, 1666), *The Rehearsal* was laid aside, probably because so many of its topical jokes had lost their point. But Buckingham was not to be denied his comic sock. He chose to rewrite the last two acts of a long-popular play, Fletcher's *The Chances*; his altered version was produced sometime late in 1666 or early in the following year.[16]

Fletcher's play was a rollicking, obscene comedy, dealing with the adventures of two young Spanish gentlemen in search of a beautiful prostitute named Constantia. They became involved with a lady bearing the same name as the prostitute, with various hot-blooded Italian gentlemen, a baby, a bawd or two, and a conjurer. The result was a typically Fletcherian hash of wild action and violent horseplay. Buckingham tied up the loose strings in the plot, eliminated needless characters and scenes, and threw the emphasis on the younger of the two comic heroes, Don John. In his hands, the Don became a typical Restoration rake, so rampant that in the presence of the voluptuous Constantia (the professional) he could hardly contain himself. More ruttish than Fletcher's hero, he was also more adept at the brisk, railing wit which was to become one of the trademarks of the Restoration comedy of manners. In 1672, John Dryden, comparing the courtly wit of his age with that of the first half of the century, wrote with authority:

> Fletcher's Don John is our only bugbear; and yet I may affirm, without suspicion of flattery, that he now speaks better, and that his character is maintained with much more vigour in the fourth and fifth acts, than it was by Fletcher in the three former.[17]

For more than a year after *The Chances*, the Wits' pens were dry. Meanwhile, with the constantly growing vogue for love-and-honor drama, the professional poets were tuning their pipes to the heroic note. There was a serious shortage of good comedies. Accordingly, Etherege shook off his crying sin, idleness, and on February 6, 1668, produced *She wou'd if she cou'd* at the Duke's Theatre. By that time the Wits (reinforced by Rochester, Mulgrave, Savile and others) were a well-known group, and a play by one of the circle was an event to be anticipated. When Pepys went to see the first performance of the new play, he found the house full, even though he was quite early, and in addition "there were 1000 people put back that could not find room in the pit." With difficulty, the diarist squeezed into an eighteen penny box, and saw what he labeled a very "silly" play. In the pit was a group of Wits: the Duke of Buckingham (recently restored to favor after his fatal duel with the Earl of Shrewsbury), Lord Buckhurst, Sedley, and Etherege himself.[18]

Perhaps the fact that the actors "had not their parts perfect" had something to do with the comedy's failure at its first performance; but even in subsequent revivals it failed to achieve much popularity. As a matter of fact, Etherege still had much to learn as a dramatist. Structurally, *She wou'd if she cou'd* is rather poor stuff. Its tissue-thin plot is woven around the central figure of Lady Cock-wood, a hypocritical harpy who would eat the cake of lechery and have her honor, too. When her expectations are disappointed by the leading gentleman of the play, Court-all, she takes out her spite in vicious plots against the other members of her circle. Defeated in her schemes, she confesses that she has been made "so truly sensible of those dangers to which an aspiring Lady must daily expose her Honour, that I am resolv'd to give over the great bus'ness of this Town [sex intrigue] and hereafter modestly confine my self to the humble Affairs of my own Family." Her reformation is not convincing.

Aside from the affairs of Lady Cockwood, the other business of the play is very slight. The love affairs of Courtall and Gatty, Freeman and Ariana, are trifling. A deal of space is given to brisk badinage among the four, and in these scenes Etherege demonstrates some skill at writing near-witty conversation. The sub-plot is a link with the past age when gentlemen could be amused by the humors of fools, in this case two country bumpkins, Sir Oliver Cock-wood, and Sir Jolly Joslin, who can think and talk of nothing but "wenching and swearing, and drinking, and tearing." There is, of course, the usual complement of pimps and prostitutes, fiddlers, waiters, and citizens' wives, and some roaring scenes in taverns and bedrooms. Etherege was still writing largely in the tradition of Caroline comedy.

Sir Charles Sedley should have profited by Etherege's experience and abstained from playwriting. However, his first full-length comedy was already in rehearsal (Pepys had heard of it as early as January 11). *The Mulberry Garden* was finally produced at the King's Theatre on May 18, 1668. Again, "great matters" were expected from "so reputed a wit." The house was "infinitely full," and the King, Queen, and "all the Court" were there.[19] Again the product fell short of the advertising.

By his contemporaries, Etherege was accused of writing comedies without plots; Sedley could have been accused of reversing the process. *The Mulberry Garden*, a derivative and imitative olio of plots, sub-plots, and counter-plots, is a pretty dull play. Two pairs of despairing lovers are at the usual cross-purposes: the two men love one girl, leaving the other out in the cold. Another heroic pair (Diana and Philander) seem to be unhappy for no reason at all. A fourth pair (Olivia and Wildish) belong to the bantering tradition, and quibble along quite happily. For each pair of girls there is a father: Everyoung, a gay cavalier, and Forecast, a dour Roundhead (the time is just before the Restoration). The two old fellows are rivals for the hand of a supposedly rich widow. There are complicated scenes of mistaken identity, horseplay, and cudgeling, and several high-flown honor debates in wretched blank verse—tedious and not brief. Finally, all the plots are sorted out after a fashion, every Jack gets his Jill, and the rich widow, who turns out to be a cast mistress, is married to a minor rake who seems to have no other function in the play.

Pepys wrote, "I have not been less pleased at a new play in my life, I think." In his opinion, the comedy had nothing extraordinary in it, of language, design, or music. No one was pleased; the King did not laugh even once. (The last fact may have affected Mr. Pepys' judgment.) Nevertheless, the play was revived a number of times, and apparently with success. In justice, one must add that it was no worse than many a comedy of the day; its measure of undeserved success was probably due to its author's eminence and courtly favor.

For the next three years, the Wits produced nothing for the stage. Etherege was in Turkey; Buckingham was busy ruling England and making love to the Countess of Shrewsbury; Sedley (let us hope) was doing penance for *The Mulberry Garden*; haughty Rochester felt himself

Mrs BARRY
in the Character of ALMIDA.

Elizabeth Barry
Courtesy of the Harvard Theatre Collection, Harvard University

William Wycherley. About 1677-1680
By Sir Peter Lely. Courtesy of the National Portrait Gallery

superior to the theatre;* and Dorset, having made his one-act contribution to the tragic muse, had settled down to writing lazy songs and satires. In the spring of 1669, Buckingham collaborated with his friend and fellow poet, Sir Robert Howard, in writing a political comedy designed to satirize Sir William Coventry, Secretary of State. But Coventry heard of the scheme and promptly sent his nephew, Harry Savile, with a challenge to the Duke. As usual, the challengers were imprisoned—Coventry in the Tower and Savile in the Gatehouse—until their tempers cooled.[20] The play was never acted, perhaps because of royal command, perhaps because Coventry declared that if any actor "did offer at anything like representing him . . . he would cause his nose to be slit." Since, only a few months earlier, the actor Kynaston had been thoroughly thrashed by hired bullies for "representing" Sedley on the stage, Coventry's threat was duly heeded.[21] Courtiers were not to be slandered by vulgar players.

The 1670's were the years of the Wits' greatest influence on the Restoration theatre, and of their greatest productivity, with eight of their plays produced or made ready for production. Already they had shown that they could equal and even at times outdo the run-of-mine professional writers. They were now a group to be feared, flattered, and propitiated.† New dramatists, trying out their plays on the town, strove to get powerful protectors, and increasingly more often during the decade plays were dedicated to Rochester, Dorset, Mulgrave, Buckingham and Sedley—

* See "An Allusion to Horace,"
>   Canst thou be such a vain mistaken thing,
>   To wish thy Works might make a Play-House ring.
>   With the unthinking Laughter, and poor praise
>   Of Fops and Ladies factious for thy Plays;
> . . . .
>   I've no Ambition on that idle score, . . .

† One of the lesser Wits, Henry Killigrew, had a considerable financial interest in the Theatre Royal. In 1678 he became associated with his half-brother, Charles, as a master partner.

the top wits of the circle. It became almost traditional to look upon the Wits as literary geniuses, whose productions were certain to elevate the stage. We find, for example, William Joyner, who in 1671 dedicated his *The Roman Empress* to Sedley, urging that the baronet, "so far plac'd above the reach of envy, would honour the Theatre with some production of this nature"—that is, a tragedy. In due time, possibly in reply to Joyner's flattering suggestion, Sedley wrote a tragedy, but, like the rest of the Wits he was by temperament better suited to the writing of comedy. And comedy it was that dominated the decade; Buckingham and Etherege hit their peak in that medium, and Wycherley swept all before him.

In the spring of 1671, a new comedy called *Love in a Wood: or, St. James's Park* appeared at the Theatre Royal. Its author was youngish William Wycherley (about thirty-one), a big, handsome man who had spent some ten years dawdling about Town, alternating between the delights of Court and the labors of the Inns-of-Court. He had no desire to be a lawyer, but his stern father, Daniel, held the purse strings and gave the orders. In 1669, Wycherley had published anonymously a burlesque *Hero and Leander*, but he was otherwise undistinguished among the horde of lesser gentry on the fringes of the Court. Tradition has it that the production of his first play gained him acquaintance among the Wits, but it is quite likely that he was already known to that circle. However, the success of *Love in a Wood* gave him prestige, the esteem and friendship of the Wits, and the dubious affections of the Duchess of Cleveland. The point of a song in the play is that "great wits and great braves" are always the offspring of trollops. As John Dennis tells the story, the Duchess drove by Wycherley in the Park one day, thrust her head out the coach window and cried, "You, Wycherley, you are the Son of a Whore," laughing heartily the while. Out of this delicate salutation grew the liaison between the budding playwright and the still blooming senior concubine of Charles II.[22]

Love in a Wood, a passable comedy, gives the impression that for years Wycherley had been noting carefully the sure-fire comic devices of the professionals. There are a few minor innovations—for example, the love-and-honor plot is in prose instead of verse—but in the main the play is built according to formula. There is the usual group of people at cross-purposes: Lady Flippant, a raffish widow who needs a rich husband; Sir Simon Addleplot, who wants a rich wife (and gets Lady Flippant instead); Dapperwit, a fool who gets a rich wife (Martha, daughter of Alderman Gripe), and finds her "six months gone with child"; Ranger, a fine gentleman, who goes sniffing after a new love; Lydia, Ranger's betrothed, who pursues him and catches him in the net of matrimony; Christine, who wants (one wonders why) and gets the ultra-heroic and over-jealous lover, Valentine; and Alderman Gripe, who pursues, is cheated of, and finally marries a prostitute, thereby frustrating Dapperwit, his new son-in-law. Like all such gulling-intrigue comedies, the play is full of bustle and confusion; characters gallop on and off the stage in full cry; there are grossly vulgar and brightly witty scenes; there is no one dominant theme.

Worthy of note, however, is the satiric force which was to become Wycherley's dramatic signature. It appears at its peak in the picture of Alderman Gripe, a lecherous old Commonwealth's-man, the very "bellows of zeal," a "conventicle of virtues," and a complete hypocrite. He is the epitome of a type-character which had been popular for a decade, but particularly in the first few years after the Restoration. Disappointed of his erotic expectations and caught in an old form of the badger game, he is forced to pay five hundred pounds. He cries, "My enemies are many, and I shall be a scandal to the faithful, as a laughingstock to the wicked." Later he bitterly regrets losing not only the money but the prostitute, out of whom he has not had his "pennyworths." When he finally decides to marry the girl, he has several reasons: he will regain his five hundred pounds; he will get heirs to exclude from his inheritance his daughter and her new husband; and "besides, 'tis agreed on all hands, 'tis cheaper keeping a wife than a wench." The picture is brilliant, but painful.

As the boon companion of the Wits, Wycherley was brought into the sunshine of royal favor, which was later to prove very warming. Immediately, however, his only material gain was a commission as lieutenant (later, as captain) in Buckingham's regiment of foot (June 19, 1672).[23] The fact that he knew nothing about military matters was of no importance.

Meanwhile, the mighty Buckingham was preparing his dramatic *magnum opus*. *The Rehearsal*, revised, improved, and brought up to date topically, was presented at last on December 7, 1671, at the Theatre Royal in Drury Lane. Known to be associated with Buckingham were two of his dependents: Thomas Sprat, his chaplain (later Bishop of Rochester), and Martin Clifford (later Master of the Charterhouse). Other collaborators have been suggested, among them Samuel Butler, author of *Hudibras*. It is quite likely that *The Rehearsal* had grown, snowball-like, from the ideas and quips of a number of the Wits, so that it was truly, as a contemporary lampoon called it, "twenty other men's Farce."[24]

The most recent editor of the play goes into rhapsodies over "the exquisite wit, the irresistible humour, the mordant satire, the inimitable parodies and banter of *The Rehearsal*."[25] With all due apologies, one must point out that a burlesque is funny only to the reader or audience intimately acquainted with that which is parodied. In spite of its learned partisans, *The Rehearsal*, though historically important and in its time undeniably clever, is today deader than the heroic rant it burlesqued. Yet so great is the power of tradition that modern anthologists continue to reprint it for the mystification of undergraduates.

The plan of the burlesque is simple and obvious. Two gentlemen, Johnson and Smith, are invited by the poet Bayes (a composite caricature, but chiefly of Dryden) to witness the rehearsal of his new play. There follows a series of incredibly wild scenes of unmotivated action, bellowing rant, horseplay and slapstick, and silly debates on love and honor. No doubt the habitual playgoers in the audience recognized the plays and themes parodied, and split with laughter. There were two kings; two usurpers; two princes; an ultra heroic fire-eater, Drawcansir; four cardinals; a general; several characters representing the sun, the moon, thunder, lightning, and the earth; some modest little melting heroines; and numerous players, soldiers, attendants, and so forth. Much as in the true heroic play, nothing makes sense. Thrusts are made at all the popular dramas of the day, and many of the less popular—some seventy in all. Throughout waddles the squab figure of Bayes, played by the comic actor John Lacy, who was coached by Buckingham (says tradition) to imitate Dryden's voice, dress, gait, and mannerisms. Tradition adds further—cruelest touch of all—that the Wits took Dryden to see the play and sat with him in a box where they could watch him squirm!

The Rehearsal did no harm to the vogue for heroic drama, but it was a vast success. It was produced again and again, revised from time to time to keep it topical, and published in numerous editions from 1672 on. In its own day it fathered several similar dramatic burlesques, and it is credited with suggesting to Sheridan, a century later, the plan for *The Critic*. As for Buckingham, in a literary sense he had reached his summit. It is reported that the King of France told Colbert, his prime minister, that unless he wrote a play "he would be out of fashion, for the chief minister of state in England had gotten a great deal of honour by writing a farce."[26] It was truly a strange and wonderful epoch, when statesmen were expected to be farceurs.

The tumult and shouting following on the production of *The Rehearsal* had barely subsided when Wycherley was a second time in the field with *The Gentleman Dancing Master*, presented at the Dorset Garden Theatre in March, 1672. The plot is built on the efforts of an impudent young jillflirt, Hippolita, to free herself from a marriage into which she is being forced by her father and to find a husband of a better complexion. Gerrard, the fine gentleman rescuer, who is forced to pose as a dancing master in order to visit Hippolita, comes as near to a sentimental attachment as Restoration cynicism allowed. The bulk of the comedy is given over to the follies and absurdities of three type-characters, familiar to the Restoration audience: Hippolita's affectedly Castilian father, James Formal (or "Don Diego"), her francophile fiancé, Nathaniel Paris (or "Monsieur de Paris"), and her prurient-minded aunt, Mrs. Caution.

Wycherley had learned something from his first experiment: the play is competent, if a bit slow-paced. It is much simpler in structure than the earlier play, lacking the tangles of intrigue so common to the contemporary stage. But it was not a success; "being lik't but indifferently it was laid by [after six days] to make room for other new ones."[27] It was probably too simple and not sufficiently lubricious for the Restoration audience. The relationship of Hippolita and Gerrard, despite vulgar Mrs. Caution's suspicions, is entirely innocent. Monsieur disappoints lewd expectations by dodging the waiting maid, Prue, who throws herself openly at him. But if the play was too clean for an audience accustomed to comedies of blatant adultery, Wycherley balanced the account in his next play, *The Country Wife*, which did not appear until 1675.

In the intervening years, the Wits' dramatic activity was

confined to patronage and the writing of occasional prologues and epilogues for other men's plays. As a line in the
epilogue to *The Gentleman Dancing Master* had said, "all
gentlemen must pack to sea." War with the Netherlands
was formally declared in March, 1672, and the slow hos-
tilities dragged themselves along until February, 1674.
Such Wits as held military posts—Buckingham, Mulgrave,
Dorset, Savile, Vaughan, Bulkeley and probably Wycherley—made a fine show of martial ardor (see Chapter III).
Rochester, no soldier if he could help it, was occupied with
personal affairs, and presumably Etherege was enjoying
his usual indolence. Sedley was getting rid of an insane
wife, and contracting a pseudo-marriage with Ann Ayscough. Left to shift for itself, the stage did quite well with
new plays by Behn, Crowne, Dryden, Duffett, Lee, Payne,
Ravenscroft, Shadwell, and Settle.

During these years Wycherley's perception of the comic
had sharpened, and his sense of the dramatic had matured.
The Country Wife, presented at the Drury Lane Theatre
in January of 1675, is by all odds his best and liveliest
comedy; indeed it is one of the best plays produced during
the Restoration period. Despite some nasty-nice prudes and
hypocrites in the audience (very tellingly dealt with by
the author in his next play, *The Plain Dealer*), the comedy
was a great success.[28]

Horner is the leading rake of the play—a maker of
cuckolds, hence a giver of horns to husbands. By pretending impotence, he gains the freedom of all boudoirs, and,
safe from husbandly suspicion, acquits himself right gal-
lantly. His paramours include Mrs. Pinchwife, Mrs.
Squeamish, Mrs. Dainty Fidget, and that most remarkable
wanton, Lady Fidget, who has so much honor in her
mouth that she has none elsewhere.

The country wife, Margery, is married to a grum old
rake, Pinchwife, who at forty-nine is satiated. She is at
once innocent and lovable, frank and dissembling, ignorant

and yet wise in the most wanton ways of her sex. She sees
no harm in a little innocent adultery; caught almost *in
flagrante*, she is not ashamed. When Horner claims impotence as his defense, and his friend Dorilant calls him
"an arrant French capon," Margery cries indignantly,
" 'Tis false, sir, you shall not disparage poor Mr. Horner,
for to my certain knowledge—" She gets no further; there
is a concerted rush to stop her foolish little mouth.

Probably the most famous episode in the play is the so-
called "china scene" (Act IV, iii)*, which abounds in such
clever *double entendre* that one can readily forgive its vulgarity. Lady Fidget and Horner are locked in an inner
room, presumably so milady may get a piece of Horner's
china, while Sir Jasper Fidget, Mrs. Squeamish, and old
Lady Squeamish talk together provocatively on the fore
stage or make insinuating remarks through the keyhole.

The play depicts the kind of life which the libidinous in
the audience (i.e., nearly everybody) could happily imagine themselves to be leading. Conventionally, Wycherley makes fun of the usual fools, such as Sparkish and Sir
Jasper Fidget, but the drift of his satire is against anyone
and anything which is opposed to the free and open playing
of the venereal game—against surly husbands who keep
charming wives locked up; against foolish women who
make much of their honor; against the nice institutions
and customs of society which hamper the devotees of Ve-

---

* In *The Plain Dealer*, Wycherley put a typical prudish remark in the
mouth of hypocritical Olivia:

Oliv.   O, believe me, 'tis a filthy play! and you may take my word for a
         filthy play as soon as another's. But the filthiest thing in that play,
         or any other play, is—
Eliza.   Pray keep it to yourself, if it be so.
Oliv.   No, faith, you shall know it; I'm resolved to make you out of love
         with the play. I say, the lewdest, filthiest thing is his china; nay, I
         will never forgive the beastly author his china. He has quite taken
         away the reputation of poor china itself, and sullied the most in-
         nocent and pretty furniture of a lady's chamber; insomuch that I
         was fain to break all my defiled vessels. You see I have none left;
         nor you, I hope.

nus; against everything, in short, which went then or now by the name of respectability. *The Country Wife* is a knavish and laughable piece of work, and one to make Mrs. Grundy scream with horror.

Whatever induced easy Etherege to break his long years of silence and write another play we shall never know— perhaps he was goaded by his fellow Wits; perhaps he was emulous of Wycherley's success; perhaps he wished to call himself to the attention of Royalty, to get a better post at Court,* or to acquire the knighthood which would make him more pleasing to the rich widow he was said to have been courting. At all events, he set to work, and on March 11, 1676, *The Man of Mode; or, Sir Fopling Flutter* was produced at the Duke's Theatre in Dorset Garden.

With this comedy, Etherege reached his climax; regrettably it was also his last literary effort. *The Man of Mode* is the brightest, gayest, wittiest comedy produced in the Restoration proper. In its brittle, polished way, it is great. Less satiric than the best of Wycherley, less humorous than the best of Shadwell, less witty than the best of Congreve, it is nevertheless nearly perfect as an example of brisk, clever, comedy of manners.

There has been much useless breaking of brains over the questions whether Dorimant, the leading rake of the play, was designed to represent Rochester, Dorset, or Etherege himself; Medley to represent Sir Charles Sedley, Fleetwood Shepherd, or Etherege himself; and Sir Fopling to stand for Sir George ("Beau") Hewitt, a pattern of Restoration foppery, or Etherege himself.[29] The important fact is that Etherege, the complete courtier, had studied the

---

* He was evidently in the service of the Duke or Duchess of York at the time the play was published. In his dedication of *The Man of Mode* "To Her Royal Highness The Duchess," he wrote, "But I hope the honour I have of belonging to You, will excuse my presumption." Since he added that the printed play was the first thing he had produced in the Duchess' service, we may take it that he had only recently been appointed—possibly in reward for *The Man of Mode*.

Wits and their ladies so well that his idealized portraits are recognizable as the patterns of mannered, aristocratic society. Here is no question of realism; Etherege seized upon and embodied in his play not the real, day by day life of Whitehall, but the life which Whitehall was pleased to imagine it led. Individual items may be factual, but the total picture is a comic illusion.

In a true comedy of manners, of course, plot is relatively unimportant, and *The Man of Mode* is comparatively simple in structure: Dorimant seeks to break off a wearisome affair with Mrs. Loveit; to seduce Bellinda; and to marry Harriet, who is "wild, witty, lovesome, beautiful and young"—and a fortune. He succeeds with his first two projects, and the impression at the end of the play is that he will achieve the third. Young Bellair, ordered to marry Harriet, marries Emilia instead, thus cheating his father, who had thought of Emilia as a possible wife for himself. The man of mode, Sir Fopling Flutter, is made to appear a fool, but is hardly chastised as his folly deserves.

The dominant note of the play is social satire. The dramatis personae are neatly divisible into the accepted and the rejected, or the admired and the scorned. Admirable from the point of view of Restoration Society are: Dorimant, the complete gentleman, gay, careless, witty, gallant, and completely amoral, and his shadows, Medley and Bellair; Harriet, Emilia, and Bellinda, emancipated jillflirts who enjoy the game of love as much as the rakes do; and old Lady Townley, who is the very spirit of well-bred urban sophistication. Scorned as inferior are: Sir Fopling, a would-be Dorimant, whom nature made a complete ass and fashion an egregious francophile; Old Bellair, a silly, doting, country gentleman; old Lady Woodvil, the country mouse to Lady Townley's town mouse; and Mrs. Loveit, whose great failure is her inability to be nonchalant when Dorimant jilts her.

In spite of the fact that very little happens, the comedy

seems to move at a headlong pace. The illusion is largely due to the qualities of Etherege's prose. His sentences are brief and at times clipped; they are polished and sharply sententious. The reader finds himself increasingly going faster than is his wont. The brisk speeches sound like epigrams, but rarely are; Etherege was a clever writer but no philosopher. Still there are ear-catching phrases like the following: "Our love is as frail as is our life, and full as little in our power"; "In love there is no security to be given for the future"; "Against a woman's frailty all our care is vain"; and "Men are seldom in the right when they guess at a woman's mind." The dialogue is, of course, overartificial, lacking in the homely human notes. The characters are amazingly quick at quip and banter, and inhumanly brittle and hard. Even in the Restoration it seems rather brutal for a successful contestant to say to the loser, as Harriet cries to Mrs. Loveit, "Mr. Dorimant has been your God Almighty long enough, 'tis time to think of another." But such contrasts are the essence of comedy.

The boundary line between satiric comedy and tragedy is ill-defined. Wycherley's fourth and last play, *The Plain Dealer* (produced in December, 1676, at the King's Theatre), is a satiric comedy by definition, but its effect is an almost tragic revelation of the inherent evil of mankind. A masterpiece of irony and invective, from its dedication (to Madam Bennet, a famous bawd) to its epilogue, it is more painful than funny.

Manly, a misanthropic gentleman, returns from a sea battle with the Dutch to find his sweetheart Olivia married to his best friend Vernish, and all his money and jewels in the clutches of the precious pair. Olivia is a beautiful and lustful Messalina, with "impudence enough to put a court out of countenance, and debauch a stews" and Vernish is her male counterpart. Convinced of Olivia's hypocrisy, Manly is still dominated by his old passion. By deceit, he possesses her twice, the first time for lust, the second time for revenge. Having run out of reasons, he turns to the lovelorn Fidelia, who, disguised in male attire, has served him faithfully as his page and even as his pander in the affairs with Olivia.

The bulk of the play is given over to the depiction of various type-characters: Novel, a pert, railing fop; Lord Plausible, a supple coxcomb; Major Oldfox, an impertinent old scribbler; and the Widow Blackacre. The first three of these were conventional enough, but the litigious Widow Blackacre was triumphantly new. Quite possibly, through her Wycherley was hitting at his own father, who was forever involved in law suits, and by whose orders Wycherley had been forced to remain so long a student of the law. Gross, vulgar, shrill and loud, the Widow is a most unpleasant figure.

In addition, there are bitter portraits of a time-serving gentleman, Freeman, the secondary lead; of a raw squire, Jerry Blackacre; of mercenary aldermen and pettifogging lawyers (Wycherley knew the breed). Only two characters escape the dramatist's invective, and they are properly outside his picture: Eliza, Olivia's cousin and confidante, whose sober common sense makes her a kind of *raisonneur* for the play; and Fidelia, who has strayed direct from romantic drama and seems a bit bewildered by her crass surroundings.

Manly himself is a tragic yet a completely unsympathetic character, and it is ironic that for generations to come his creator was to be known as "Manly" Wycherley, or "the Plain Dealer." Surly, contentious, moody and passionate, Manly has ideals and morals, yet he makes no serious attempt to live up to them. He hates all mankind except himself; professing to be a complete pessimist, he can still be disillusioned. He is proud, intolerant, quarrelsome, and vindictive. At the end of the play, just after he has satisfied his goatish lust and won his ignoble revenge, he is rewarded with the love of Fidelia Grey and with a fortune of ten thousand pounds a year. Irony can go little further.

Unlike *The Country Wife* and *The Man of Mode* there is nothing in *The Plain Dealer* to make sin and sex attractive. Where Etherege (and Wycherley, too, in his earlier plays) judged his characters and accepted or rejected them according to the standards of a highly sophisticated society, Wycherley in his last play held up his characters against an ideal standard of human behavior, and rejected them all. In one play, at least, he was a truly great satirist, and that play is a classic of its kind.

The ribald Restoration, we learn on good authority, was properly doubtful what reception to give to *The Plain Dealer*. But "Villiers Duke of Buckingham, Wilmot Earl of Rochester, the Earl of Dorsett, the Earl of Mulgrave ... Mr. Savile, Mr. Buckley, Sir John Denham, Mr. Waller &c"—in short, most of the Court Wits—"by their loud approbation of it, gave it both a sudden and a lasting reputation."[30] It has maintained that reputation for two and a half centuries.

It must have been the authority of the Wits which also managed to get Sedley's second play acted, and to keep it on the boards for a number of performances. *Antony and Cleopatra*, produced at the Dorset Garden Theatre in February, 1677, represents the first attempt at tragedy by any of the Wits since the translation of *Pompey* in 1663. To put it mildly, the attempt was a failure.

Inevitably, Sedley's effusion invites comparison with the plays of Shakespeare and Dryden on the same subject. Usually comparisons are only odious, but in this case they are appalling. Shakespeare's episodic drama of world politics and middle-aged passion is not well constructed, but it is still a magnificent example of Renaissance romance. Dryden's neo-classic illustration of the theme that the world is well lost for love is well-knit and vigorous, less appealing than Shakespeare's play, but a great poetic drama nonetheless. Sedley's effort is puerile. His theme is obscure; his plot is chaotic; his characters are stereotyped. His world-conquering Antony is a weakling; his Cleopatra squeaks. Their gelid passion is subordinated to the petty intrigues and betrayals of minor characters. In his invincible inventiveness, Sedley made the Egyptian Photinus a knave who lusts after Iras and betrays his queen; he turned the Roman Thyreus into a milksop, hopelessly enamored of Cleopatra; he made Caesar's counselor, Mecaenas, also a lover, smitten by the fading charms of Octavia. In such a medley of love-making and petty intrigue, Antony and Cleopatra are dwarfed. They are stilted figures, given brief space upon the stage to be by turns jealous, accusing, defensive, and withal rather silly. By comparison with Shakespeare and Dryden, Sedley was a scald rhymer who at best could only ballad a great love story out o' tune. One looks in vain for the gleam of clear light, and listens hopelessly for the ring of authentic verse.

Sedley's *Antony and Cleopatra*, however, was "acted often"—at least until it was superseded by Dryden's version in December, 1677. Some years later (perhaps inspired by the work of the greater poet) Sedley recast his play as a classical tragedy with choruses between the acts—and entitled it "Beauty the Conqueror." Apparently it was never produced.[31]

Sometime in 1678, the Earl of Rochester climbed down from his high horse and tried his hand at scenes and machines for the stage. By a nice irony, the Wit who had attacked the heroic play so often in his satires, chose to work in that form himself. His first attempt was a brief scene, written probably in the summer of 1678,[32] and intended for a play to be called "The Conquest of China," by his friend Sir Robert Howard. Rochester's fragment, which dealt with a battle between the amazonian Empress of China and the Tartars, is competent enough, but too conventional to be distinctive. Howard's play was never produced.

Perhaps it was this fleshing of his pen which gave Rochester larger ideas. Sometime in the same year, probably, he began work on an alteration of Fletcher's *Valentinian*. A prompt copy of the play seems to have been prepared early in 1679, but it is doubtful if it was produced then.[33] Rochester was ill during the greater part of the year, and there was still some work to be done on the alteration. In February, 1684, nearly four years after Rochester's death, his play was given a magnificent production at the King's Theatre, and "The well performance, and the vast interest the Author made in Town, Crown'd the Play, with great Gain of Reputation, and Profit to the Actors."[34] Even in death, a Wit could draw crowds, but, indeed, in many ways the alteration is an improvement over the original.

Rochester's reason for choosing *Valentinian* out of the lumber room of old plays is easy to guess. To a man who was above all a satirist, the parallel between the courts of Valentinian and Charles II must have been tempting. While much that Rochester did to Fletcher's play was designed to compress and unify its loose structure or to add to its heroic sentiment,[35] he neglected no opportunity to emphasize the resemblance between the lustful Roman, Valentinian, and England's Old Rowley.[36] He added so considerably to the lubricity of the earlier version that, a few years later, in self-defense, Aphra Behn cited his play as worse than anything she had written. She referred particularly to Valentinian's appearance on the stage "all loose and Ruffled a moment after the Rape" of Lucina,[37] but she might have listed several other passages as well.

At some time during his last years, Rochester must have planned a comedy; little more than a page of it exists in manuscript, but that little is promising.[38] Many reputable historians, on very slender evidence, credit him also with the authorship of *Sodom, or The Quintessence of Debauchery*, a vulgar and worthless piece of pornography which was certainly never acted upon the public stage. It is quite likely that this was only one of the many obscene writings which were attributed to Rochester for want of a better culprit.[39]

By the end of 1680, the dramatic heyday of the Wits was over. Rochester and Scroope were dead; Etherege and Wycherley were silent; and Dorset and Mulgrave had gone in for politics and preferment. Buckingham, after the failure of the Popish Plot and the defeat of the Whigs, retired from politics and spent several years trying to convince the King and Court that he was essentially harmless; perhaps for that reason he took to writing for the stage again. The most extensive job he undertook (probably in 1682-83) was an alteration of Fletcher's *Philaster*. At least, a revision of that play entitled *The Restauration: or Right will take Place* is printed under his name in a 1715 edition of his works. If Buckingham was really the author (and there is a good deal of evidence to that effect) all one can say in charity is that the Duke lacked both cunning and collaborators. It is sufficiently depressing to see the famous derider of heroic plays giving in to the trend of the times and trying to make an old tragi-comedy conform to contemporary standards of heroism, sentiment, and decorum; it is worse to watch his struggles with blank verse. Undeniably, Buckingham was a Wit, but that he was not a dramatic poet is conclusively proved by *The Restauration*.

Fortunately for Buckingham's reputation, the alteration was never produced. It is quite likely that it was submitted to the United Company and rejected—perhaps because of its lack of merit, perhaps because its author was still considered a dangerous Whig.[40]

Sometime also during his last years, Buckingham wrote a few short dramatic dialogues, probably not intended for the public stage: "A Conference between the Duke of Buckingham and Father Fitzgerald," "The Battle of Sedgmoor," and "The Militant Couple." These are little essays, cast in dialogue form, and rather well done; Buckingham was at his best in prose and very likely the Court was much amused at his squibs circulated in manuscript. But he remained in disgrace, and after the accession of James II he gave up the struggle for courtly favor, retired to his Yorkshire estates, and spent his declining days among his horses and hounds.

In May, 1687, the last of the Wits' plays, Sedley's *Bellamira, or The Mistress*, was produced at the King's House in Drury Lane. Most of the top Wits were dead or scattered, and Sedley was doggedly carrying on alone. There was no longer a claque at the playhouse, no circle of Wits to overawe the playgoers. Only Etherege was still loyal and partisan—and diplomatic. From his post in distant Ratisbon, he wrote, "my witty Friend Sir C——S——y's *Bellamira* gave me that intire Satisfaction that I cannot read it over too often."[41]

Bellamira is a blend, composed of nine parts Terence (*The Eunuch*), one part Sedley, and a dash of Shakespeare (*Henry IV*, Part 1). Well shaken, the mixture is mildly palatable but far from exhilarating. The title character, Bellamira, a lady of pleasure, is kept by Keepwell, a doting fool, pursued by Dangerfield, an impotent, boastful ex-captain, and caressed by Merrywell, a fat tun of a man. She betrays Keepwell, plays Falstaffian tricks on Dangerfield, and lies once with Merrywell. Her protégée Isabella, a romantic lost lady, is loved and ravished by Keepwell's younger brother Lionel, who is disguised as a eunuch. A duel between Isabella's brother and Lionel is averted by apologies and a hasty marriage, and all ends happily. Merrywell marries his ward, Thisbe, for whose presence in the play there seems to be no further reason. The comedy has no ascertainable social or satirical significance, and almost no wit. It is, however, mildly entertaining; obviously, therefore, it is the best of Sedley's dramatic work.

With *Bellamira* the Wits' career upon the stage came to

a not very glorious end.* It was just as well. Already, in 1687, the tide of reaction against wit and eroticism had begun to flow. "Respectable" people were going to see plays; clergymen were inveighing against the license of the stage; and, a decade later, Jeremy Collier was to lead the forces of reformation in a notable crusade against dramatic obscenity and profaneness. Sentimentalism, for the average man the normal escape from crude reality, was coming in like a fog with the tide, and with it came pudicity.

In such an atmosphere the Restoration Wits would have stifled; with soft, tender sentiment they had nothing to do. Only the cynical interpretation of experience was valid, and therefore their plays were as cynical as their songs. Since metaphysical speculation seemed empty, they dealt with no profundities. Since their own particular society was obviously well-ordered, they discussed no problems. Since love was a matter not of soul but of body, only lust was important. Characters were seen and drawn with sharp lines and in strong colors. A man was a wit and a gentleman, or a knave, fop, dullard, gull or fool. A woman was a prude, a hoyden, a flirt or a strumpet, but never a ministering angel. The motives of human action were simple— greed, lust, and revenge. In their occasional ventures into romantic (i.e., heroic) drama, the Wits drew pictures of complex, overblown honor, but surely with tongue in cheek. In their world an honorable man was one who was true to his friends, lent them money, listened to their brags, drank with them, and seconded their duels. But between man and woman there was no honor; there was only

---

* Mulgrave's division of Shakespeare's *Julius Caesar* into two plays, "The Tragedy of Julius Caesar" and "The Tragedy of Marcus Brutus" is worth no more than a footnote. Why he chose to halve the original and rewrite some of Shakespeare's best verse is a question that perhaps only Pope could have answered. Mulgrave (Duke of Buckingham in 1703) seems to have committed his mayhem around 1710. Neither of the still twitching segments was ever performed. (See H. B. Charlton, "Buckingham's Adaptation of *Julius Caesar* and a note in the *Spectator*," MLR, XVI [1921], 171.)

pursuit, conquest and enjoyment. For the most part they enjoyed the spectacle of man the ruttish simian scratching his itches; only Wycherley seems ever to have felt revolted, but *The Plain Dealer* was the result.

The Wits' plays fitted into the framework of Restoration drama in only a superficial way. They dealt with the same themes and characters as those used by the professional playwrights, but almost always with a difference. Buckingham struck out boldly against the tide with *The Rehearsal*; Wycherley offended the Town twice, once with the bald obscenities of *The Country Wife*, and again with the savage satire of *The Plain Dealer*. And there is no real counterpart in the period for the mannered style and brittle characters of Etherege's *The Man of Mode*. Sedley, the poorest dramatist of the lot, was also the most typical of his theatrical generation.

The Wits produced no great plays in the sense in which *Hamlet* is great. Their subject matter was too limited, their themes too trivial. Yet within their narrow range they wrote with gusto for their own amusement and satisfaction, and left one burlesque and three comedies which are classics of their kind.

Censures of the Poets

IN his "Epistolary Essay from M.G. to O.B. upon their Mutual Poems" (*ca.* 1669),[1] Rochester laid down the two main planks of his literary platform: (1) he would write to please himself and pay no heed to the "saucy Censurers" of the Town, and (2) he would criticize the writings of others on the arrogant assumption that only his judgment was sound. Perhaps none of his friends would have stated the matter so bluntly, but they surely had the same independent spirits and highly developed egos. The Court Wits considered themselves Apollo's vicegerents; they were the cocks of Mount Parnassus. By virtue of birth and education they, and they alone, were qualified to pass judgment on the poor-fed poets of the Town. They were the lawmakers of poetry, competent to give advice to Apollo himself. Scores of sycophantic poetasters and criticasters confirmed them in their bumptious belief.

Rarely, a professional poet dared to rebel openly against the tyrants at Whitehall. John Dryden, a courageous soul, fought them cautiously on two occasions. In his preface to *The State of Innocence* (1677) he struck at all hypercritics who imposed their judgment on their inferiors, pretended "to reform our poetry," and ridiculed heroic plays. "There is some difference," he wrote "between a laugher and a critic." This was temerarious, but Dryden was careful to mention no names. In his preface to *All for Love* (1678) he wrote more trenchantly. He surely had the Court Wits in mind, for he had recently suffered from their attacks in "An Allusion to Horace" and "A Session of the Poets."

He described his critics as those who were called "witty men, either by the advantage of their quality, or by common fame," and "men of pleasant conversation (at least esteemed so) and endued with a trifling kind of fancy, perhaps helped out with some smattering of Latin." Ambitious to distinguish themselves from the herd of gentlemen by their poetry, they had set themselves up as judges of literature, and "from hence it comes that so many satires on poets and censures of their writings, fly abroad." Lacking knowledge and skill, unable to distinguish between judgment and mere liking, the dilettante Wits were disqualified for criticism. "Poets themselves," Dryden asserted, "are the most proper, though I conclude not the only critics."[2]

To the Restoration reader Dryden's idea that the poet was the most proper critic was no novelty; many English poets had also been critics—Sidney, Jonson, Davenant, Cowley, and Dryden himself—to name some of the more famous. The Court Wits, themselves, would have agreed with Dryden, for it must be remembered that they were all poets. Every courtier who wrote a paper of verses was at once made free of Parnassus and therefore qualified as a critic. Dryden's strictures fell on deaf ears.

Most of the critical judgments handed down by the Wits were not set forth on paper. As acknowledged connoisseurs, their opinions were repeated widely at the Court and in the coffeehouses, and their reactions were studied in the theatres. Samuel Pepys once found himself seated near Sir Charles Sedley at the Duke's house; he was "mightily taken with" the way in which Sir Charles "did at every line take notice of the dulness of the poet and the badness of the action," evidently at full voice. At a later time Pepys went to see a revival of Beaumont and Fletcher's *The Maid's Tragedy* but was distracted by a wit combat between the same Sir Charles and two talkative ladies, and "by that means lost the pleasure of the play wholly, to

which now and then Sir Charles Sedley's exceptions against
words and pronouncing were very pretty."³ In the same
vein, an apocryphal story about the Duke of Buckingham
is at least characteristic. "Being present at the first representation of one of Dryden's pieces of heroic nonsense,
where a lover says,

My wound is great, because it is so small,

the Duke cried out,

Then 'twould be greater, were it none at all."*⁴

The Wits were not formal critics in the sense of those
who studied and analyzed literature, defined its terms,
drew nice distinctions between Fancy and Judgment, di-
lated upon Decorum, and argued learnedly for or against
the Three Unities. Dryden's pictures of Lord Buckhurst
as Eugenius and Sir Charles Sedley as Lisidieus in his
Essay of Dramatic Poesy must not be taken too seriously.
No doubt the Wits had read Hobbes and certainly they had
studied their master, Horace. Some of them even had some
smatterings gleaned from Rapin, Bossu, and Boileau, and
could put up a good front in conversation. But in poetry
as in philosophy they were empiricists. Speculation was
amusing but rather futile; common-sense told them what
was good and what was bad. They knew comparatively
little about art, but they knew what they liked. On the
whole, their practical taste served them well. Their sense
of humor saved them from the banalities of the excessively
serious-minded. They paid due tribute to "the Rules" and
"the Ancients" without worshiping either; they thought
"Sense" (i.e., substance) more important than form or
florid decoration; they approved of neatness, clarity, and

---

* See Buckingham's squib upon two lines from Dryden's *The Conquest
of Granada:*

> For as old Selim was not mov'd by thee
> Neither will I by Selim's Daughter be.

A Py a Pudding, a Pudding a Py,
A Py for me, and a Pudding for thee:
A Pudding for me, and a Py for thee,
And a Pudding-Py for thee and me!

brevity, and despised romantic luxuriance, turgidity, and bombast. Among English poets of the past they admired chiefly Ben Jonson, Beaumont and Fletcher, Shakespeare, Denham and Cowley. Among their contemporaries they admired old Waller and themselves. In the flood of Restoration writings they rarely found anything to praise; perhaps it was more fun to find fault.

Lacking the objective and impartial attitude of the true critic (who was very rarely found among Restoration men of letters), the Wits frequently confused poetry and personality. In their eyes it was impossible for an enemy to write well. Charges of false grammar or logic, faulty rhymes, fustian, and nonsense were indiscriminately mingled with charges of personal meanness, dishonesty, and incontinence. This practice was not by any means peculiar to the Wits; it was a disease of the times. In the turbulent literary controversies of the late seventeenth century it is always a question whether the participants were moved by personal animus or by critical conviction. Pope was the lineal heir of the Restoration, and *The Dunciad* had antecedents.

I

IN their younger days at least, the Wits were united in their hatred for what passed in the Restoration as heroic poetry, dramatic and epic. Buckingham's famous collaborative *The Rehearsal* (see Chapter VI) is a standard example of their attack on the fustian of ultra-romance on the stage. Perhaps the most famous of their attacks on nondramatic heroic poetry was instigated by the publication in May, 1669 of the Honorable Edward Howard's long heroic poem, *The Brittish Princes*, which abounded in the worst faults of its kind. Within a few weeks, eight satiric poems from the pens of the Court Wits and their associates were circulating in manuscript.[5]

It is quite possible that all eight poems resulted from a single session at the Duke of Buckingham's London residence, Wallingford House. Those present for a convivial occasion would have been the Duke himself; his three noble guests, Lords Buckhurst, Rochester, and Vaughan; his three retainers, Thomas Sprat, his chaplain; Martin Clifford, his secretary; and Samuel Butler, who seems to have been in the Duke's service at the time, or at least under his patronage. Present also would have been Thomas Shadwell, a professional dramatist who seems to have been at the time on intimate terms with the Wits.

We can imagine Buckingham, a man "too much enclined to Burlesque,"[6] proposing a wit contest with *The Brittish Princes* as the subject, perhaps taking the lead with his squib "On Two Verses from the Same," which he reduced to utter nonsense. Butler wrote an ironic compliment on Howard's improvements upon history; Sprat congratulated the poet on his pseudo-learning and his ability to ignore chronology; Clifford made much of Howard's inventiveness of episodes and language. Vaughan and Shadwell wrote slight, mocking compliments. Rochester scolded the poet for his temerity in publishing his epic, a very "uncivil" action. Buckhurst produced the best satire of the lot, a poem which was echoed and quoted for many years.[7] Under the sesquipedalian title "To a Person of Honour, upon his Incomparable, Incomprehensible Poem, called *The Brittish Princes*," Buckhurst brought together some memorable quips:

> Come on, you critics, find one fault who dare;
> For, read it backward, like a witch's prayer,
> 'Twill do as well; throw not away your jests
> On solid nonsense that abides all tests.
> Wit like tierce-claret, when't begins to pall,
> Neglected lies, and's of no use at all,
> But, in its full perfection of decay
> Turns vinegar, and comes again in play.
> Thou hast a brain, such as it is indeed;

On what else should thy worm of fancy feed?
Yet in a filbert I have often known
Maggots survive, when all the kernel's gone.
This simile shall stand in thy defence,
'Gainst such dull rogues as now and then write sense.
Thy stile's the same, whatever be thy theme,
As some digestions turn all meat to phlegm.
He lyes, dear Ned, who says thy brain is barren,
Where deep conceits, like vermin breed in carrion.
Thy stumbling founder'd jade can trot as high
As any other Pegasus can fly.
So the dull eel moves nimbler in the mud,
Than all the swift-finn'd racers of the flood.
    As skilful divers to the bottom fall,
Sooner than those that cannot swim at all,
So in the way of writing, without thinking,
Thou hast a strange alacrity in sinking.
Thou writ'st below ev'n thy own nat'ral parts,
And with acquired dullness, and new arts
Of study'd nonsense, tak'st kind readers hearts.
Therefore, dear Ned, at my advice, forbear
Such loud complaints 'gainst critics to prefer,
Since thou art turn'd an arrant libeller:
Thou sett'st thy name to what thy self dost write;
Did ever libel yet so sharply bite?

Howard seems to have made some reply to the general onslaught of the Wits, perhaps in a paper of verses that has been lost, perhaps in his ponderous, belligerent preface to *The Womens Conquest* (1670). He drew three sharp retorts. Butler wrote a lengthy "Palinodie" (a mock-formal retraction), attacking Sir Edward's wit, sense, and learning, and concluding that the paper that gentleman had written on was thereby the better fitted for base uses. Buckhurst included Howard's plays in a new satire and blasted their author as "Thou damn'd antipodes to common sense." Shadwell had earlier pilloried Howard as "Poet Ninny" in *The Sullen Lovers* (1668); now Rochester picked up the dramatic character and used it as the title of one of his most vicious libels, "On Poet Ninny."

He sneered at Howard's attempt to fight back, at his "Cap'ring Person . . . With dismal look and Melancholly Meen," and at his lack of wit,

> For of all Folly, sure the very Top,
> Is a conceited Ninny and a Fop.

This was literary criticism.

For years to come, *The Brittish Princes* was a name to conjure with when bad writing was discussed, and Edward Howard joined his brother Sir Robert (the "Sir Positive At-all" of *The Sullen Lovers*) in the picture gallery of Restoration dunces. Perhaps the brothers consoled each other, for Sir Robert, too, had suffered from the pens of the Wits. In May or June of 1667, Sir Robert had written a heroic beast-allegory, *The Duel of the Stags* (printed in 1668), in which the two combatant monarchs of the forest seem to symbolize Buckingham and King Charles. At the time, Buckingham was in hiding under suspicion of high treason, and it is possible that Sir Robert, who was his political ally, wrote the poem to show him the fatal results of a conflict between the duke and the King. But neither good intentions nor the dedication of the poem to Buckingham could save Sir Robert from the ribald Wits. An obscene parody appeared, in which the royal stags were diminished to vulgar lice, and the magnificent forest of their battle was reduced to the intimate pilosity of a prostitute. A short version of this, entitled "The Duel," was ascribed to Harry Savile; a longer one, entitled "The Duel of the Crabs," was attributed to Buckhurst. Probably the two young men collaborated.[8]

II

THE Wits' supercilious attitude toward professional poets is well illustrated by "A Session of the Poets" (*ca.* December, 1676), otherwise known as "A Trial of

the Poets for the Bays." "A Session," which owes its title
and form to a genre first developed by the Cavalier poet
Sir John Suckling,[9] was inspired by three years of name-
calling among the leading contemporary writers of heroic
plays. The poem has been variously attributed to Buckingham, Rochester, and "Anon," but it was probably written
by a group of the Wits in some kind of collaboration.[10]

In the spring of 1673, Elkanah Settle's heroic play, *The
Empress of Morocco*, was given an elaborate amateur production at Court,*[11] and in the same year the play was
published, with a boastful preface in which Settle made
some slurs on a number of his brother professionals. They
were not slow to reply: in 1674, Dryden, Shadwell, and
John Crowne joined in producing an abusive pamphlet
entitled *Notes and Observations on the Empress of Morocco*. This Settle tried to turn into a boomerang with his rejoinder in the same year, *Notes and Observations on the
Empress of Morocco Revised*. Dryden and Crowne by
now had enough of this futile skirmishing, but Shadwell
carried on the *poetomachia* valiantly in his adaptation of
Newcastle's *The Triumphant Widow* (November, 1674),
in which he caricatured Settle as a foolish heroic poet. Settle
then, in his postscript to *Love and Revenge* (1675), attacked Shadwell alone, and drew in return some ill-tem-
pered remarks in Shadwell's preface to *The Libertine*
(1676). It was Settle's lengthy and peevish review of the
whole quarrel in his preface to *Ibrahim* (1676) which
seems to have been the immediate inspiration for "A Session of the Poets."

The battle of the prefaces had lasted three years and
apparently the Wits had observed it with superior amuse-

* The fact that both Mulgrave and Rochester had written prologues is
not to be interpreted as showing their approval of either the author or his
play. As courtiers they could hardly have refused to contribute to such a
gala occasion; and it is noteworthy that their verses were merely conventional witticisms and compliments to the audience, with no reference whatever to the play.

ment. From time to time their chief speaker, Rochester, had attacked one or all of the combatants, scarifying each with Olympian impartiality. In 1673, perhaps in collaboration with Buckingham, he had written "Timon, a Satyr," in which he had ridiculed Settle's *Empress of Morocco*, Crowne's *Charles the Eighth* and *Pandion*, and Dryden's *Indian Emperor*. In a long epilogue to Sir Francis Fane's *Love in the Dark* (1675), he had devoted much heavy-handed sarcasm to heroic dramas in general and to Shadwell's heroic opera *Psyche* (February, 1675) in particular. In *An Allusion to Horace* (1675-76), he had rebuked Crowne, Settle, and Dryden, among others. It was time now to put the whole tribe of heroic poets in their places.

The circumstances of the writing of "A Session" can only be conjectured, of course. We know that Rochester's lodge at Woodstock, where he was Ranger and Keeper of the Park, was a customary retreat for the Wits. In a letter to his wife from there (undated, but just before Christmas and possibly in 1676), Rochester speaks of his regret at not having brought the countess with him, for "since these rakehells are nott here to disturb us you might have past yr devotions this Holy season as well in this place as att Adderbury."[12] Apparently the "rakehells" had just departed. We also know from a comment by Henry Savile (in a letter to Rochester in 1677) that libels of the type of "A Session" had been composed at Woodstock, especially when an "assembly" of the Wits had been there.[13]

We may imagine, then, the Wits and near-Wits sitting about a long table in the great hall at Woodstock, with bumpers of wine before them and a log burning in the fireplace. The talk turns to the latest event in the little war of the theatres: Settle's publication of *Ibrahim* with an impertinent preface which was almost immediately withdrawn. Some Wit proposes a satire, a general attack upon the whole tribe of professional poets, that "unwitty Generation" as Rochester called them later. The device of a "session" or "Trial" of poets before the Court of Apollo, in the style of Sir John Suckling, is suggested by another. Perhaps Suckling's original is dug out of the bookshelves and passed around as a model. Possibly someone has a copy of the anonymous "The Session of the Poets, to the Tune of Cock Laurel" (*ca.* 1665), in which Buckhurst, Sedley, and Etherege had been given brief mention. Then the process of composition begins. Perhaps the Wits take turns writing, each one dealing with a different poet; perhaps one of them (Rochester himself?) acts as amanuensis and scribbles the couplets as his ribald friends suggest them.

The result is a loose, disorganized blend of many styles and points of view. The couplets limp or gallop, perhaps in accordance with the inspiration or the metrical skill of the various composers. Occasional confusion of thought and phrase further supports the theory of hilarious cooperative authorship. Consider for example this passage:

> Poet Settle, his Tryal was the next came about.
> He brought him an *Ibrahim* with the Preface torn out,
> And humbly desir'd he might give no Offence:
> Dam him, cries Shadwell, he cannot write Sense:
> And B-ll-cks, cry'd Newport, I hate that dull Rogue;[14]

Now there was no Newport among the Restoration poets— none, therefore, who had a right to be at the fictitious session summoned by Apollo. But Francis (Frank) Newport was a minor courtier, a drinking companion of Killigrew, Savile, and Rochester. He was given to scandalous behavior and lewd talk. It is quite possible that he, was one of the gathering at Woodstock, and that he interjected his drunken comment at just the right time to get it set down by the Muses' Secretary!

"A Session" mentions only two of the Court Wits, Etherege and Wycherley; perhaps they were the only ones absent when the libel was composed. Etherege is praised for his "Fancy, Sense, Judgment, and Wit" and scolded gently for his "crying Sin, Idleness." Wycherley is denied the bays only because as a "Gentleman Writer" he is "too good for the place," which could go only to "a Trader in Wit." Dryden too is dismissed briefly as "that ancient Grave Wit, so long lov'd and feared," and is given leave to retire from the stage and turn priest.

Thereafter, the major poets dealt with in succession are Shadwell, Lee, Settle, Otway, Crowne, and Aphra Behn. Shadwell is ridiculed for his pretensions to wit, and for "his Guts, his Paunch, and his Tallow," a commonplace gibe. Lee, a harmless man but an ultra-heroic poet, is told that he drinks too much and has strained his throat in his efforts at the high heroic tune. Otway, brutally labeled the "Scum of a Play-house," is reminded of his mange and lice. Crowne, for whom someone seems to have had a deep aversion, is told that he lacks "Sense of Smart," is "past Sense of Shame," and should continue to "be dull to the end of the Chapter." Aphra Behn puts in a double claim to the laurel because of her poetry and her personal charms, but she is rudely informed that on the second claim she should "have pleaded a Dozen years since." Three lesser authors clamor for attention, but Apollo, "tir'd with their tedious Harangue," sees in the crowd the kindly face of Tom Betterton, the famous actor-manager, and gives him the laurel on the general ground that, by his polishing and revising of plays for production, he was the best of poets,

> And was the great'st Wonder the Age ever bore,
> Of all the Play-Scriblers that e'er writ before,
> His wit had most Worth, and Modesty in't,
> For he had writ Plays, yet ne'er came in Print.

A lame and impotent conclusion. No doubt inspiration had flagged.

In the strictest sense, of course, "A Session of the Poets" is not criticism. Its intention is not impartial judgment but castigation; the clamorous "Sons of the Muses" must be put in their places. They had become public nuisances with their airs and affectations, their quarrels and their pretensions as men of letters. They must be reminded that they were, after all, mere entertainers.

III

ROCHESTER'S "An Allusion to Horace" (or "Horace's Tenth Satire of the First Book Imitated")[15] involves a controversy with John Dryden which has long been the subject of confused and sometimes malicious conjecture. Edmond Malone, Dryden's famous editor, bent on vilifying Rochester, wrote a good deal of nonsense on the subject, and subsequent writers have accepted Malone's hasty statements with little question.[16]

Of the relations between Dryden and Rochester we know with certainty only a few facts. In March, 1673, Dryden's *Marriage-à-la-Mode* was published with a fulsome dedication to Rochester. This in itself means very little. During the course of his career, Dryden dedicated plays to a total of nineteen people of high rank—knights, barons, earls, dukes, and duchesses; he repeated himself only once. In acknowledgment of the dedication Rochester wrote Dryden a letter (which has disappeared), whereupon Dryden sent him a lively, gossipy epistle.[17] Sometime later in the same year came the Rochester-Buckingham "Timon, a Satyr," containing some cutting remarks about Dryden's *The Indian Emperor*. Next, late in 1675, appeared Rochester's "Allusion to Horace," devoted chiefly to an attack on Dryden. Henry Savile, in March or April, 1676, relayed the poet laureate's anger to Rochester who, acknowledging that he was "out of favour" with Dryden, refused to go into the matter further. The final word was Dryden's thinly veiled attack on Rochester in his preface to *All for Love* (1678). These are all the facts we have.[18] Malone's conjectures that Rochester had helped Dryden get his post as poet laureate, that he had later turned against Dryden for accepting the patronage of his enemy, Mulgrave, and that he had maliciously brought forward Settle and Crowne in turn to displace Dryden at Court, are based on guess work and unreliable tradition.[19]

It is doubtful if Dryden and Rochester were ever more than acquaintances. Dryden was sixteen years the older of the two, and, as he himself admitted, his conversation was "slow and dull," his "humour saturnine and reserved."[20] Rochester was the direct opposite in temper; he was one of those who (in Dryden's words) "endeavour to break jests in company, or make reparties." Moreover, there was a vast gulf, difficult for the modern mind to comprehend, between a glittering nobleman and a mechanic poet, a mere "Trader in Wit." In view of the deference accorded Dryden in later years, when wits and nobles alike thronged about him at Will's Coffee-house, and in view of his elevation today to the place he so richly deserves as one of the greatest English men of letters, it seems to us almost incredible that Rochester, a far lesser poet, should not have sought his company; but we must remember that Dryden had not as yet (in 1675) attained his full stature as a poet. If the acceptance of the dedication of a play makes for patronage (Dryden's letter makes no mention of the customary gift of money), Rochester was once Dryden's patron, but there is nothing to show that he ever considered Dryden his protégé or his friend. There was no reason in the world why he should not have written satires on a mere professional poet of the day.

From the autumn of 1675 to the summer of 1676, Rochester was rusticating at Woodstock, reading Livy (and probably his favorite Horace), and writing critical and satirical verses on any subject that chanced to amuse him. It is difficult to say why he chose to direct an imitation of Horace's famous tenth satire at Dryden. Perhaps, considering himself to be, like Horace, the spokesman for the literati of his age, he wished to make Dryden the scapegoat for the swarm of hasty, half-literate, popular writers of the Restoration. Perhaps someone had actually challenged him to amplify some past aspersions on Dryden, for, even though he closely follows the Horatian model, he may have been addressing some real person and referring to some actual conversation, when he begins his satire,

> Well, Sir, 'tis granted, I said Dryden's Rhimes
> Were stol'n, unequal, nay, dull many times;
> What foolish Patron is there found of his,
> So blindly partial, to deny me this?
> But that his Plays, embroider'd up and down
> With Wit and Learning, justly pleas'd the Town,
> In the same Paper I as freely own.*

After brief jibes at Crowne, Settle, and Otway, he proceeds to give all dramatic poets some sound advice:

> ... within due Proportion circumscribe
> What e'er you write, that with a flowing Tide,
> The Style may rise; yet in its Rise forbear
> With useless Words, t'oppress the weary'd Ear.
> Here be your Language lofty, there more light,
> Your Rhetoric with your Poetry unite:
> For Elegance sake, sometimes allay the Force
> Of Epithets, 'twill soften the Discourse;
> A Jest in Scorn points out, and hits the Thing
> More home, than the Morosest Satyr's Sting.

Thereafter he takes up one by one a number of poets and dramatists, gentleman amateurs and traders in wit. "Refin'd Etherege" is a true original; Flatman is a poor imitation of Cowley; Lee is guilty of abominable fustian; "hasty Shadwell and slow Wicherley" are the only writers of true comedy; Waller "in Panegyric does excel Man-

---

* "To be sure I did say that the verses of Lucilius run on with halting foot. Who is a partisan of Lucilius so in-and-out of season as not to confess this? And yet on the self-same page the self-same poet is praised because he rubbed the city down with much salt." Trans. by H. R. Fairclough, *Horace, Satires*, etc., Loeb Classics, London, 1936.

kind"; Buckhurst, "the best good Man, with the worst
natur'd Muse,"* is to be chosen for "pointed Satyr" and
for "Songs and Verses mannerly obscene"; while Sedley
is masterly at love songs.

Having thus praised his friends and denounced most of
the professional poets, Rochester turns his attention to
Dryden again. He sneers at the laureate's attempts to write
in the erotic vein of Sedley, but admits

> . . . to be just, 'twill to his Praise be found,
> His Excellencies more than Faults abound:
> Nor dare I from his sacred Temples tear
> The Laurel, which he best deserves to wear.

This is very high praise from a Court Wit, and it should
be remembered by those who accuse Rochester of sheer
malice and prejudice. However, it is praise which is quickly
tempered by censure; Dryden's critical prefaces must have
annoyed the vicegerent of Apollo, for he continues,

> But does not Dryden find ev'n Johnson dull?
> Beaumont and Fletcher uncorrect, and full
> Of lewd Lines, as he call 'em? Shakespeare's Stile
> Stiff and affected? To his own, the while,
> Allowing all the Justice that his Pride
> So arrogantly had to these deny'd?
> And may not I have leave impartially
> To search and censure Dryden's Works, and try
> If those gross Faults his choice Pen doth commit,
> Proceed from want of Judgment, or of Wit?
> Or if his lumpish Fancy does refuse
> Spirit and Grace to his loose slattern Muse?
> Five Hundred Verses ev'ry Morning writ,
> Prove him no more a Poet, than a Wit.

---

* "an insolent, sparing, and invidious panegyric," wrote Dryden to
Dorset in 1693, "where good nature, the most godlike commendation of
a man, is only attributed to your person, and denied to your writings." This
was not, however, as Dryden claimed, all the commendation that Rochester's
"self-sufficiency could afford to any man"; he said much finer things about
Dryden himself, as see above. (Dryden, *Essays*, II, 18-19.)

In the total perspective of Dryden's work, this seems unfair, but Rochester, of course, had seen only the earlier poems and heroic plays. Apparently Dryden had failed to measure up to Rochester's artistic ideal of brevity, polish, and perfection as expressed in this passage from the "Allusion" (for which there is no parallel in Horace),

> To write what may securely stand the Test,
> Of being well read over thrice at least;
> Compare each Phrase, examine ev'ry Line,
> Weigh ev'ry Word, and ev'ry Thought refine.

Perhaps Dryden's Muse was not a loose slattern, but in his early works at least she was sometimes in dishabille.

Rochester, like Horace, was an aristocrat in esthetics. "Should I be troubled," he wrote,

> . . . when the poor-fed Poets of the Town,
> For Scraps and Coach-room cry my Verses down?
> I loathe the Rabble, 'tis enough for me,
> If Sidley, Shadwel, Shephard, Wicherley,
> Godolphin, Butler, Buckhurst, Buckingham,
> And some few more, whom I omit to Name,
> Approve my Sense, I count their Censure Fame.*

Dryden was a sensitive man, and he did not take kindly to Rochester's reflections. Like one present-day editor, he must have looked upon the "Allusion" as "a pert and foppish set of verses, malicious and grum."[21] Certainly its strictures were severe, but as a self-appointed reformer of poetry, Rochester could hardly afford to be gentle.

The "Allusion" was probably circulated anonymously in manuscript, and it must have taken some time before the author was identified. Rochester's reaction to the news of Dryden's displeasure is characteristic not only of him but

---

* It is tempting to speculate that Rochester may have written the "Allusion" for the amusement of a party of friends who had come to Woodstock to console him in his exile, and that the names chosen for his tribunal of taste represent the men present at the time. Horace lists fourteen names to Rochester's eight. Notably missing from the list is the name of the Earl's close friend and correspondent, Henry Savile.

of the privileged class to which he belonged. In April, 1676, he wrote to Savile,

> You write me word, That I'm out of favour with a certain Poet, whom I have ever admir'd for the disproportion of him and his Attributes: He is a Rarity which I cannot but be fond of, as one would be of a Hog that could fiddle, or a singing Owl. If he falls upon me at the Blunt, which is his very good Weapon in Wit, I will forgive him, if you please, and leave the Repartee to Black Will, with a Cudgel.[22]

Dryden did not fall upon Rochester "at the Blunt." His only retort to his noble critic, in his preface to *All for Love* two years later, was so cleverly disguised that Rochester must have been helpless to answer it. Dryden never mentioned the earl by name; instead he professed to believe that the "Allusion" had been written by some nameless scribbler, a "rhyming judge of the twelvepenny gallery," who had hidden himself "behind the lion's skin."[23] With this attack the controversy ended. Perhaps Dryden may be said to have won on points.

IV

JOHN SHEFFIELD, Earl of Mulgrave, also considered himself to be a supreme legislator for Parnassus, but little besides his conceit qualified him for the job. He had so far distinguished himself as a man of letters only by a few weak songs and the harsh "Essay on Satire." Perhaps he wrote *An Essay on Poetry* in 1682 to prove to his fellow Wits that he was a scholar and critic; perhaps he wrote it to dazzle the eyes of Princess Anne, whom he was at the time presumptuously courting.[24] At any rate, in writing a verse essay on poetry he was in tune with his times.

The late seventeenth century was growing more and more self-conscious about its art. Dryden was not the only one to write prefaces to plays; long prefatory essays, in which the brain child was defended by citations from Aristotle, Longinus, Horace, Boileau and any other authority the author could think of, became almost the rule. Plays suffered from multiple paternity. From France, the three militant leaders of neo-classicism, Rapin, Boileau, and Le Bossu, had launched their critical invasion of England; by the early seventies they had established their literary bridgehead and were pouring in reinforcements. In England, by the eighties, Rymer (translator of Rapin) had set up his standard as the leader of the new order; with Dryden's help, Sir William Soames was translating Boileau's *Art Poetique*; and essays and satires on poetry were pouring from dozens of lesser pens. Mulgrave's *Essay on Poetry* and Roscommon's *Essay on Translated Verse* (1684) were two of the important predecessors of Pope's *Essay on Criticism* and the triumph of regularity.

Mulgrave's *Essay* was not quite, as Robert Wolseley called it, a blend of "Scraps of Bossu, Rapin, Boileau, Mr. Dryden's Prefaces, and Table Talk," new cast "in the mould of a flat unmusical verse."[25] It was not original; the tracks of Boileau are everywhere set deep; but Mulgrave was sensible enough to avoid the most extreme of the neo-classic strictures, and what he had to say to the would-be poet was usually harmless. But Mulgrave unquestionably wrote "flat, unmusical verse," and Pope found it necessary to tune up a number of his lines.

Mulgrave begins his *Essay* modestly enough, with a quatrain in praise of poetry:

> Of all things in which Mankind does most excel,
> Nature's chief Master-piece is writing well;
> And of all sorts of Writing none there are
> That can the least with Poetry compare.*[26]

---

* Here is Pope's version of the quatrain:
> Of all those Arts in which the Wise excel,
> Nature's chief Master-piece is Writing well:
> No Writing lifts exalted Man so high,
> As sacred and Soul-moving Poesy:

He then discusses briefly the various forms of verse. He admits that no kind of poetry "requires a nicer Art" than the song, but instead of giving rules or suggestions for the writing of lyrics he goes off at a tangent with a jibe at his dead enemy, Rochester, the author of "Nauseous Songs," and "Bare Ribaldry, that Poor Pretence to Wit." He gives short and rather commonplace commentaries on the elegy, the ode, and the satire. He pays a mild tribute to Dryden's satiric gift, and seems to admit rather grudgingly that at times Dryden writes almost as well as himself:

> The Laureat here may justly claim our Praise,
> Crown'd by Mac-Fleckno with immortal Bays;
> Tho prais'd and punish'd for another's Rhimes,
> His own deserve as great Applause sometimes.*

Next, Mulgrave calls upon his Muse "to give Instructions that concern the Stage." Here he merely summarizes a number of neo-classic precepts. The dramatic poet should observe the three unities, of course. He should avoid soliloquies if he can, and if he finds them necessary he should make them brief. Figures of speech should be used only in descriptive passages, never in ordinary dialogue, which should always be natural. A good plot is the first and sometimes the only requisite for a successful play. Characters must be human and typical, not perfect and individual, and they must be suited to the capabilities of the players. The poet should avoid "Sheer-Wit," or quibbling and jesting; his aim in comedy should be for real humor. To prove his points, Mulgrave exposes a short "View on this wrong side of Sence," a brief parody of a typical heroic drama. His horrible example is mildly amusing.

---

* The "another's Rhimes" refers, of course, to Mulgrave's "Essay on Satire," for which Dryden was beaten in Rose Alley. Very wisely, Pope deleted the second of the two couplets. Of course, Mulgrave may not have intended his lines to convey such a supercilious meaning; he was often a very inept poet. The "sometimes," for example, may have been merely his effort to find a rhyme.

The poem reaches its climax and conclusion with a eulogy of epic poets, who dwell on the very top of Parnassus. Alas, only Homer and Virgil have climbed the peak; all others have failed. If there is any man who has Fancy, Reason, Judgment, Discernment, and a profound knowledge of all science,

> Let such a Man begin without delay,
> But he must do much more than I can say,
> Must above Cowley, nay and Milton too prevail,
> Succeed where great Torquato, and our greater Spencer fail.*

A modern reader finds little to admire in the *Essay on Poetry*, yet for half a century numerous writers testified to its beauties and wisdom. Roscommon hailed Mulgrave as the author

> whose correct Essay
> Repairs so well our old Horatian way.

Dryden admitted that he had read the *Essay* "over and over, with much Delight, and as much Instruction." Bishop Burnet praised it as "clear Sense, joined with home, but gentle Reproofs," and hoped that it would have good effects. Addison listed it with Roscommon's *Essay on Translated Verse* and Pope's *Essay on Criticism* as masterpieces of their kind. Lansdowne hailed Mulgrave and Roscommon as two lights which had risen "to clear our Darkness, and to guide our Flight." Pope, who later edited Mulgrave's works for final publication, paid tribute to the *Essay* in his own *Essay on Criticism*, even quoting a line with approval: "Nature's chief Masterpiece is writing well."[27] Charles Gildon, however, outdid everybody in his long-winded commentary, *The Laws of Poetry, as laid down by the Duke of Buckinghamshire in his Essay on Poetry* (1721). He padded out Mulgrave's poem of nine-

---

* Pope changed the last couplet to read,

> Must above Tasso's lofty Flights prevail,
> Succeed where Spencer, and ev'n Milton fail.

Cowley's reputation had faded by the eighteenth century.

teen pages with two hundred and forty pages of abject flattery. The reader can scarcely escape the suspicion that John
Sheffield's wealth and power as Earl of Mulgrave, Marquis of Normanby, and Duke of Buckinghamshire had
something to do with the success of the *Essay*.

In December, 1718, when Laurence Eusden, a poetical
nonentity, was appointed poet laureate as a reward for a
flattering ode to Newcastle, then Lord Chamberlain, the
aging Duke of Buckinghamshire remembered the days of
his youth, when "Sessions" of the poets were in vogue.
In imitation, he wrote "The Election of a Poet Laureate"
in galloping, hudibrastic verse. Except for an occasional
shot at a minor poetaster of the day, the satire is mild and
undistinguished. Eusden is finally brought forth to claim
the laurel as the King's gift, and immediately

> Apollo begg'd pardon, and granted his Claim;
> But vow'd tho, till then he ne'er heard of his Name.

Undistinguished as it is, the "Election" does give us a
final view of Mulgrave's conceit. He is very careful to let
the reader know that he himself could have been poet
laureate if he had chosen.

> When BUCKINGHAM came, he scarce car'd to be seen,
> Till PHOEBUS desir'd his old Friend to walk in:
> But a Laureat Peer had never been known;
> The Commoners claim'd that Place as their own.
>
> Yet if the kind God had been ne'er so inclin'd
> To break an old Rule, yet he well knew his Mind,
> Who of such Preferment would only make Sport,
> And laugh'd at all Suitors for Places at Court.

V

A FEW miscellaneous verse-criticisms by the Wits de-
serve little more than passing mention. The Earl of
Dorset's "The Duel" (1687), an attack on two minor

poets, Phillip, Lord Wharton, and Robert Wolseley, who had been conducting their own little war in couplets, is reminiscent of "A Session of the Poets"; it was designed to check and rebuke the quarrelsome dunces of poetry.[28] In 1700, perhaps remembering the earlier chorus of attacks on Edward Howard, Sir Charles Sedley joined Richard Steele, the Earl of Anglesey and other wits in a hue and cry after Sir Richard Blackmore, the physician-author of *A Satyr against Wit*.[29] A fair sample of Sedley's lampoon is this couplet,

> Thy Satyr's harmless; 'tis thy Prose that kills,
> When thou prescrib'st thy Potions and thy Pills.

Probably the Wits wrote other verse criticisms which have been lost or cannot be identified. The anonymous "Advice to Apollo, 1678"[30] has all the earmarks of one of their cooperative poems, and, in spite of the discrepancy of the appended date, it may have been the poem to which Savile referred in a letter to Rochester on November 1, 1677,

... and now I am upon poetry I must tell you the whole tribe are alarumed att a libell against them lately sent by the post to Will's coffe house. I am not happy enough to have seen it, but I heare it commended and therefore the more probably thought to be composed att Woodstock, especially considering what an assembly either is yett or att least has been there, to whom my most humble service, if they are yett with you.[31]

"The Advice," a series of appeals to Apollo to "strike" all poetasters who dare aspire to the writing of satire, gives high praise to Rochester and Dorset, and ridicules Dryden, Mulgrave, Sir Carr Scroope, and Fleetwood Shepherd. The first three satirized were all at odds with Rochester, and the slur at Shepherd may have been punishment for his absence from the convivial gathering. This, of course, is only conjecture, but we know that Buckingham and "other nobles" had been visiting Rochester at Woodstock

since mid-October, 1677, and that Shepherd had been expected but had failed to appear.[32]

The Wits wrote very few poems of compliment on
literary themes. Their prologues and epilogues sometimes
rang the changes on the conventional praise of Beaumont
and Fletcher, Ben Jonson, and Shakespeare, but on their
contemporaries they were usually either satirical or silent.
In 1668, Lord Buckhurst wrote a congratulatory ode to
Sir Thomas Sydserff on the printing of the latter's *Tarugo's
Wiles*. Lord Vaughan wrote a highly complimentary poem
to Dryden on the publication of *The Conquest of Granada*
in 1672.[33] When the famous philosopher Thomas Hobbes
died early in 1680, his old friend John Aubrey, the antiquarian, tried to persuade a number of poets to write commendatory odes. Dryden, Waller, Dorset, and Vaughan
agreed, and the last two promised to engage Mulgrave and
Rochester, but in the end only Mulgrave complied.[34] "On
Mr. Hobbs and his Writings" (possibly polished by Pope)
is one of his best poems.

In conclusion, it must be remembered that although the
Wits' written (and, no doubt, spoken) literary criticisms
were predominantly censorious, their actions often belied
their words. As we have seen earlier, they were—particularly Dorset—patrons and encouragers of poets and
playwrights. Apparently they recognized and applauded
artistic merit, and (as dozens of professional writers testified in prefaces and dedications) they helped the struggling
beginner in a variety of ways. It is difficult to determine
how much help they gave. Certainly Dryden owed a good
deal to Dorset and Mulgrave. The well-known story that
Dorset and Shepherd found Prior reading Horace in his
uncle's tavern, and saw to it that he was properly educated,
may be apocryphal, but it is true that Prior looked upon
both Wits as his beneficent patrons.[35] According to tradition, Oldham was "discovered" by Dorset, Rochester, and
Sedley; but what material benefits their patronage brought

him it is impossible to learn.[36] According to another tradition, even Milton was "discovered" (but certainly not patronized) by the Wits, when Dorset happened upon a copy of *Paradise Lost* at a bookseller's and introduced it to his friends.[37] Certainly a group of critics who could be interested by such diverse literary talents as those of Milton, Dryden, Prior, and Oldham were catholic in their taste and uninhibited by poetic formulas. Perhaps they wrote censoriously, not because they found all contemporary letters unworthy, but chiefly because they regarded themselves as lawmakers of poetry, curbs to impertinence, and castigators of folly.

Epilogue

SIR GEORGE ETHEREGE refused to believe that the golden days were gone. At fifty-two he hated middle age and dreaded the thought of growing old. There would be no possets and night-caps for him; he was resolved to "blaze to the last." From his diplomatic retreat in Germany he wrote often to his old friends among the Court Wits, seeking to prove by his sprightly reminiscences that he was still young in spirit. He reminded Dorset of their long-forgotten adventures with the fair Cuffley, the subject of four erotic verse-epistles many years before. He reminded Mulgrave of a past episode involving a mysterious "Lady in the Garret," and was mildly bantered in return for thinking lascivious thoughts at his age.[1]

The changes that were taking place among his old associates surprised and disturbed him. He was shocked at the news of Buckingham's "retiring into Yorkshire," at only fifty-eight, "and leading a sedate contemplative life there." As a constant rake himself he could not understand how men of wit could reform. In 1687 he wrote sadly to Henry Guy,

> The women need not rail at our changing; few of us have the gift to be constant to ourselves. Sir Charles Sedley sets up for good hours and sobriety; my Lord Dorset has given over variety and shuts himself up within my Lady's arms, as you inform me . . .

With such remarkable alterations going on in England, how could he know what tune to sing in his letters? He wrote to Lord Middleton,

I know you are Mr. Secretary still, but I know not whether you are still the same Lord Middleton I left you. You may be grown as temperate as Sir Ch[arles] Sedley and as uxorious as my Lord Dorset; 'twould be a fine way then to make my court to you to talk of wine and women.

He was determined to "persevere to the end of debauchery," and perhaps he was a bit boastful of his wickedness. In 1687, when John Dryden published his great religious poem, *The Hind and the Panther*, Etherege wrote to Middleton, "What a shame it is to me to see him a saint and remain still the same devil."[2]

The old days could never be recaptured: the mad, bawdy riots at Epsom and Tunbridge, the carouses at Woodstock and Knole, the intrigues at Whitehall, and the witty debates at the Dog and Partridge. With bigoted James II on the throne the days had passed when wit was a way of preferment, and the Court circle had disintegrated. Rochester and Scroope had died before Etherege went to Ratisbon; Buckingham and Savile died while he was abroad. Sedley had indeed reformed under the influence of a good woman, Ann Ayscough; and Lord Dorset's second marriage (in 1685), at forty-two, to seventeen year old Lady Mary Compton seems to have had a settling effect upon the rake who had always sought "variety." Lord Vaughan also had taken a second spouse (in 1682) and was living quietly. Mulgrave had married his first wife in 1686, and although for a while the match had promised to be one continuous storm, "numps" was soon "in the stocks in earnest."[3]

The other Wits were aging, if not reforming. Poor Wycherley, released from prison in 1686 with his health and memory impaired, had no heart for either marriage or debauchery. Bulkeley, forty-eight in 1686, was growing staid and settled at Court. Killigrew, just under the half-century mark, and with very little fire left, was still a courtier, but rapidly becoming an old beau. Shepherd, the same age as Etherege, was content to drift along as Dorset's companion and major-domo. And Henry Guy, at fifty-five still a bachelor, was more interested in money than in lechery. Etherege was the pitiful last of the rakes.

It is possible that even Etherege reformed at the end. Sometime before his death on or about May 10, 1692, he is said to have turned Catholic. Perhaps he did so to please his exiled master, James II, whom he had joined in France; perhaps he experienced a true conversion and died in bed with all the rites of the church. Oldys' picturesque story that Etherege, soundly drunk, fell down a flight of stairs and broke his neck, is too good to be true. It is just the way he would have wished to die, at the climax of a debauch.[4]

Since most of the Wits had reformed or dropped into comparative obscurity, their deaths caused only perfunctory comment, and we know very little about the cause or the manner of their passing. In August, 1680, Sir Carr Scroope was reported at Tunbridge Wells, "in no good condition," and with "reason to fear so much pain as he is threatened with." In November he died of his mysterious malady.[5] Savile died in France in 1687, after an agonizing surgical operation.[6] Shepherd expired in August, 1698, at Copt Hall, after a long illness.[7] Although no one seems to be sure, Bulkeley may have died in the same year.[8] In August, 1701, Sir Charles Sedley gave up the ghost "like a philosopher, without fear or superstition."[9] Henry Killigrew was buried at St. Martin's in the Fields on December 16, 1705.[10] Dorset died of somewhat premature old age on January 26, 1706, and even toward the last he was reported as driveling more sense than other men talked.[11] Henry Guy won the prize for longevity; he was a few months short of eighty in February, 1711, when he tired of amassing wealth in this world and set forth to try his skill in another, leaving an estate of more than a hundred thousand pounds.[12] John Vaughan, now Earl of Carbery, returning home from a visit to his banker one day in January, 1713, "sickened and died presently," presumably leaving his affairs in order.[13] After years of suffering from palsy, gravel, and other diseases, Wycherley died, almost in his sleep, on the last day of December, 1715.[14] The proud Earl of Mulgrave lived to be almost seventy-three, and then, in 1721, he was no doubt transported to Heaven in a special chariot.[15]

The two greatest sinners among the Wits, the Duke of Buckingham and the Earl of Rochester, true to their eccentric and flamboyant characters, could not leave the world without creating a last sensation. Each met the fell sergeant, Death, with the church's indulgence clutched in his hand. Respectable folk were much edified.

In his retreat in Yorkshire, Buckingham caught a chill one spring day from sitting on the damp ground after a fox hunt. The chill developed into a fever and thence into a "mortification." The Duke was put to bed in a tenant farmer's house at Kirkby Moorside, and Lord Arran (Buckingham's cousin) summoned doctors who within three days knew there was no hope. They bade the aging sinner take care for his soul. Accordingly Lord Arran summoned a neighboring parson, who appeared (very much flustered) at seven o'clock on the morning of April 16, 1687. When asked what his religion was, Buckingham answered, "It is an insignificant question, for I have been a shame and disgrace to all religion; if you can do me any good, do." The honest parson said prayers. After some further urging by Lord Arran that his cousin "might die as a Christian," Buckingham consented to receive the Sacrament. He was in some fear, "for all this time he was not ready to take death to him, but in a few minutes he became calm and received the Sacrament with all the decency imaginable, and in an hour afterwards he lost his speech, and so continued till eleven that night, when he died."

Contrary to popular belief, Buckingham had never been

an atheist, but the fact that he died in the communion of the Church of England was taken as evidence of conversion. A letter which he wrote to Dr. Isaac Barrow during his illness shows that he was truly repentant for his sins.[16]

Rochester had a longer time to die in, and a greater battery of clergymen to beat him into more abject submission. Some years earlier he had expressed a skeptical attitude toward the after life in a translation of "The Latter End of the Chorus of the Second Act of Seneca's *Troas*,"

> After Death nothing is, and nothing Death;
> The utmost Limits of a Gasp of Breath.
> Let the ambitious Zealot lay aside
> His Hopes of Heav'n (whose Faith is but his Pride);
> Let slavish Souls lay by their Fear,
> Nor be concern'd which way, or where,
> After this Life they shall be hurl'd;
> Dead, we become the Lumber of the World;
> And to that Mass of Matter shall be swept,
> Where things destroy'd, with things unborn are kept;
> Devouring Time swallows us whole,
> Impartial Death confounds Body and Soul.
> For Hell and the foul Fiend that rules
>   The everlasting fiery Gaols,
> Devis'd by Rogues, dreaded by Fools,
> With his grim griesly Dog that keeps the Door,
>   Are senseless Stories, idle Tales,
> Dreams, Whimseys, and no more.

But now Rochester was faced with the grim reality, and the weakness of his body sapped the strength of his mind.

Prostrate at Woodstock from late April until July 26, 1680, he endured the ministrations of Dr. Fell, the Lord Bishop of Oxford, Dr. Marshall, minister of the parish of Woodstock, Robert Parsons, his mother's zealous chaplain, and the great Gilbert Burnet, a passionate proselyter and debater, who had been working on him since the previous October. The odds were overwhelming. Moreover, to the efforts of the clergymen were added the tearful prayers of his wife and his mother. Elizabeth even joined bribery to entreaty, offering to renounce her allegiance to the Catholic Church if he would abjure his Deism.

The combination was too much for a dying man. On June 19, Rochester signed his "Dying Remonstrance," a statement of his contrition and reformation written in rolling periods which sound suspiciously like the eloquence of Robert Parsons. Six days later, the courtier who had formerly sought only the company of the wicked and witty wrote to Dr. Burnet, "I begin to value Churchmen above all men in the World, and you above all the Churchmen I know in it." A few days before his death, he took the Sacrament, and his wife joined him in the ceremony. Thereafter he lay quietly, awaiting death, and once the watchers at his bedside heard him praying devoutly. "And on a Monday about Two of the Clock in the Morning, he died, without any Convulsion, or so much as a Groan."[17]

His body had hardly grown cold before the happy clergymen began to capitalize upon his reformation. In the autumn of the year, Robert Parsons rushed into print his *A Sermon Preached at the Funeral of the Rt. Honourable John Earl of Rochester*, a small volume which included the Earl's "Dying Remonstrance." This very popular treatise was reprinted many times in succeeding years, and was translated into French and German. Parsons was followed closely by Burnet in the same year with *Some Passages of the Life and Death of the Right Honourable John Earl of Rochester*, an even more famous book which in the course of two centuries went through more than thirty editions in English, four in German, two in French, and one in Dutch. The lesser Parnassians were also busy: John Oldham, Anne Wharton, Aphra Behn, Thomas Flatman, Samuel Holland, Samuel Woodforde, and one "Unknown Hand" mourned Rochester's death and hailed his apotheosis. Last came the unctuous moralizers with such titles as *The Libertine Overthrown: or a Mirror for Atheists (ca.*

1690), *The Hazard of a Death-Bed Repentance* (1728), *The Contrast: or the Last Hours of an Impenitent and a Converted Infidel* (1806), and *The Repentance and Happy Death of the Celebrated Earl of Rochester* (1814). Finally, in 1840, the convert was canonized in a seventy-page pamphlet called *The Conversion of the Earl of Rochester*, published by the British Tract Society. Fame had no more to offer.[18]

By 1721 all the Court Wits of the Restoration were dead, and their reputations as poets and critics were dying. The eighteenth century remembered them as a literary circle only vaguely. Old John Dennis, who had been a child in their heyday, indulged in nostalgic reminiscences of them as the top wits and critics of the days of Charles II, but in Pope's superior phrase they were merely some of "the Mob of Gentlemen who wrote with Ease."[19] The collectors of anecdotes and letters, the hack biographers and venal publishers, and the writers of literary forgeries found them still interesting and sometimes profitable. Some of their songs were still sung; some of their plays were revived occasionally; a few of their satirical squibs and critical dicta were quoted with varying degrees of approval from time to time throughout the century; and their reputations as rakes lived on and grew.

The good that men do turns to dust with their bodies. The noble efforts of Buckingham for religious toleration were quickly forgotten, and remembered was his liaison with Lady Shrewsbury and his fatal duel with her husband. The Earl of Dorset's years of service to the state and his lifelong patronage of poets faded into the background, and his brief affair with Nell Gwyn was highlighted as never before. What little good there was in Rochester's life was ignored, and the tales of his erotic exploits were lushly rewritten to titillate the susceptible. The lesser Wits—Scroope, Savile, Guy, Bulkeley, Shepherd, Killigrew—were forgotten except when their names appeared as companions in accounts of the scandalous doings of the top Wits. Vaughan, one-time governor of Jamaica, was known to history as little more than a name; Mulgrave was hardly remembered at all. Whatever was good in the lives and writings of Sedley, Etherege, and Wycherley was ignored; their songs had a brief half-life; and *The Country Wife* was altered by Garrick into a moral farce.

There were other rakes in the eighteenth century and after; there were even some who combined poetry with the life of pleasure. But the unusual combination of circumstances which produced the Court Wits of the Restoration —a closely knit, aristocratic society, a violent reaction against enforced morality, a cynical *carpe diem* philosophy, and a monarch who, himself a Wit, valued and protected his witty companions—has never been duplicated.

THE following biographical summaries are not designed to be exhaustive. Accounts of those Wits who have been extensively written about are confined to the more important events in their lives. The lesser Wits, especially those who do not appear in the *Dictionary of National Biography*, are given fuller treatment. Included in each account are the names and dates of separately printed poems, plays, essays, and "works" published during the writer's lifetime, or shortly after his death. All dates are given according to the modern calendar.

Buckingham, George Villiers, Duke of
(Born January 30, 1628, died April 16, 1687)

1628, August 30, became second duke on the death of his father. Educated at Court with the Prince of Wales and the Duke of York.

1641, Trinity College, Cambridge.

1645, joined King's forces at Oxford. After defeat at Lichfield, was sent abroad with his brother Francis. Lived chiefly at Florence and Rome.

1648, joined Lord Holland in an abortive uprising. Escaped to Holland.

1649, September, Order of the Garter, Gentleman of the Bedchamber, and colonel of a regiment of horse.

1650, April, Member of the Privy Council; accompanied Charles II to Scotland; Secretary of State and General of the Eastern Division of England.

1651, September, defeat of Scots at Worcester; Buckingham hid in Nottinghamshire; escaped to Holland in October.

1654, fought with Turenne against Spain.

1657, returned to England, tried to make peace with Cromwell and get back his estates. September 7, married Mary Fairfax.

1658, committed to Tower for leaving estates without permission; released on February 23, 1659.

1661, Lord Lieutenant of Yorkshire; in favor at Court.

1662, May 1, Member of the Privy Council.

1663, given patent for making flint glass; built factory at Lambeth; sought to "manage" Frances Stuart for the King.

1666, June, with the fleet, but left when denied a command. Beginning of affair with Lady Shrewsbury. October, quarrel and near-duel with Ossory. December, similar affair with Dorchester. Banished in late December for coming to Court without the King's permission.

1667, January, accused of plotting against the King; dismissed from Privy Council and Bedchamber; went into hiding. In June, surrendered and sent to Tower; examined July 1; exonerated and restored to places. July, brawl with Killigrew at the Duke's Theatre. (*The Chances* probably produced during this year, perhaps in February.)

1668, January 16, fatal duel with the Earl of Shrewsbury. February-March, proposed Toleration Act voted down. June, Master of the Horse.

1669, March, challenged by Sir William Coventry. Involved in intrigue for the Treaty of Dover.

1670, July, sent to France with condolences on the death of the Duchess of Orleans; returned in September. December 31, with other members of the Cabal signed treaty with France.

1671, February, son born to Buckingham and Lady Shrewsbury; died in infancy and buried in Westminster Abbey. June 7, Buckingham installed as Chancellor of Cambridge. December 7, *The Rehearsal*.

1672, summer, sent with Arlington and Halifax to attempt peace between France and Holland.

1673, July, quarrel with Ralph Montague.

1674, January, Commons attacked Buckingham; he was removed from all Court appointments, and separated from Lady Shrewsbury.

1675, April, helped defeat new Test Act. October, fought again for an Act of Toleration.

1677, February 15, called for a dissolution of Parliament; sent to the Tower with three other lords. July 2, released. Made his submission to Parliament on January 28, 1678.

1678, October, with Shaftesbury helped prosecute alleged Popish plotters.

1678-80, engaged in minor plots to get back in power. Palace intrigue to "manage" Miss Lawson as the King's mistress.

1682, final defeat of Country Party; Buckingham retired from public affairs.

1685, *A Short Discourse upon the Reasonableness of Men's having a Religion or Worship of God.*

1686, retreated to Helmsley, Yorkshire.

1704, *The Miscellaneous Works of His Grace George, late Duke of Buckingham,* 2 vols. Also 1715, 1721, 1754, 1775.

Bulkeley, Henry

(Born *ca.* 1638, died *ca.* 1698)

1654, April 12, at Gray's Inn.

1657, Queen's College, Cambridge.

1664, May 20, ensign in His Majesty's Guards, in Ireland. November, seriously wounded while acting as second in a duel.

1668, June 1, killed Stephen Radford in a duel at Dublin; convicted of manslaughter; pleaded his clergy and was pardoned.

1672, December 28, a captain in the Guards in Ireland.

1673, July 4, with Lord Buckhurst in a brawl outside the King's Theatre in London. Now in Lord Mulgrave's regiment. November 13, reported about to marry Sophia Stuart.

1675, January 30, sent to the Tower for challenging Lord Ossory; released on February 11. May 24, sworn in as Master of the King's Household.

1677, December 3, a duel with Lord Ossory. December 17, a brawl with Etherege in a tavern.

1679, elected to Parliament from Anglesey. In years 1679-81, he was Member from Beaumaris.

1683, December 12, Groom of the Bedchamber to the King.

1685-87, Member from Beaumaris.

1689, accompanied James II to France.

1690, December 24, returned from a "visit" to France; arrested for high treason but quickly released. Seems to have lived in England thereafter, while his wife was with the exiled Court.

1691, July, skirmish with Doctor Frazier, brother of the Countess of Monmouth.

1697, January 7, bargained to marry his eldest daughter to Charles Viscount Clare. Had two sons and four daughters. His daughter Anne married in 1700 James Fitzjames, Duke of Berwick, a natural son of James II.

Carbery, John Vaughan, Earl of
(Born July 18, 1639, died January 16, 1711)

1656, July 23, Christ Church, Oxford.

1657, September 15, to France, probably on a grand tour.

1658, at Inner Temple.

1661, April, Knight of the Bath.

1661-79, Member of Parliament from borough of Carmarthen.

1667, March 7, inherited courtesy title of lord on the death of his brother Francis. November, took an active part in impeaching Clarendon.

1670, dedicatory verses to Dryden's *Conquest of Granada*.

1673-74, colonel of a regiment of foot.

1674, April, patent as Governor of Jamaica. October, death of first wife, Mary Browne. December, sailed for Jamaica.

1675, March 13, arrived at Jamaica.

1677, March, returned to England.

1679-81, Member of Parliament for Carmarthen County.

1681, September, went with Dorset and Shepherd to visit Savile at Paris.

1682, August 8, married Anne Savile.

1683-84, Member of the Admiralty Commission. October 3, son George baptized; buried May 7, 1685.

1685, January 28, member of the Royal Society. President from 1686 to 1689.

1686, June, inherited title and estates of Carbery.

1688, December, joined other lords in inviting William of Orange to England.

1689-90, Member of the Admiralty Commission. July, death of second wife; survived by a daughter, Anne.

1716, verses on Edward Howard, in Dryden's *Miscellany*, III, 73.

Dorset, Charles Sackville, Earl of
(Born January 24, 1643, died January 29, 1706)

1661, March 28, elected to Parliament from East Grinstead. December, appointed Deputy Lieutenant of Kent.

1663, June 16, episode at the Cock Tavern, with Sedley. October, *Pompey the Great*.

1664, December, with the fleet; *The Noble seamans complaint to the Ladies at Land*.

1667, affair with Nell Gwyn.

1668, September, Groom of the Bedchamber to the King.

1669, July, on a mission to France, with Savile. December 26, Gentleman of the Bedchamber.

1670, May, another mission to France. June 4, joint Lord Lieutenant of Sussex. July, mission to France, with Sedley.

1672, May, with the fleet.

1763, birth of a natural daughter, Mary.

1674, June, marriage to Lady Falmouth.

1675, April 4, inherited title and estates of Earl of Middlesex.

1675, birth of a natural daughter, Katharine.

1677, August 27, inherited title and estates of Earl of Dorset.

1679, September 12, death of first Lady Dorset.

1685, June, marriage to Lady Mary Compton.

1687, January 18, birth of a son, Lionel.

1688, January, removed as Lord Lieutenant of Sussex. April 24, birth of a daughter, Mary.

1689, February, appointed Lord Chamberlain, and reappointed as Lord Lieutenant.

1691, August 6, death of second Lady Dorset.

1692, February 2, Order of the Garter.

1695, May 12, one of seven regent lords in King William's absence.

1697, April 19, resigned as Lord Chamberlain.

1699, January 11, a Fellow of the Royal Society.

1704, October, married Anne Roche.

1714, *The Works of the Earls of Rochester, Roscommon, Dorset,* etc., 2 vols. Also 1718, 1721, 1731, 1739.

1749, *The Works of the Most Celebrated Minor Poets,* Vol. 1 and Supplement.

Etherege, Sir George

(Born 1634 or 35, died *ca.* May 10, 1692)

1664, March, *The Comical Revenge.*

1668, February 6, *She wou'd if she cou'd.* August, went to Turkey as secretary to Sir Daniel Harvey.

1671, summer, returned from Turkey. September, a fight with Colonel Ashton.

1676, March 11, *The Man of Mode.* June, brawl at Epsom which resulted in the death of Captain Downes.

1677, December, tavern brawl with Bulkeley.

1680, January 14, hurt in the fall of the roof of a tennis court. About this time married to Mary Arnold; possibly knighted before the marriage.

1685, August 30, went to Germany as minister to Ratisbon.

1688, presumably went to France to join James II.

1704, *The Works of Sir George Etherege, containing his Plays and Poems.* Also 1715, 1723, 1735.

Guy, Henry

(Born June 16, 1631, died February 23, 1711)

1648, at Gray's Inn.

1652, at the Inner Temple.

1663, September 28, Master of Arts, Oxford.

1670 (*ca.*), one of the farmers of the excise in the north.

1670-81, Member of Parliament from Hedon.

1674, Cupbearer to the Queen.

1675, July 6, Groom of the Bedchamber to the King.

1679, Secretary to the Admiralty Commission.

1685-87, Member from Hedon. Returned again for 1689-95 and 1702-8.

1690, March, a Commissioner of the Customs.

1691, June, Secretary of the Treasury.

1695, February, imprisoned in the Tower for bribery. April, resigned as Secretary of the Treasury.

Killigrew, Henry

(Born April 9, 1637, died December, 1705)

1660, July, in a duel at Heidelberg.

1661, Page of Honor to the King.

1662, Groom of the Bedchamber to the Duke of York. Married Lady Mary Savage (Sedley's sister-in-law).

1666, October 21, banished from the Court for insulting Lady Castlemaine.

1667, July 20, quarreled with Buckingham at the theatre; fled to France.

1668, March 19, rumor of trouble in France. May 30, back in England. October, back in France again.

1669, May 18, beaten by Lady Shrewsbury's footmen. September 30, made peace with Buckingham and Lady Shrewsbury. In favor at Court again.

1674, October 22, Groom of the Bedchamber to the King.

1677, February 8, his servant stabbed in the room next to the King's chamber; Killigrew suspected. October 29, death of his wife. December 11, banished from the Court for insulting Nell Gwyn.

1678, became a master partner (with his brother Charles) in the Theatre Royal.

1693, January 30, fought a duel with Mr. Chamberlain.

1694, July, a member of the Commission to regulate hackney coaches. November, appointed jester to the King.

1695, May, turned out of the Commission to regulate hackney coaches.

Mulgrave, John Sheffield, Earl of

(Born April 7, 1648, died February 24, 1721)

1658, succeeded to earldom on the death of his father.

1666, a volunteer with the fleet.

1667, June 13, captain of a troop of horse.

1669, November, quarreled with Rochester.

1673, February, Gentleman of the Bedchamber to the King. Given command of *The Royal Katherine*. December, appointed colonel of the "Old Holland" regiment.

1674, April 23, Order of the Garter. May 15, commissioned as Governor of North Yarmouth. September, affair with Mall Kirke. October, wounded in a duel with Mr. Felton.

1675, July, wounded in a duel with Percy Kirke.

1677, August, in France with his regiment.

1679, December 2, Lord Lieutenant of the East Riding of Yorkshire and Governor of Hull.

1682, banished for courting Princess Anne. *Essay on Poetry.*

1685, July 24, Privy Councillor. October 20, Lord Chamberlain; held office until 1689.

1686, March 18, married Ursula, Lady Conway. November 22, on Court of High Commission.

1689, *A Letter from the Earl of Mulgrave to Dr. Tillotson.*

1694, May 3, Privy Councillor again. May 10, Marquis of Normanby.

1695, *The Temple of Death. A Poem.*

1696, *The Character of Charles II.*

1699, March 12, married Katherine, Lady Gainsborough.

1702, April 21, Lord Privy Seal.

1703, March, Duke of Buckinghamshire.

1704, married Catherine, illegitimate daughter of James II and Katherine Sedley, and divorced wife of the Earl of Anglesey.

1705, resigned all Court appointments with Whig triumph.

1710, Privy Councillor and Lord Steward of the Household.

1721, *The Works of the Most Noble John Sheffield, late Duke of Buckingham, Published by his Grace in his Lifetime* (Curll's unauthorized edition).

1723, *The Works of John Sheffield, Earl of Mulgrave, Marquis of Normanby, Duke of Buckingham,* 2 vols. Also 1724, 1726, 1729 ("corrected"), 1740, 1752, 1753, etc.

Rochester, John Wilmot, Earl of

(Born April 1, 1647, died July 26, 1680)

1660, January 18, Wadham College, Oxford. M.A. on September 9, 1661.

1661, November 21, left England for a foreign tour.

1665, May 26, abducted Elizabeth Malet. Imprisoned in the Tower until June 19. July 15, with the fleet. September 12, back at Court.

1666, March 21, Gentleman of the Bedchamber to the King. July 20, with the fleet again.

1667, January 29, married Elizabeth Malet. June 13, captain of a troop of horse.

1668, February 28, Gamekeeper for the county of Oxford.

1669, March, went to France after a quarrel with Tom Killigrew. June 29, in a brawl at Paris. August, Anne Wilmot baptized. November, Rochester quarreled with Mulgrave.

1671, January 2, Charles Wilmot baptized.

1672, October 30, deputy lieutenant for Somersetshire.

1674, February 27, Ranger and Keeper of Woodstock Park. July 13, Elizabeth Wilmot baptized.

1675, January 6, Malet Wilmot baptized. June 26, affair of the sundial in the Privy Garden.

1676, June 17, brawl at Epsom.

1677, November, Alderman of Taunton.

1678, *Epigram upon my Lord All-Pride.*

1679, *A Satyr Against Mankind.*

1680, *Poems on Several Occasions: By the Right Honourable the E of R,* "Antwerpen." Also 1685, 1701, 1712.

1682, *A Pastoral Dialogue between Alexis and Strephon.*

1685, *Valentinian: A Tragedy.*

1691, *Poems, &c. On Several Occasions: with Valentinian, a Tragedy.* Also 1696, 1705, 1710, 1714.

Savile, Henry

(Born 1641-2, died October 16, 1687)

1657, April 21, Christ Church, Oxford.

1661, toured southern Europe with Henry Sidney and the Earl of Sunderland.

1665, Groom of the Bedchamber to the Duke of York.

1666, September, with the fleet.

1667, October, failed of election to Parliament from Rye.

1669, March 4, sent to prison for carrying a challenge from Coventry to Buckingham. Freed on March 20. July 23, to France on a diplomatic mission with Buckhurst.

1670, July, again in France, with Buckingham, Buckhurst, and Sedley. August, sent to Florence on a mission. Returned to England in September.

1671, September, attempt to win Lady Northumberland frustrated. Probably went to France.

1672, May, with the fleet at the battle of Solebay. Temporary secretary to the Duke of York. *A true Relation of the Engagement of His Majesties Fleet under the command of His Royal Highness with the Dutch Fleet, May 28 1672.* October (to February, 1673) envoy extraordinary to France.

1673, June 6, Groom of the Bedchamber to the King.

1674, December, quarreled with Mulgrave.

1675, June 26 to July 8, stormy voyage with the King to the Isle of Wight.

1676, March, banished from Court for disrespect to the Duke of York. May, banished again for the same cause.

1677, April, elected to Parliament from Newark.

1678, May, dismissed from Court for voting against Lauderdale. July 15, sent to France to settle the Duchess of Cleveland's affairs.

1679, February 27, envoy extraordinary to France. July, *Advice to a Painter to Draw the Duke by*.

1680, Vice-Chamberlain to the King.

1682, January 20, sixth commissioner of the Admiralty. March, replaced as envoy to France.

1684, May 11, Admiralty Commission dismissed.

1687, March, opposed policies of James II and lost Court appointments. July, went to Paris for an operation.

Scroope, Sir Carr

(Born 1649, died November, 1680)

1664, August 26, Wadham College, Oxford.

1667, January 16, created a baronet. February 4, Master of Arts.

1672, May, petitioned for grant of lands in the King's gift.

1675, August, younger brother killed by Sir Thomas Armstrong.

1676, March, prologue and song for Etherege's *The Man of Mode*. Beginning of satiric war with Rochester.

1676, November, quarrel with Cary Frazier.

1677, March, prologue for Lee's *The Rival Queens*.

1678, June, quarrel with Nell Gwyn.

1679, March, song for Lee's *Mithridates*.

1680, joined the Whigs; member of the Green Ribbon Club.

1684, "Elegy the Fourth," from Ovid's *Amores*, Book I, and "The Parting of Sireno and Diana," from Montemayor's *Diana*, in *Miscellany Poems by the Most Eminent Hands*.

1704, "A Satire upon the Follies of the Men of the Age," in Buckingham's *Works*, I, 47.

Sedley, Sir Charles

(Born March, 1639, died August, 1701)

1645, September, to April, 1648, in France.

1656, March 22, Wadham College, Oxford. April 18, inherited the title on the death of his older brother.

1657, February 9, married Katherine Savage. December 21, Katherine Sedley born.

1663, June 16, affair at the Cock Tavern. October, *Pompey*.

1665, November 25, went to France.

1667, July, living with Buckhurst and Nell Gwyn at Epsom.

1668, May, elected to Parliament from New Romney. *The Mulberry Garden*. September, with the King on a progress.

1669, January, Kynaston beaten for imitating Sedley on the stage.

1670, July, diplomatic trip with Buckingham, Buckhurst, and Savile.

1672, sent insane wife to a convent in France (she died there on July 1, 1705). April, went through a form of marriage with Ann Ayscough. Natural son Charles probably born this year.

1677, February, *Anthony and Cleopatra*.

1679, March, re-elected from New Romney; again in October.

1680, January, escaped death when the roof of a tennis court collapsed.

1681, March, re-elected from New Romney (not in Parliaments of 1685 and 1689).

1687, May, *Bellamira*.

1690, March, re-elected from New Romney.

1695, November, defeated, but returned to Parliament because his opponent vacated the seat.

1698, December, re-elected from New Romney.

1702, *Miscellaneous Works of Sir Charles Sedley*.

1707, *The Poetical Works of the Honourable Sir Charles Sedley Baronet, with Large Additions never before made Publick.*

Shepherd, Sir Fleetwood

(Born January 6, 1634, died September 6, 1698)

1650, November 19, Magdalen Hall, Oxford.

1655, March 10, B.A. at Christ Church, Oxford.

1657, at Gray's Inn. June 11, M.A. at Christ Church.

1664, December 14, by intervention of the King relieved from the necessity of entering the church.

1665 (*ca.*), became a steward and companion to Buckhurst.

1676 (*ca.*), tutor to the Earl of Burford, son of Nell Gwyn.

1681, went with Dorset to visit Savile in Paris.

1694, April 25, Gentleman Usher of the Black Rod; knighted.

1698, "The Countess of Dorset's Petition to the late Queen Mary for Chocolate," in *Poems on Affairs of State*, 1698 (Part 3), 233.

1704, "Upon an Old Affected Court Lady," and "The Calendar Reformed," in Buckingham's *Works*, 1, 82, 217.

1716, a mock elegy, a mock prophecy, and an "Epitaph on the Duke of Grafton," in *Poems on Affairs of State*, 1716, 1, 249, 251, 259.

Wycherley, William

(Born 1640, died December 31, 1715)

1655, a student at Angoumois, France.

1660, March, returned to England. May, at Queen's College, Oxford. November 10, at Inner Temple.

1664, January 31, with Sir Richard Fanshaw on an embassy to Spain; returned in February. Summer, with the fleet.

1666, at Inner Temple again.

1669, *Hero and Leander, in Burlesque.*

1671, spring, *Love in a Wood.* Intimacy with the Duchess of Cleveland.

1672, March, *The Gentleman Dancing Master.*

1675, *The Country Wife.*

1676, December, *The Plain Dealer.*

1678, autumn, journey to France in search of health.

1679, spring, return to England, by way of Holland. September, married Letitia, widowed Countess Drogheda.

1681, January, death of first wife. Law suits to get possession of her jointure; resultant poverty.

1682, in Newgate for debt.

1683, *Epistles to the King and Duke.*

1685, July 7, committed to Fleet Prison, for debt.

1686, spring, released on payment of debts by James II and Mulgrave.

1689, went to live at Clive.

1697, May, inherited life interest in his father's estate.

1704, *Miscellany Poems.*

1715, married Elizabeth Jackson, eleven days before his death.

1729, *The Posthumous Works of William Wycherley, Esq.*

BIBLIOGRAPHY OF WORKS
FREQUENTLY CITED

Aubrey, John
>   'Brief Lives,' chiefly of Contemporaries, set down by John Aubrey between the Years 1669 and 1696, ed. Andrew Clark, 2 vols., Oxford, 1898.

Behn, Aphra
>   Miscellany, Being a Collection of Poems by Several Hands, London, 1685.
>   The Works of Aphra Behn, ed. Montague Summers, 6 vols., London, 1915.

Boswell, Eleanore
>   The Restoration Court Stage (1660-1702), Harvard University Press, Cambridge, 1932.

Brown, Thomas
>   The Works of Mr. Thomas Brown (5th edition), 4 vols., London, 1720.

Bryant, Arthur
>   King Charles II, London, 1931.

Buckingham, George Villiers, Duke of
>   The Miscellaneous Works of His Grace George, Late Duke of Buckingham, 2 vols., London, 1705-7.

Bulstrode, Sir Richard
>   The Bulstrode Papers, Extracts from Newsletters written to Sir Richard Bulstrode . . . 1673-1675, London, 1897.

Burghclere, Lady Winifred
>   George Villiers: Second Duke of Buckingham, 1628-1687, London, 1903.

Burnet, Gilbert
>   Bishop Burnet's History of His Own Time, 6 vols., Oxford, 1823.
>   Some Passages of the Life and Death of the Right Honourable John Earl of Rochester, London, 1680.

Cartwright, Julia (Mrs. Henry Ady)
>   Madame: A Life of Henrietta, Daughter of Charles I and Duchess of Orleans, New York, 1901.

> *Sacharissa: Some Account of Dorothy Sidney, Countess of Sunderland, Her Family and Friends, 1617-1684*, London, 1893.

Chancellor, E. Beresford
> *The Restoration Rakes* (Vol. II, *The Lives of the Rakes*), New York, 1926.

"Choyce Collection, A," MS miscellany, The Ohio State University Library.

Clarendon, Edward Hyde, Earl of
> *The Life of Edward Earl of Clarendon . . . written by himself*, 3 vols., Oxford, 1761.

(CSPD) Calendars of State Papers, Domestic Series.

Dennis, John
> *The Critical Works of John Dennis*, ed. Edward Niles Hooker, 2 vols., Johns Hopkins Press, Baltimore, 1939-43.

Dorset, Charles Sackville, Earl of
> *The Works of the Most Celebrated Minor Poets*, 3 vols., London, 1751 (I, 125-139; III, 26-41).

Downes, John
> *Roscius Anglicanus*, ed. Montague Summers, London, 1928.

Dryden, John
> *Miscellany Poems: Containing Variety of New Translations . . . Together with Several Original Poems* (4th edition), 6 vols., London, 1716.

> *The Works of John Dryden*, ed. Sir Walter Scott, revised and corrected by George Saintsbury, 18 vols., Edinburgh, 1882.

> *Essays of John Dryden*, ed. W. P. Ker, 2 vols., Oxford University Press, Oxford, 1926.

Essex, Arthur Capel, Earl of
> *Essex Papers* (Vol. I, 1672-79), ed. Osmund Airy, The Camden Society, 1890.

> *Selections from the Correspondence of Arthur Capel Earl of Essex, 1676-1677* (Vol. II of *Essex Papers*), ed. Clement Edwards Pike, The Camden Society, 1913.

Etherege, Sir George
> *The Works of Sir George Etheredge, Plays and Poems*, ed. A. Wilson Verity, London, 1888.

> *The Dramatic Works of Sir George Etherege*, ed. H. F. B. Brett-Smith, 2 vols., New York, 1927.

> *The Letterbook of Sir George Etherege*, ed. Sybil Rosenfeld, London, 1928.

Evelyn, John
    Diary of John Evelyn, ed. Henry B. Wheatley, 4 vols., London, 1906.
Hamilton, Count Anthony
    Memoirs of Count Grammont, ed. Gordon Goodwin, 2 vols., London, 1903.
Harris, Brice
    Charles Sackville, Sixth Earl of Dorset: Patron and Poet of the Restoration, University of Illinois Press, Urbana, 1940.
(HMC) Reports of the Royal Commission on Historical Manuscripts. Reports One through Ten are cited in the notes by number, prefixed HMC. The following are cited by short titles, prefixed HMC.
    Marquis of Bath
    Earl of Dartmouth
    Sir William Fitzherbert
    R. Rawdon Hastings
    J. M. Heathcote, Esq.
    J. Eliot Hodgkin, Esq.
    Laing MSS
    S. H. Le Fleming, Esq.
    Lord Montagu of Beaulieu
    MSS in Various Collections
    Marquis of Ormonde
    Duke of Portland
    Duke of Rutland
    Stuart Papers
Hatton
    Correspondence of the Family of Hatton . . . 1601-1704, ed. Edward Maunde Thompson, The Camden Society, 2 vols., 1878.
Johnson, Samuel
    Lives of the English Poets, ed. George Birkbeck Hill, 3 vols., Oxford, 1905.
Lauderdale, John Maitland, Earl of
    The Lauderdale Papers, ed. Osmund Airy, 3 vols., The Camden Society, 1884-85.
Luttrell, Narcissus
    A Brief Relation of State Affairs from September 1678 to April 1714, 6 vols., Oxford, 1857.
Marvell, Andrew
    The Poems & Letters of Andrew Marvell, ed. H. M. Margoliouth, 2 vols., Oxford, 1927.

Mulgrave, John Sheffield, Earl of
> *The Works of John Sheffield, Earl of Mulgrave, Marquis of Normanby, and Duke of Buckingham* (3rd edition, "corrected"), 2 vols., London, 1740.

Nicoll, Allardyce
> *A History of Restoration Drama, 1660-1700*, Cambridge University Press, London, 1923.

Pepys, Samuel
> *The Diary of Samuel Pepys*, ed. with additions by Henry B. Wheatley, 9 vols., London, 1893.

Pinto, Vivian De Sola
> *Sir Charles Sedley, 1639-1701. A Study in the Life and Literature of the Restoration*, New York, 1927.
> *Rochester: Portrait of a Restoration Poet*, London, 1935.

(POAS) *Poems on Affairs of State from the Time of Oliver Cromwell to the Abdication of K. James Second, Written by the Greatest Wits of the Age*, 4 vols., London, 1716.

Porritt, Edward
> *The Unreformed House of Commons: parliamentary representation before 1832*, Cambridge, 1909.

Prinz, Johannes
> *Rochesteriana: Being some Anecdotes concerning John Wilmot, Earl of Rochester*, Leipzig, 1926.
> *John Wilmot Earl of Rochester: His Life and Writings* (Palaestra, No. 154), Leipzig, 1927.

Prior, Matthew
> *Dialogues of the Dead and other Works in Prose and Verse*, ed. A. R. Waller, Cambridge, 1907.

Radcliffe, Alexander
> *The Ramble: An Anti-Heroic Poem*, London, 1682.

Rochester, John Wilmot, Earl of
> *Collected Works of John Wilmot Earl of Rochester*, ed. John Hayward, London, 1926.
> *The Rochester-Savile Letters, 1671-1680*, ed. John Harold Wilson, The Ohio State University Press, Columbus, 1941.

Savile, Henry
> *Savile Correspondence. Letters to and from Henry Savile, Esq.*, ed. William Durrant Cooper, The Camden Society, 1858.

Sedley, Sir Charles
> *The Poetical Works of the Honourable Sir Charles Sedley Baronet, with Large Additions never before made Publick*, London, 1707.

The Poetical and Dramatic Works of Sir Charles Sedley, ed. Vivian De Sola Pinto, 2 vols., London, 1928.

Sprague, Arthur Colby
Beaumont and Fletcher on the Restoration Stage, Harvard University Press, Cambridge, 1926.

Summers, Montague
A Bibliography of the Restoration Drama, London, 1934.
The Playhouse of Pepys, New York, 1935.

Walpole, Horace
A Catalogue of the Royal and Noble Authors of England, Edinburgh, 1796.

Williamson, Sir Joseph
Letters Addressed from London to Sir Joseph Williamson . . . in the years 1673 and 1674, ed. W. D. Christie, 2 vols., The Camden Society, 1874.

Wood, Anthony
Athenae Oxonienses. An Exact History of All the Writers and Bishops who Have Had their Education in the University of Oxford, ed. Philip Bliss, 4 vols., London, 1813.
Fasti Oxonienses, or Annals of the University of Oxford, ed. Philip Bliss, 2 vols. in 1, London, 1815.
The Life and Times of Anthony Wood, Antiquary of Oxford, 1632-1695, Described by Himself, ed. Andrew Clark, 5 vols., Oxford, 1891-1900.

Wycherley, William
The Complete Works of William Wycherley, ed. Montague Summers, 4 vols., London, 1924.

NOTES

IN the following reference notes, short titles and a few abbreviations (*CSPD*, *POAS*, HMC) are used for books listed in the bibliography. Unless otherwise noted, poems and plays quoted or cited in the text will be found in the author's "Works" as listed in the bibliography. Modern periodicals are referred to by the following abbreviations:

ELH	*Journal of English Literary History*
LTLS	*[London] Times Literary Supplement*
MLN	*Modern Language Notes*
MLR	*Modern Language Review*
N&Q	*Notes and Queries*
PMLA	*Publications of the Modern Language Association of America*
PQ	*Philological Quarterly*
RES	*Review of English Studies*
SP	*Studies in Philology*

THE COURT WITS

1. For a study of the King as a personality, see Bryant, *Charles II*.
2. Clarendon, *Life*, III, 646.
3. "The Lovers Session," *POAS*, II, 157.
4. Dryden, *Essays*, I, 14, 15, 72, 77, 190.
5. Etherege, *Letterbook*, p. 416.
6. Marvell, *Poems & Letters*, II, 329.
7. Wood, *Athenae*, IV, 627.
8. Dennis, *Works*, II, 277.
9. For a discussion of Restoration marriage customs, see Arthur Bryant, *The England of Charles II*, London, 1935, Chapter III.
10. *Savile Correspondence*, p. 121.
11. HMC, *Ninth Report*, p. 448a.

12. Pepys, July 7, 1667. For the prices of numerous commodities, see the invaluable Pepys and also Gladys Scott Thomson, *Life in a Noble Household, 1641-1700*, London, 1937.

13. For the details of a typical university education, see Charles Edward Mallet, *A History of the University of Oxford*, 3 vols., New York, 1924, Vol. ii.

14. For a summary of the conflicting philosophies of the seventeenth century, see Louis I. Bredvold, *The Intellectual Milieu of John Dryden*, University of Michigan Press, Ann Arbor, 1934, Chapters ii and iii.

15. William Congreve, *The Way of the World* (1700), iii, i.

16. *Rochester-Savile*, p. 34.

17. Mulgrave, *Works*, ii, 55.

18. Rochester, *A Satyr Against Mankind*.

19. Mulgrave, *Works*, ii, 202.

20. Dryden, *Mac Flecknoe*.

21. *Rochester-Savile*, p. 49.

22. Etherege, *The Man of Mode* (1676), iv, ii.

23. "The Town-Life," *POAS*, i, 192.

24. *Savile Correspondence*, pp. 107-8. Savile's satire is reprinted in Marvell, *Poems & Letters*, i, 197-200.

25. See preface to Volume iv, *POAS*.

26. See Prinz, *Rochester*, pp. 146-51; Behn, *Works*, vi, 148, 151, 178; Harold Brooks, "Attributions to Rochester," *LTLS* (May 9, 1935), p. 301.

27. "The Trial of the Poets for the Bays" and "Timon, a Satyr," usually attributed to Rochester, and "Satyr upon the Follies of the Men of the Age," by Scroope.

28. Wood, *Fasti*, ii, 294.

29. Behn, *Miscellany*, preface to "Seneca Unmasqued."

30. *Rochester-Savile*, p. 37.

31. Buckingham, *Works*, i, 82, 217; *POAS*, i (Part 2), 249, 251, 259; Harris, *Dorset*, p. 154.

32. Dryden, *Miscellany*, iii, 74.

33. See Prinz, *Rochester*, p. 283. Prinz attributes the letter to Robert Bulkeley.

34. "The Session of the Poets, to the Tune of Cock Laurel," *POAS*, i, 207.

35. Killigrew's talent for description is vouched for by Muddiman, the journalist. See HMC, *Bath*, ii, 153.

36. Harris, *Dorset*, pp. 173-214.

THE WITS IN PRIVATE LIFE

1. Dryden, *Works*, IV, 373.
2. HMC, *Seventh Report*, p. 488.
3. Wood, *Life and Times*, II, 560.
4. Marvell, *Poems & Letters*, II, 311.
5. HMC, *Seventh Report*, p. 486.
6. *Rochester-Savile*, p. 52.
7. *Essex Papers*, I, 281.
8. *Savile Correspondence*, p. 58.
9. HMC, *Tenth Report* (Part V), pp. 67-68.
10. HMC, *Heathcote*, p. 170.
11. *CSPD*, 1673, July 4, p. 420; *Williamson Letters*, I, 87.
12. HMC, *Rutland*, II, 27.
13. *Essex Papers*, I, 295; HMC, *Rutland*, II, 42.
14. *Rochester-Savile*, p. 52.
15. HMC, *Seventh Report*, p. 200.
16. Burghclere, *Buckingham*, pp. 158-60, 192-94.
17. HMC, *Third Report*, p. 117.
18. Luttrell, *Brief Relation*, III, 25.
19. HMC, *Seventh Report*, p. 488; *Essex Papers*, I, 281.
20. HMC, *Rutland*, II, 27; *Essex Papers*, I, 261.
21. *Bulstrode Papers*, I, 303.
22. Marvell, *Poems & Letters*, II, 318.
23. *Bulstrode Papers*, I, 304.
24. *Savile Correspondence*, p. 39.
25. Mulgrave, *Works*, II, 32-33.
26. Harris, *Dorset*, p. 77.
27. Mulgrave, *Works*, II, 6-8.
28. *Hatton Correspondence*, I, 68; HMC, *Seventh Report*, p. 513.
29. *Miscellanies: by . . . The Late Lord Marquis of Halifax*, London, 1700, p. 18.
30. Burghclere, *Buckingham*, pp. 190, 295.
31. Etherege, *Letterbook*, pp. 161, 293, 328, 338.
32. Wycherley, *Complete Works*, I, 54ff.
33. Harris, *Dorset*, pp. 58-60, 78, 79.
34. For comments on Mrs. Bulkeley, see HMC, *Rutland*, II, 42; HMC, *Ormonde*, n.s., V, 242; "Choyce Collection," pp. 198, 239, 284.
35. C. H. Collins Baker, *Lely and the Stuart Portrait Painters*, London, 1912, I, 172.

36. See the detailed study of the Duchess (formerly Countess of Castlemaine) by Philip W. Sergeant, *My Lady Castlemaine*, Boston [1911].
37. Prinz, *Rochester*, pp. 41-56. For some wild inventions, see Prinz, *Rochesteriana*.
38. Burghclere, *Buckingham*, p. 244.
39. Pepys, March 29, 1669.
40. Harris, *Dorset*, pp. 34, 35, 53, 89.
41. Mulgrave, *Works*, II, 341. In his will (*Works*, II, 361) Mulgrave provided for three natural children: Charles, Sophia, and Charlotte.
42. See *The Conduct of the Earl of Nottingham*, ed. W. A. Aiken, Yale University Press, New Haven, 1941, p. 43, and *Essex Papers*, I, 140.
43. Pepys, July 29, 1667.
44. Summers, *Playhouse*, p. 18.
45. Pinto, *Sedley*, pp. 126-31.
46. Etherege, *Letterbook*, p. 240.
47. *Rochester-Savile*, p. 71.
48. *CSPD*, 1676-77, November 25, 1676, p. 433; Cartwright, *Sacharissa*, p. 234.
49. Wycherley, *Collected Works*, I, 35-36.
50. Burghclere, *Buckingham*, pp. 209-10.
51. Etherege, *Letterbook*, pp. 338, 416.
52. HMC, *Laing*, p. 405; Aubrey, *Brief Lives*, II, 34.
53. HMC, *Seventh Report*, p. 467; *Hatton Correspondence*, pp. 133-34; *Essex Papers*, II, 59.
54. Pepys, October 23, 1668.
55. Etherege, *Letterbook*, pp. 383-84.
56. HMC, *Portland*, III, 356.
57. Prinz, *Rochesteriana*, p. 15.
58. *Rochester-Savile*, p. 46.
59. Quoted by Pinto, *Sedley*, pp. 308-9.
60. Pepys, July 1, 1663. There is no evidence that Batten was at the trial.
61. Wood, *Athenae*, IV, 732, and *Life and Times*, I, 476-77, and II, 335-36. For Wood's confusion about the justices, see *N&Q*, Ninth Series, VIII (1901), 157.
62. *Diaries and Letters of Philip Henry*, ed. M. H. Lee, London, 1882, p. 158.
63. Johnson, *Lives*, I, 303-4.
64. Chancellor, *Restoration Rakes*, p. 165.

65. Pepys, January 17, 1668.

66. Burghclere, *Buckingham*, pp. 192-95, and HMC, *Ninth Report*, II, 36.

67. Joseph Spence, *Anecdotes, Observations, and Characters, of Books and Men*, ed. S. W. Singer, London, 1858, p. 124.

68. John Langhorne, *Letters Supposed to have passed between M. De St. Evremonde and Waller*, London, 1769, Letter IV.

69. Macaulay, *History of England*, London, 1850, II, 318.

70. Hamilton, *Grammont*, I, 108-11; II, 3.

71. A reprint of the memoir is prefixed to Quilter Johns, *The Poetical Works of John Wilmot Earl of Rochester*, London, 1933.

72. Cf. Ralph Straus, *The Unspeakable Curll*, London, 1927, p. 205, and Prinz, *Rochester*, p. 354.

73. An anonymous correspondent in *LTLS* (June 13, 1942, p. 300) suggests that the author of the memoir might have been one Thomas Alcock, who had claimed to be "a servant of the earl and a sharer in his pranks."

74. M. E. D. Forgues, in "John Wilmot, Comte de Rochester," *Revue des deux mondes*, X (1857), 855, commented, apropos the "Innkeepers" yarn, that it was a story "que La Fontaine à le riguer pu rimer."

THE WITS IN PUBLIC LIFE

1. *Rochester-Savile*, p. 41.

2. *Savile Correspondence*, p. 37.

3. W. J. Thoms, *The Book of the Court*, London, 1844, p. 32.

4. *CSPD*, 1675-76, September 13, 1675, p. 293.

5. *CSPD*, 1667, August 22, p. 408.

6. For information on Court posts, their incumbents, duties, and pay, see Edward Chamberlayne, *Angliae Notitiae*, London, 1674.

7. For example, in 1668, a futile attempt was made to reduce the number of bedchamber servants to eight of each rank. See *CSPD*, 1667-68, March 16, 1668, pp. 291-92.

8. HMC, *Seventh Report*, p. 468, and HMC, *Rutland*, II, 37-38.

9. Prinz, *Rochester*, p. 254.

10. Pepys, April 29, 1663.

11. See Robert J. Allen, "Two Wycherley Letters," *LTLS*, April 18, 1935, p. 257.

12. Burghclere, *Buckingham*, pp. 275-77.
13. Harris, *Dorset*, pp. 31-33.
14. Pinto, *Rochester*, pp. 51-57.
15. HMC, *Hastings*, II, 159.
16. Mulgrave, *Works*, II, 17.
17. Burghclere, *Buckingham*, p. 263.
18. Harris, *Dorset*, p. 32.
19. Mulgrave, *Works*, II, 6; II, 325-29; I, 78-86.
20. Burghclere, *Buckingham*, p. 225; Pinto, *Sedley*, pp. 113-16.
21. *Bulstrode Papers*, I, 108, 114, 118.
22. *CSPD*, 1670, September 3, p. 421.
23. *Savile Correspondence*, pp. xviii-xxiii.
24. Etherege, *Letterbook*, pp. 62, 293, 414-15, 416.
25. Clarendon, *Life*, III, 844-45; Pepys, November 16, 1667.
26. HMC, *Dartmouth*, pp. 25-26. For the details of Vaughan's experiences at Jamaica, see numerous references in *Calendars of State Papers Colonial*, 1674-78.
27. HMC, *Seventh Report*, p. 508.
28. See, for example, George Macaulay Trevelyan, *England under Queen Anne*, London, 1930-34, III, 147.
29. See Sir Courtenay Peregrine Ilbert, *Parliament: its history, constitution, and practice*, London [1911], pp. 120ff, and Ned Ward, *The London Spy*, ed. Arthur L. Hayward, London, 1927, pp. 145-50.
30. Porritt, *Commons*, pp. 123, 222.
31. *Ibid.*, pp. 51, 58.
32. *Savile Correspondence*, p. 47.
33. Porritt, *Commons*, p. 566.
34. Arthur Bryant, *Samuel Pepys, The Years of Peril*, New York, 1935, p. 252.
35. Clarendon, *Life*, I, 495.
36. *Savile Correspondence*, p. 45.
37. Pepys, October 21, 1666.
38. *Lauderdale Papers*, II, 132-42; *Rochester-Savile*, pp. 58-66.
39. Pepys, November 16, 1667.
40. Pinto, *Sedley*, pp. 175-201.
41. *Williamson Letters*, II, 106.
42. Burghclere, *Buckingham*, pp. 279, 286.
43. The speech is printed in Buckingham, *Works*, II (Part 2), 10.
44. For an account of the marriage, see Wycherley, *Complete Works*, I, 54ff.
45. Prinz, *Rochester*, p. 266.

46. Chancellor, *Restoration Rakes*, p. 262.
47. Pinto, *Sedley*, p. 77.

LETTERS OF WIT AND FRIENDSHIP

1. For Rochester's letter to Savile, see *Rochester-Savile*, p. 33. For his letter to Lichfield, see Prinz, *Rochester*, p. 273. My attempt to reconstruct Rochester's method of writing is based upon a study of the originals of some of his letters in B. M. Harleian 7003.
2. See J. G. Muddiman, *The King's Journalist, 1659-1689*, London, 1923.
3. See *Essex Papers, Hatton Correspondence, Lauderdale Papers, Williamson Letters*, Cartwright, *Madame*, and *Sacharissa*. See also, *Conway Letters: The Correspondence of Anne, Viscountess Conway, Henry More, and their Friends, 1642-1684*, ed. Marjorie Hope Nicolson, London, 1930; *The Letters of Dorothy Osborne to Sir William Temple*, ed. G. C. Moore Smith, Oxford, 1928; *Letters of Rachel, Lady Russell*, Philadelphia, 1854; *Memoirs of the Verney Family During the Seventeenth Century*, eds. Frances Parthenope Verney and Margaret M. Verney, 2 vols., London, 1907.
4. On the history and development of the letter in the seventeenth century, see Benjamin Boyce, *Tom Brown of Facetious Memory*, Harvard University Press, Cambridge, 1939; Katherine Gee Hornbeak, *The Complete Letter Writer in English, 1658-1800*, Smith College Studies, Northampton, 1934; Elbert N. S. Thompson, *Literary Bypaths of the Renaissance*, Yale University Press, New Haven, 1924.
5. HMC, *Hodgkin*, p. 67.
6. *Rochester-Savile*, pp. 37, 50.
7. HMC, *Bath*, II, 153.
8. Etherege, *Letterbook*, pp. 199, 239.
9. Dryden, *Works*, XVIII, 87. For Dryden's letters to Rochester and Etherege, see *The Letters of John Dryden*, ed. Charles E. Ward, Duke University Press, Durham, 1942, pp. 7, 26.
10. In MS Eng. 636F (Harvard Library) this poem is entitled "To My Lord Mulgrave from Rochester: An Epistolary Essay from M.G. to O.B."
11. Wycherley, *Collected Works*, II, 243, 245.
12. *Poems on Several Occasions: By the Right Honourable, The E of R[ochester]*, Antwerpen [1680], pp. 77-88.

13. Etherege, *Letterbook*, pp. 62-63, 80-82, 346-48.
14. See the King's letters as quoted by Cartwright, *Madame*, especially pp. 207, 209.
15. Prinz, *Rochester*, p. 253.
16. Robert J. Allen, "Two Wycherley Letters," *LTLS*, April 18, 1935, p. 257.
17. Pinto, *Sedley*, pp. 152-53.
18. *Rochester-Savile*, p. 33.
19. *Ibid.*, p. 56.
20. HMC, *Bath*, II, 172.
21. Etherege, *Letterbook*, p. 140.
22. Robert J. Allen, "Two Wycherley Letters," *LTLS*, April 18, 1935, p. 257.
23. *Rochester-Savile*, p. 50.
24. Prinz, *Rochester*, pp. 281-82.
25. *Rochester-Savile*, p. 71.
26. *Savile Correspondence*, p. 95.
27. Cartwright, *Madame*, p. 228.
28. Etherege, *Letterbook*, p. 337.
29. Cartwright, *Madame*, p. 153.
30. Etherege, *Letterbook*, pp. 69, 327.
31. *Ibid.*, p. 161.
32. Harris, *Dorset*, pp. 58-59, 76.
33. Prinz, *Rochester*, p. 264.
34. Burghclere, *Buckingham*, pp. 88-89.
35. Rochester, *Collected Works*, p. 268.
36. Harris, *Dorset*, p. 91.
37. J. Harold Wilson, "Etherege's 'Julia,'" *MLN*, LXII (1947), 40.
38. Etherege, *Letterbook*, pp. 328, 338.
39. *Savile Correspondence*, p. 146.
40. Prinz, *Rochester*, p. 279.
41. *Rochester-Savile*, p. 53. For the identity of the actress, see Boswell, *Court Stage*, p. 123.
42. Etherege, *Letterbook*, p. 357.
43. *Rochester-Savile*, p. 65.
44. Cartwright, *Sacharissa*, p. 245.
45. *Savile Correspondence*, p. 159.
46. *Ibid.*, pp. 15, 151, 114.
47. *Rochester-Savile*, p. 54.
48. *Ibid.*, p. 67.
49. *Savile Correspondence*, p. 235.

50. *Diary of the Times of Charles II, by the Honourable Henry Sidney*, ed. R. W. Blencowe, 2 vols., London, 1843, I, 140.
51. *Savile Correspondence*, pp. 232, 123.
52. *Rochester-Savile*, p. 58.
53. *Ibid.*, p. 54.
54. *Savile Correspondence*, pp. 143, 213.
55. *Ibid.*, p. 301.

LOVE SONGS TO PHYLLIS

1. See Elizabeth Hazelton Haight, *Romance in the Latin Elegiac Poets*, New York, 1932.
2. For the theories about Lucasta, see Cyril Hughes Hartmann, *The Cavalier Spirit, and Its Influence on the Life and Work of Richard Lovelace (1618-1658)*, London, 1925, pp. 71-76.
3. Wood, *Life and Times*, II, 42-43; and Buckingham's "The Lost Mistress, a Complaint against the Countess of ——."
4. Pinto, *Sedley*, pp. 126, 128-31.
5. Harris, *Dorset*, pp. 82-83.
6. Pinto, *Rochester*, pp. 60-76.
7. Bryant, *Charles II*, p. 169.
8. Pepys, October 23, 1668.
9. Evelyn, *Diary*, October 21, 1671.
10. *Rochester-Savile*, p. 49.
11. Etherege, *Letterbook*, p. 209.
12. *Rochester-Savile*, p. 61.
13. See Cyrus Lawrence Day and Eleanore Boswell Murrie, *English Song-Books, 1651-1702*, Oxford University Press, Oxford, 1940.
14. *Odes of Anacreon*, trans. Nathan Haskell Dole, Boston, 1903.
15. Rochester's "Upon Drinking in a Bowl" and "Anacreontic."
16. *The Poems of Catullus*, trans. Horace Gregory, New York, 1931.
17. Dryden, *Essays*, I, 230-31.
18. *Ibid.*, II, 19.
19. For studies of early seventeenth century amatory verse, see Lu Emily Pearson, *Elizabethan Love Conventions*, University of California Press, Berkeley, 1933, and Douglas Bush, *English Literature in the Earlier Seventeenth Century, 1600-1660*, Oxford University Press, Oxford, 1945.
20. From *The Comical Revenge; or, Love in a Tub* (1664), II,

iii. The last four verses, not usually included with reprints of the song, appear in the same scene and are sung by the same character.

21. From Lee's *Mithridates* (1678). It appears also in *Choice Ayres and Songs* (1681), with music by Grabu.

22. *The Guardian*, No. 16, March 30, 1713.

23. Dryden, *Miscellany*, v, 130.

24. The poem was first printed in *Familiar Letters: Written by The Right Honourable, John, late Earl of Rochester, To The Honourable Henry Savile, Esq.*, etc. (2nd edition), London, 1697, I, 169. See also J. H. Wilson, "Rochester: an Overlooked Poem," *N&Q*, CLXXXVII (1944), 79.

25. Buckingham, *Works*, II (Part 2), 56.

26. Sedley, *Poetical Works*, p. 139.

27. See *Pope's Own Miscellany*, ed. Norman Ault, London, 1935. In various early miscellanies, this poem appears as "The Perfect Enjoyment." Charles Gildon (*The Laws of Poetry*, London, 1721, p. 92) assigned it to Mulgrave.

28. Sedley, *Poetical Works*, p. 139.

29. "Remedy of Love," Nahum Tate's *Poems by Several Hands*, London, 1685, p. 103.

30. Modern apologists have taken it for granted that numerous vulgar poems were fathered upon the Wits by unscrupulous booksellers. Such an assumption should not be used as a reason for denying the authorship of a poem merely because it is obscene. As Robert Wolseley pointed out in his preface to Rochester's *Valentinian* (1685), the poet did not design his obscene songs "to be sung for Anthems in the King's Chappel" . . . nor "for the Cabinets of Ladies, or the Closets of Divines . . . but for the private Diversion of those happy Few, whom he us'd to charm with his Company, and honour with his Friendship."

31. Prior, "A Satyr Upon the Poets," *Dialogues*, p. 56.

32. Preface to Sedley's *Poetical Works*.

33. Dryden, *Works*, IV, 372.

34. Behn, *Miscellany*, p. 49.

35. Harris, *Dorset*, p. 239.

36. See Etherege, *The Man of Mode; or, Sir Fopling Flutter* (1676), IV, ii.

37. Radcliffe, *The Ramble*, p. 21.

38. Behn, *Miscellany*, preface to "Seneca Unmasqued."

39. *The Works of Mr. John Oldham*, London, 1710, p. 152.

40. Pepys to Hewer, November 2, 1680, *Letters and The Second Diary of Samuel Pepys*, ed. R. G. Howarth, London, 1933, p. 105.
41. *POAS*, II, 371.

LIBELS AND SATIRES

1. Burnet, *History*, I, 486.
2. Burnet, *Rochester*, p. 25.
3. Dryden, *Essays*, II, 79-80.
4. See Brice Harris, "Captain Robert Julian, Secretary to the Muses," *ELH*, x (1943), 294.
5. Walpole, *Noble Authors*, p. 204.
6. Dryden, *Essays*, II, 19.
7. Brown, *Works*, I, 27.
8. Prinz, *Rochester*, p. 280.
9. "Answer to the Satyr on the Court Ladies, 1680," "Choyce Collection," p. 74.
10. Hamilton, *Grammont*, II, 2, 57, 114.
11. See Dorset's "A Faithful Catalogue of our most Eminent Ninnies."
12. *Rochester-Savile*, p. 72.
13. HMC, *Rutland*, II, 31.
14. Walpole, *Noble Authors*, p. 206.
15. "The Prophecy," "Choyce Collection," p. 239.
16. Buckingham, *Works*, I, 47.
17. *Memoirs of Thomas, Earl of Ailesbury*, London, 1890, I, 13.
18. "The Answer" is attributed to Rochester in various editions of his poems. It is attributed to Scroope in "A Collection of Poems" (Harvard, Eng. 636F) and in *Roxburghe*, IV, 569.
19. For satires containing attacks on Scroope, see *POAS*, I, 155, 180, 200; I (Continued), 37, 240; III, 126, 132; and *Roxburghe*, IV, 583. Probably one of Rochester's attacks on Scroope has been lost. On April 25, 1678, John Verney (HMC, *Seventh Report*, p. 470) wrote that he was enclosing with his letter Rochester's "verses on Sir Carr Scroope at large." Rochester's "On the Supposed Author," etc., must have been written early in 1677.
20. Although the "Familiar Epistle" is usually assigned to Buckingham, and is certainly in his rough style, it was sometimes attributed to Dryden by his contemporaries. It is printed as his in Dryden's *Miscellany*, VI, 359. Perhaps it was of this

poem that Shadwell was thinking when in his "Satyr to his Muse" (1682) he represented Dryden as saying,

On Scroope my Blunderbuss of Satyr fir'd,
In cool blood call'd him Fool, Knave, Coward too.

And Aubrey (*Brief Lives*, II, 279) wrote of the "bitter satyricall verses made on Sir Carr Scroope, viz—'Thy brother murdered'—etc." To this Wood added a marginal note: "4 or 6 verses made against him by Driden or somebody else."

21. See HMC, *Le Fleming*, p. 121; HMC, *Seventh Report*, p. 465a; *CSPD*, 1675, September 9, October 8.

22. J. J. Jusserand, *A French Ambassador at the Court of Charles II*, London, 1892, p. 151.

23. HMC, *Rutland*, II, 31, 37; Cartwright, *Sacharissa*, p. 257; HMC, *Ormonde*, n.s., V, 324.

24. Mulgrave, *Works*, II, 11. But see also the report in the *House of Lords Journal* for November 23, 1669. Evidently Rochester had been so eager to keep his appointment with Mulgrave that he had broken his parole to an officer of the House rather than risk losing his honor as a duelist.

25. The poem was apparently printed under this title about 1679 (*Roxburghe*, IV, 575). In early editions of Rochester's poems it was sometimes called "A very Heroical Epistle in Answer to Ephelia." In Rochester's *Collected Works* (p. 107) it appears as "To a Lady that Accused Him of Inconstancy."

26. *Rochester-Savile*, p. 73.

27. See J. H. Wilson, "Rochester, Dryden, and the Rose-Street Affair," *RES*, XV (1939), 294.

28. *Roxburghe*, IV, 567. In Rochester's *Collected Works* (p. 64) the poem appears as "Monster All-Pride."

29. For Mulgrave and the Princess Anne, see HMC, *Seventh Report*, p. 498. The original "Ovid to Julia" appeared in Behn's *Miscellany* as "By an unknown Hand," however, Brice Harris ("Aphra Behn's *Bajazet to Gloriana*," *LTLS*, February 9, 1933, p. 92) proved that the poem was written by Aphra Behn herself. The later version of the poem appears in Dryden's *Miscellany*, II, 80. The name "Bajazet" must have been applied to Mulgrave before 1680, for in the edition of Rochester's poems of that year "Ephelia to Bajazet" (by Etherege?) is given as the title of the poem in which "Doll-Common" reproached Mulgrave for deserting her.

30. Sybil Rosenfeld (Etherege, *Letterbook*, p. 69) failed to identify Mulgrave as "numps."

31. *The Conduct of the Earl of Nottingham*, ed. W. A. Aiken, Yale University Press, New Haven, 1941, pp. 43-44.

32. Maurice Irvine in "Characters in Mulgrave's 'Essay upon Satire,' " *SP*, XXXIV (1937), 533, contends that the "beastly Brace" are Portsmouth and Nell Gwyn. However, the antitheses between the two are clear: Cleveland, notorious for her infidelity, has jilted Charles; Portsmouth, known to be strong for the French interest, has sold him; Cleveland, a brazen creature, affects to laugh; Portsmouth, a lachrymose lady, affects to weep. Neither description fits Gwyn.

33. Marvell, *Poems & Letters*, II, 329.

34. *Rochester-Savile*, pp. 56, 57.

35. Hayward (Rochester, *Collected Works*, p. 128) prints this poem with the title date 1678. But there is an unmistakable reference to the poem on January 26, 1673/4, in *Williamson Letters*, II, 132.

36. Buckingham, *Works*, I, 29, 34.

37. *Ibid.*, I, 24, 29.

38. See Chalmers' *English Poets*, London, 1810, VIII, 344, and Harris, *Dorset*, p. 235.

39. Buckingham, *Works*, I, 82.

40. *POAS*, I (Continued), 32, 33.

41. Buckingham, *Works*, II (Part 2), 14; reprinted by Harris, *Dorset*, p. 81.

42. For a discussion of the type and a list of examples, see *Roxburghe*, IV, 546.

43. *POAS*, III, 158. A longer version appears in "Choyce Collection," p. 33.

44. *POAS*, I, 260.

45. Maurice Irvine, "Characters in Mulgrave's 'Essay upon Satire,' " *SP*, XXXIV (1937), 533.

46. See Marvell, *Poems & Letters*, I, 197.

47. James Welwood, *Memoirs of the Most Material Transactions*, etc., London, 1743, p. 130.

48. For various versions of this quip, see *LTLS*, October 4 to November 1, 1934, pp. 675, 715, 735, 755.

49. In Dryden, *Miscellany* (I, 273), "The Nature of Women" is titled also "A Translation of Part of the Fourth Eclogue of Mantuan." Actually it is an imitation rather than a trans-

lation of the famous Fourth Eclogue of Baptista (Mantuanus) Spagnolo.

50. The quotation is from *The Works of the Earls of Rochester, Roscommon and Dorset*, etc., London, 1739. Hayward (Rochester, *Collected Works*, p. 126) omits the last four lines.

51. See *Rochester-Savile*, pp. 13-15. The satire must have been written before March 23, 1676, when it was mentioned in a letter from Sir Ralph Verney (HMC, *Seventh Report*, p. 467).

52. See John F. Moore, "The Originality of Rochester's *Satyr against Mankind*," *PMLA*, LVIII (1943), 393.

53. C. H. Collins Baker, *Lely and the Stuart Portrait Painters*, London, 1912, I, 212.

54. *Rochester-Savile*, p. 60.

55. Prinz, *Rochester*, p. 95. Prinz's stricture would apply more accurately to Pope's imitation, "Upon Silence."

56. James Carkasse, *Lucida Intervalla* (*ca.* 1678-79). For this quotation I am indebted to Prof. Charles E. Ward.

57. *Rochester-Savile*, p. 46.

58. Mulgrave, "An Essay on Satire."

59. Wycherley, *The Country Wife*, II, i; Congreve, *The Way of the World*, I, i.

60. See Prinz, *Rochester*, p. 276.

61. MS versions of the two "Answers" are in B. M. Harleian 6207. Griffith's reply appears in *The Works of John Earl of Rochester*, etc., 1714, p. 59, immediately after the poem to which it is an answer. It appears also in *POAS*, II, 432, but as by "Dr. P[oco]ck." For dates of printing see Prinz, *Rochester*, p. 309.

62. Radcliffe, *The Ramble*, p. 4.

63. Brown, *Works*, I, 27.

PATTERNS FOR THE STAGE

1. Brown, *Works*, III, 37-38.

2. Toward the end of the century, it appears that arrangements were made whereby the author received the profits of the third, sixth, and perhaps ninth performances. See Nicoll, *Restoration Drama*, p. 343.

3. Shadwell, *The Sullen Lovers* (1668), III, i.

4. See also Shadwell's dedication of *The Squire of Alsatia* to

Dorset, Dryden's dedication of *The Assignation* to Sedley, and of *Aurenge-Zebe* to Mulgrave. Although it was common practice to dedicate plays to noblemen, it was only to the Wits that the playwrights acknowledged literary indebtedness.

5. Dennis, *Works*, I, 290.
6. Rochester, "An Allusion to Horace."
7. See Wycherley, *Complete Works*, I, 53, 56. In his preface to *Bellamira*, Sir Charles Sedley wrote that a friend (possibly Shadwell) liked the play in manuscript. "I told him . . . that if he cou'd get it acted under his own or another's Name, I wou'd finish it for him. But for I know not what reasons he could not do it; and I was oblidg'd to own it my self, or my friend had lost his third day." Apparently the "friend" received all the profits of the third day.
8. Denham, prologue to *The Sophy* (1641).
9. Rochester, "An Allusion to Horace," and "The Session of the Poets."
10. Sir Edward Filmer was the eldest son of Sir Robert Filmer of East Sutton, Kent. He had some small reputation as a poet; see HMC, *Seventh Report*, p. 531. Sidney Godolphin (1645-1712), third son of Sir Francis Godolphin of Somersetshire, was an adept courtier and politician; he had a distinguished career in public office.
11. The story of *Pompey* is told by Harris, *Dorset*, p. 24, and Pinto, *Sedley*, pp. 79-83. For Mrs. Philips, see Philip Webster Souers, *The Matchless Orinda*, Harvard University Press, Cambridge, 1931. For dates of production, see Summers, *Bibliography*, p. 104.
12. For a discussion of the two versions, see Dorothy Canfield Fisher, *Corneille and Racine in England*, Columbia University Press, New York, 1904, pp. 51-64.
13. *The Comical Revenge* was produced in March, 1664. Pepys saw it on January 5, 1665. On October 29, 1666, after seeing it again, he called it "a silly play." He saw it once more on April 29, 1668, without comment.
14. Downes, *Roscius Anglicanus*, p. 25.
15. Eleanore Boswell, in "Sir George Etherege," *RES*, VII (1931), 207, suggested that Etherege was appointed to a Court post in 1668 to give him prestige as a member of the ambassadorial mission to Turkey. In a list of the Duke of York's pensioners (1682), a payment of one hundred pounds

to Etherege is noted. This may have been on a long-standing annuity. See HMC, *Hodgkin*, p. 19.

16. Pepys saw what is generally believed to be Buckingham's version of *The Chances* on February 5, 1667; however, the play might have been produced some months earlier. For evidence on the date and an analysis of the alteration, see Sprague, *Beaumont and Fletcher*, pp. 31-33, and 221-27.

17. Dryden, *Essays*, I, 174.

18. Pepys, February 6, 1668.

19. Pepys, May 18, 1668.

20. For the Buckingham-Howard collaboration, see Pepys, May 1, 4, 6, 22, 1669. See also Summers, *Playhouse*, p. 178.

21. The story of the Sedley-Kynaston affair is told by Pepys on February 1 and 2, 1669.

22. For the story of Wycherley and the Duchess of Cleveland, see Dennis, *Works*, II, 409.

23. See Wycherley, *Complete Works*, I, 38. Evidently the dramatist quickly became intimate with Buckingham. On August 24, 1672, he served as witness to a deed of gift of a glass works which Buckingham was turning over to his mistress, Lady Shrewsbury. See Eleanore Boswell, "Footnotes to Seventeenth Century Biographies," *MLR*, XXVI (1931), 345.

24. "The D. of B's Litany," *POAS*, III, 83.

25. *The Rehearsal*, ed. M. Summers, London, 1914, p. xiv.

26. HMC, *Sixth Report*, p. 368.

27. Downes, *Roscius Anglicanus*, p. 32.

28. See Summers, *Playhouse*, pp. 318-20. In 1936, *The Country Wife* was produced successfully in New York. No one seems to have been shocked.

29. For a summary of the conflicting claims for character representation, see Etherege, *Dramatic Works*, I, pp. xxiii-xxv. Harris (*Dorset*, pp. 67-69) reasons that the most trustworthy of the early commentators, John Dennis, who claimed to remember "the first acting this Comedy," gives Dorimant as Rochester and Medley as Fleetwood Shepherd, but Harris makes out a good case for Dorimant as a composite portrait of Dorset and Rochester. See Dennis, *Works*, II, 248-49.

30. Dennis, *Works*, II, 277.

31. See Sedley, *Dramatic Works*, I, 190.

32. See J. H. Wilson, "The Dating of Rochester's 'Scaen,'" *RES*, XIII (1937), 455.

33. For arguments that the play was produced in 1679, see Summers, *Playhouse*, pp. 290-91.

34. Downes, *Roscius Anglicanus*, p. 40.

35. See Sprague, *Beaumont and Fletcher*, pp. 167-78.

36. J. H. Wilson, "Rochester's *Valentinian* and Heroic Sentiment," *ELH*, IV (1937), 265; and "Satiric Elements in Rochester's *Valentinian*," *PQ*, XVI (1937), 41.

37. Aphra Behn, preface to *The Lucky Chance* (1687).

38. Pinto, *Rochester*, p. 125.

39. For arguments in favor of Rochester as the author of *Sodom*, see Prinz, *Rochester*, pp. 172-77, and Summers, *Playhouse*, pp. 296-97. For arguments to the contrary, see Rodney M. Baine, "Rochester or Fishbourne: A Question of Authorship," *RES*, XXII (1946), 201. A corrupt version of *Sodom* is available in *Kryptadia*, Vol. IX.

40. See Sprague, *Beaumont and Fletcher*, pp. 187-95, and Arthur Mizener, "George Villiers, Second Duke of Buckingham, His Life and a Canon of His Works," unpublished thesis, Princeton, 1934, pp. 396-408.

41. Etherege, *Letterbook*, p. 421. Although the letter is addressed to Buckingham, it must have been written after Buckingham's death.

CENSURES OF THE POETS

1. The poem must have been written sometime between the publication of Howard's *The Brittish Princes* (May, 1669) and November, 1669, when Rochester and Mulgrave fell out.

2. Dryden, *Essays*, I, 188, 195, 196.

3. Pepys, October 4, 1664, and February 18, 1666.

4. Walpole, *Noble Authors*, p. 227.

5. All but Shadwell's poem are printed together in Dryden's *Miscellany*, III, 68-74. The first poem in the collection is by Butler, although it is here attributed to Waller. For Shadwell's poem see A. J. Bull, "Thomas Shadwell's Satire on Edward Howard," *RES*, VI (1930), 312. Mr. Bull's claim that a poem on the same subject in *POAS* (1687) is by Dryden is denied by Hugh MacDonald in *A Dryden Bibliography*, Oxford University Press, Oxford, 1936, p. 192, n. For Buckingham's share in the attack on Howard, see Arthur Mizener, "George Villiers, Second Duke of Buckingham," unpublished thesis, Princeton University, 1934, p. 283.

6. Prior, *Dialogues*, p. 187.
7. Harris, *Dorset*, p. 45. A. E. Case showed that Dorset's poem was "The Model for Pope's Verses *To the Author of a Poem intitled 'Successio.'* ", in *MLN*, XLIII (1928), 321.
8. For *The Duel of the Stags* see Dryden's *Miscellany*, II, 131. Savile's version of the parody is in Dryden's *Miscellany*, IV, 282; Buckhurst's version is in *POAS*, I, 20. See also Harris, *Dorset*, pp. 47-48. For Howard's rather unconvincing denial that the *Duel* had any political significance, see Charles E. Ward, "An Unpublished Letter of Sir Robert Howard," *MLN*, LX (1945), 119.
9. For a list of "Sessions," see Hugh MacDonald, *A Journal from Parnassus*, London, 1937, Introduction.
10. For the arguments on the authorship and date of "A Session," see J. H. Wilson, "Rochester's 'A Session of the Poets,' " *RES*, XXII (1946), 109.
11. For the date and details of production of *The Empress of Morocco*, see Boswell, *Court Stage*, p. 131.
12. Prinz, *Rochester*, p. 267.
13. *Rochester-Savile*, p. 49.
14. The text quoted here is from Buckingham's *Works*, I, 41.
15. The poem appears under either title in a number of eighteenth century editions of Rochester's works. The text quoted here is from *The Works of John Earl of Rochester*, etc., 1714, p. 87.
16. Edmond Malone, *The Critical and Miscellaneous Prose Works of John Dryden*, London, 1800, I, 121-35.
17. Dryden, *Works*, XVIII, 91.
18. For the attack on Dryden in Rose Alley, see Chapter VI.
19. Although Malone was aware that the "pretended" biographical account of Rochester prefixed to Curll's edition of *The Works of . . . Rochester and Roscommon*, 1707, was not by St. Evremonde, he accepted its statements without question.
20. Dryden, *Essays*, I, 116.
21. Montague Summers, *Dryden, the Dramatic Works*, London, 1932, IV, 510.
22. *Rochester-Savile*, p. 41.
23. For an analysis of Dryden's preface, see Frank L. Huntley, "Dryden, Rochester, and the Eighth Satire of Juvenal," *PQ*, XVIII (1939), 269.
24. HMC, *Seventh Report*, pp. 480, 498.
25. Preface to Rochester's *Valentinian*, 1685.

26. This and following quotations are from *An Essay on Poetry* (2nd edition), London, 1691.

27. Quotations from all the authors cited are modestly prefixed to the 1740 edition of Mulgrave's *Works*.

28. Harris, *Dorset*, pp. 110-11.

29. Pinto, *Sedley*, pp. 231-32.

30. *POAS*, I, 199.

31. *Rochester-Savile*, p. 49.

32. HMC, *Le Fleming*, p. 141.

33. Dryden, *Works*, IV, 31.

34. Harris, *Dorset*, p. 80.

35. *Ibid.*, pp. 105-8.

36. Prinz, *Rochester*, pp. 87-89.

37. Pinto, Sedley, pp. 93-95.

EPILOGUE

1. Etherege, *Letterbook*, pp. 190, 240, 357. Cuffley appears as "Castle" in Miss Rosenfeld's transcription of the manuscript, but see H. F. B. Brett-Smith's review in *RES*, V (1929), 227.

2. *Ibid.*, pp. 411, 303, 317, 227.

3. *Ibid.*, pp. 69, 354.

4. *Ibid.*, p. 18; Dorothy Foster, "Sir George Etherege: Collections," *N&Q*, CLIII (1927), 472.

5. Cartwright, *Sacharissa*, p. 289; Wood, *Fasti*, II, 294.

6. *Savile Correspondence*, p. xxiii.

7. Harris, *Dorset*, p. 216.

8. See John and J. A. Venn, *Alumni Cantabrigienses*, Cambridge University Press, Cambridge, 1922-44.

9. Pinto, *Sedley*, p. 234.

10. Hamilton, *Grammont*, II, 237.

11. Harris, *Dorset*, p. 226.

12. Luttrell, *Brief Relation*, VI, 695.

13. HMC, *Seventh Report*, p. 508.

14. Wycherley, *Collected Works*, I, 62.

15. Johnson, *Lives*, II, 173.

16. Burghclere, *Buckingham*, pp. 393-400.

17. Prinz, *Rochester*, pp. 217-38, 294, 297; Burnet, *Rochester*, p. 158.

18. Prinz, *Rochester*, pp. 419-20, 414-18, 437-39.

19. Pope, *The First Epistle of the Second Book of Horace: To Augustus*, 1737.

Index

CN